AT THE END OF THE STREET IN THE SHADOW

AT THE END OF THE STREET IN THE SHADOW

ORSON WELLES AND THE CITY

Matthew Asprey Gear

WALLFLOWER PRESS
LONDON & NEW YORK

A Wallflower Press Book

Wallflower Press is an imprint of
Columbia University Press
publishers since 1893
New York

cup.columbia.edu

Copyright © 2016 Matthew Asprey Gear
All rights reserved

Wallflower Press® is a registered trademark of Columbia University Press

A complete CIP record is available from the Library of Congress

ISBN 978-0-231-17340-7 (cloth : alk. paper)
ISBN 978-0-231-17341-4 (pbk. : alk. paper)
ISBN 978-0-231-85090-2 (e-book)

Cover image: Orson Welles photographed in Paris in 1952, by Fred Brommet

∞

Columbia University Press books are printed on permanent
and durable acid-free paper.
This book is printed on paper with recycled content.
Printed in the United States of America

c 10 9 8 7 6 5 4 3 2 1
p 10 9 8 7 6 5 4 3 2 1

This book is for my mother

Contents

Acknowledgements ix
INTRODUCTION 1

PRELUDE
A NUISANCE IN A FACTORY | Hollywood: 1939–48, 1956–58 13

WELLES'S U.S.A.
1. THE DECLINE AND FALL OF THE LINCOLN REPUBLIC 21
2. AN EMPIRE UPON AN EMPIRE | *Citizen Kane* (1941) 33
3. THE DARKENING MIDLAND | *The Magnificent Ambersons* (1942) 49

PAN-AMERICA
4. DARKNESS AND FEAR | The Early Anti-fascist Thrillers 77
5. THE RAUCOUS RAGGLE-TAGGLE JAMBOREE OF THE STREETS
   It's All True (unfinished, 1942) 99
6. RATLINE TO MAIN STREET | *The Stranger* (1946) 125
7. PORT TO PORT | *The Lady from Shanghai* (1947) 145
8. THE BORDER | *Touch of Evil* (1958) 163
9. RETURN TO THE PERIPHERY | *The Other Man* (unproduced, 1977) 181

INTERLUDE
A FREE MAN IS EVERYWHERE | Europe & Beyond: 1947–55, 1958–85 . . . 193

POSTWAR EUROPE
10. SKIES AND RUBBLESCAPE | *Mr. Arkadin/Confidential Report* (1955) . . . 203
11. LOST IN A LABYRINTH | *The Trial* (1962) 225

IMMORTAL STORIES
12. TO ADORE THE IMPOSSIBLE 243
13. IN THE LAND OF DON QUIXOTE 257

Index 283

Acknowledgements

I am grateful to the Orson Welles scholars who generously shared their time and ideas with me during the research for and writing of this book: James Naremore, Jonathan Rosenbaum, Stefan Drössler, Josh Karp, and Scott Simmon. I also want to thank Kate Hutchens at the Special Collections Library at the University of Michigan and David Frasier at the Lilly Library at Indiana University for their hospitality and help during my research visits in January and February 2014, respectively. This book builds on the *Touch of Evil* chapter of my PhD thesis, completed at Macquarie University, Sydney, in 2011. Further funding from the university allowed me to make a research trip to the Filmmuseum München and present a preliminary version of the chapter on *Mr. Arkadin* at the 'Screen' conference at the University of Glasgow in the summer of 2013. I also want to thank Peter Doyle, Noel King, Theodore Ell, Yoram Allon at Wallflower Press, Gary Morris at *Bright Lights Film Journal*, Ray Kelly at wellesnet.com, Luc Sante, Will Straw, Adrian Martin, Clive Sinclair, the late Lester Goran, Kathryn Millard, Mark Evans, Nicole Anderson, Iván Zatz, and from the early days Bill Wrobel and Adriano.

Many thanks to Soledad Rusoci for her support throughout the writing of this book. Thanks also to Julie Asprey, Luke Asprey, Clare Anderson, Jace Davies, Amanda Layton, Ben Packham for his early insights into *Citizen Kane*, and in Buenos Aires Sabrina Díaz Bialos, Ignacio Bosero, Arthur Chaslot, Valeria Meiller, and Nuestra Señora de los Candados.

Matthew Asprey Gear
Biblioteca Nacional de Maestros, Buenos Aires
September 2015

INTRODUCTION

1.

We could begin almost anywhere. He seems to have visited all the cities so precociously early that every return was tinged with *saudade* – that untranslatable Portuguese word signifying nostalgic longing and the sweet sadness of loss. In fact, he picked up the word in Rio de Janeiro during what he later remembered as "the last great carnival in that greatest of carnival cities".[1] In the words of Bill Krohn, Orson Welles was "a man of many nostalgias".[2]

So let's begin in Vienna, close to the Cold War border but also the former heart of the Austro-Hungarian Empire, one of several politically obsolete cultures Welles gently lamented during his forty-five years in cinema. In 'New Wien', a short travel segment he made for television in the late 1960s, our corpulent guide puffs a cigar and trails a billowing *lodenmantel* – "purely utilitarian", he insists – through the wintry solitude of the city.[3] Welles peers through the front window of Demel, "the greatest of all the great Viennese pastry shops", and remembers how "when the world was young I used to run riot in there. How sweet it was". The grand opulence of Welles's hotel suite is merely *de rigueur* – "here at the Hotel Sacher that's the way it is". He wonders "how much pink champagne must have been poured here into how many pretty ladies' slippers", and remarks that late at night one can still "seem to hear again the clop clop of the horse-drawn Fiakers bringing the old playboys back". He remembers from his "own childhood days the formidable Frau Sacher herself".

As a child Welles was an international gadabout – "the best cities were certainly Budapest and Peking", he recalled[4] – who dubiously claimed early acquaintance with such world figures as Sarah Bernhardt and Harry Houdini. The latter taught him magic "as a favour" to his father.[5] He also recalled a particularly boring lunch in 1920s Bavaria seated beside Adolf Hitler. However accurate these unverifiable memories, Welles's absurdly interesting early life was an education in history, culture, and the panoply of human types.

His 1969 homage to his fantasy Vienna – an invitation to warm in the afterglow of faded glories – is hardly a radical, interrogative film essay on this city's dynamic culture and history. Instead, Welles explains:

> Your true Vienna lover lives on borrowed memories. With a bittersweet pang of nostalgia he remembers things he never knew, delights that only happened in his dreams. The Vienna that *is* is as nice a town as there is. But the Vienna that never was is the grandest city ever.[6]

The mode of nostalgic reverie was hardly reserved for Vienna. It was, in fact, Welles's characteristic approach to the past. His explanation to Peter Bogdanovich around the same time has been frequently quoted:

> Even if the good old days never existed, the fact that we can *conceive* of such a world is, in fact, an affirmation of the human spirit. That the imagination of man is capable of creating the myth of a more open, more generous time is not a sign of our folly. Every country has its "Merrie England," a season of innocence, a dew-bright morning of the world. Shakespeare sings of that lost Maytime in many of his plays, and Falstaff – that pot-ridden old rogue – is its perfect embodiment.[7]

It's also characteristic that this Vienna segment, and the television special of which it was to be a part, *Orson's Bag* (aka *One-Man Band*), was never broadcast. And although he certainly appeared in front of the Riesenrad Ferris wheel he'd immortalised by his role in Carol Reed's *The Third Man* (1949), Welles made only part of the segment on location in Vienna itself. He shot other parts in Zagreb, another former Austro-Hungarian city but by then a northern outpost in Josip Broz Tito's Socialist Federal Republic of Yugoslavia. Other parts were filmed in Los Angeles.[8]

It was typical of Welles's happy embrace of fakery to shoot parts of a documentary purportedly about 'Vienna' in other cities. In this period he worked independently across Europe by what has been called 'patchwork'. Alternating between multiple projects over long periods in different places, Welles funded stages of production via the film and television industries of various countries, when necessary with his acting income, or else by siphoning the resources of other directors' projects through special arrangement or by subterfuge. No other major filmmaker of the time worked in this way, and certainly none with Welles's ambition. Disenchanted with Hollywood, he invented both the methods and aesthetic forms of an independent personal cinema.

'New Wien' was not his first use of Zagreb as urban imposter. In 1962 he filmed parts of Franz Kafka's *The Trial* in Zagreb as a substitute for inaccessible Prague. Yet the mood is starkly different. For *The Trial* Welles said he wanted a "modern European city, yet with its roots in the Austro-Hungarian Empire",[9] but in fact most of the Zagreb locations centred not on relics of the dual monarchy under which Kafka was born but instead on its Modernist architecture – symbols of the grim autocratic future Kafka did not live to see. Many of the interior spaces of this unnamed cinematic city were created inside the empty Gare d'Orsay in Paris. Welles created an expressionist labyrinth that mirrors the unfathomable bureaucracy of the legal system, self-reflexively defying spatial logic.

The city's stunning blend of Austro-Hungarian ambience, *fin-de-siècle* industrialism, and the symbols of modern conformity provided the spatial context for a dystopian fable about power and human dignity – quite a contrast to a catalogue of Viennese pastries. But in fact such strict segregation of modes is rare. Most of Welles's cinematic cities are the context of both nostalgia and politics: we see this in his New York (*Citizen Kane*, 1941), his Munich (*Mr. Arkadin*, 1955), and his bordertown 'Los Robles' (*Touch of Evil*, 1958).

2.

[A] work of art is good to the degree in which it expresses the mind of the person who created it. I always feel very involved with my scripts, ideologically. I'm not interested in them as scripts, it's their ideological basis I'm interested in. I hate rhetoric in a play, or moralizing speeches, but nonetheless the moral basis of a play is the essential thing, in my view [...] I think every artist has an obligation to criticize his own civilization.

– Orson Welles, 1958[10]

This book is a study of Orson Welles as a poet and critic of the city. It is structured around key themes in his film work: historical and contemporary urban change; fascism, racism, and the corruption of institutional power; anti-nationalism and the utopian promise of cosmopolitanism; and romantic nostalgia for archaic forms of urban culture.

This approach situates Welles in a tradition of experimental twentieth-century artists who sought to reimagine cities in their work, often through an approximation of subjective urban experience, and often in the service of a critical or ideological motive. This particularly Modernist project sometimes embraced grandly synoptic ambitions: examples outside cinema include novels by James Joyce, Andrei Bely, Alfred Döblin, and John Dos Passos.

In cinema this synoptic ambition is most evident in the 'city symphony' cycle epitomised by Walter Ruttland's *Berlin: Symphony of a Metropolis* (1927) and Dziga Vertov's *Man with a Movie Camera* (1929). But innovations in reimagining the city on film also occurred in narrative-based contexts: in German Expressionism, the Hollywood gangster cycle of the 1930s, and in film noir. Mike Davis has written that distinct from such explicitly avant-garde films as the city symphonies, which were comparable to the innovations of other mediums in their "mappings of the metropolis", Golden Age Hollywood films (including the film noir) "generally preferred to meet the city on the familiar terms of literature (and, later, of commercial photography and advertising)".[11]

By contrast, Orson Welles, maverick experimentalist, usually sought the emphatically cinematic in his creation of cities on film, even when adapting literary works. Welles's very first cinematic city was a New York of about 1910, invented for a series of silent film sequences intended to be screened during his stage production of William Gillette's *Too Much Johnson* (1938). The project was made entirely outside Hollywood and its industrial norms. Welles apparently worked without a script for these sequences.[12] Even in the brief period when Welles had access to the resources of Hollywood studios, he constantly sought new approaches to 'mapping the metropolis'.

Unlike filmmakers who repeatedly made films set in a single city, Welles adopted an approach that was staggeringly internationalist and broadly historical – the United States' port cities, its industrializing midland, and its borderland with Mexico; the wild tumult of Carnaval in Rio de Janeiro and the impoverished fishing communities of Fortaleza; the medieval streets and public taverns of fifteenth-century London; Pamplona's enduring fiesta; and Munich's postwar rubblescape.

Throughout this study I have avoided the term 'represented' cities in favour of the 'imagined' or 'cinematic'. Although Welles preferred to shoot his films on location – he acknowledged that "stone is better than cardboard"[13] – he seems to have had a limited impulse towards mere representation, towards mere spatial verisimilitude. On location, at the level of the individual shot and the creation of *mise-en-scène*, he embellished and transformed real urban spaces through art direction (notably the introduction of props and detritus to fixed structures), false perspective, expressionist lighting, camera techniques, and optical effects. Through montage the spatiality of these actual locations proved infinitely malleable; moreover, Welles frequently combined shots from totally different locations and conceived new soundscapes in post-production. These efforts to reimagine urban space on film served Welles's dramatic, thematic, and ideological purposes.

In his introduction to the anthology *Cinema and the City: Film and Urban Societies in a Global Context* (2001), co-editor Mark Shiel promotes an interdisciplinary approach to film studies at "the nexus *cinema-city*". He writes approvingly of the 'spatial turn' since the 1970s in leftist social and cultural theory, which is to say the emphatic examination of the relationship of space to power. Shiel argues that "cinema is the ideal cultural form through which to examine spatialization precisely because of cinema's status as a peculiarly spatial form of culture". He advocates critically approaching cinema as a "spatial system" rather than a textual one because "spatiality is what makes [cinema] different [as a cultural form] and, in this context, gives it a special potential to illuminate the lived spaces of the city and urban societies".[14]

With this critical approach in mind, I argue that Welles contributed significantly to the language of cinema as a 'spatial system' through his innovations in *mise-en-scène*, extended takes, montage, and sound, and additionally in his quest for synoptic visions of urban space. Fortunately this exclusively urban prism of analysis focuses a broad spectrum of light on Welles's sprawling, uncontainable oeuvre. Apart from such unfinished works as his sea thriller *The Deep* (1967–68) and most of *Don Quixote* (from 1957), Welles was principally an urban-based filmmaker. For that reason this book can double as a general critical survey of his movies. But inevitably the prism emphasises some films and individual sequences over others, and by necessity sometimes downplays what I consider to be major work (for example, *F for Fake*, 1974) in favour of the minor (*Nella terra di Don Chisciotte*, 1964). Nevertheless, I hope this different approach stimulates a fresh discussion of what is most valuable in Welles's work.

3.

Is Orson Welles rightly to be considered a Hollywood filmmaker at all? His difficult position within that category has often sustained negative critical judgments in the United States – a prodigy in a lifelong decline from the height of *Citizen Kane* to the indignity of endorsing cheap wine on television. But really, Welles abandoned trying to reconcile his artistic practice to the Hollywood industrial model after less than a decade (1939–1948), with occasional unsatisfying return visits to gauge his compatibility with new evolutions of the industry. After the miracle of total artistic control on *Citizen Kane*, every one of his subsequent American studio features was significantly (and sometimes disastrously) weakened by studio-ordered reediting, rewrites, and reshoots. Welles embarked on a heroic struggle for artistic independence in Europe, where he was able to complete to his satisfaction *Othello* (1952), *The Trial* (1962), *Chimes at Midnight* (1965), *The Immortal Story* (1968), *F for Fake*, and *Filming 'Othello'* (1978). Only *Mr. Arkadin* was finished by others.

But even in Europe Welles operated on the fringes of commercial filmmaking and for decades was cursed by limited theatrical distribution of his work back in the United States. In subsequent decades those films were often tied up in rights disputes and only occasionally commercially available (if at all), and sometimes in very inferior editions. This led to the effective invisibility of some of Welles's most important work. The ongoing lack of a containable, finite Welles canon – shrink-wrapped and barcoded for purchase – has sustained those negative assessments of his career trajectory. Jonathan Rosenbaum, one of Welles's most radical champions, has aptly characterised Welles as an "ideological challenge" to what he calls the "media-industrial complex".[15] The breadth of Welles's achievement isn't easily quantified. It's an ever-evolving debate.

In 1959, after losing final cut on his final Hollywood studio film, *Touch of Evil*, Welles published an essay in *Esquire* magazine, 'Twilight in the Smog', which asserts his estrangement from the industry and analyses Los Angeles's failings as a city of culture:

> According to the map, Hollywood is a district attached but not belonging to the City of Los Angeles. But this is not strictly accurate: Los Angeles – though huge, populous and rich – has never quite made it as a city. It remains a loose

and sprawling confederation of suburbs and shopping centers. As for downtown Los Angeles, it's about as metropolitan as Des Moines or Schenectady.

The metropolitan air is what one misses. Neither the theatre nor its artists are at their best in a suburb. Or a gigantic trailer camp. Whether we work before a camera or behind the footlights, actors are, by nature, city people. Hollywood is most precisely described as a colony. (Colonies are notoriously somewhat cut off from reality, insular, bitchy and cliquish, snobbish – a bit loose as to morals but very strict as to appearances.) One expects a colony to be an outpost of empire. Hollywood might be called an outpost of civilization (a word which means, after all, 'city culture'), but it's also the heart of its own empire of the movies: a capital without a city, yet among its colonies are numbered the great cities of the world.

What is best in any branch of theatre must always have a certain flavor of tradition. Dear, shabby old Times Square, for instance, has its roots in Rome and the Middle Ages. It was, after all, a kind of marketplace, and in the old tradition. The saloons and bars of the Broadway area are still the sorts of places where show folk have always gathered in Athens and Madrid, in London and Paris and Peking. But Hollywood, which boasts the largest population of actors ever concentrated in a single community, is also the first show town in history without a pub or a bistro in the traditional sense. In California the tradition of the Mermaid Tavern has given way to the country club. A rigidly standardized middle-class suburbia is replacing the raucous and circusy traditions of the recent past.

Welles identified with a bohemian tradition of players:

Right down to this last moment in a long, long history, show folk have been kept quite firmly segregated from respectability. Significantly, the theatre profession had no contact (or contamination) with the middle class. Indeed, it's just recently that we began to employ that very middle-class word, 'profession.' This was when the mention of art began to embarrass us, and this was the beginning of our fall from grace: when we suddenly aspired to the mediocre rank of ladies and gentlemen. Before that, and in common with all other artists, we had no rank at all, and stood in our own dignity outside of protocol.[16]

Around the same time Welles told *Cahiers du cinéma* that "sentimental bourgeois morality makes me sick".[17] In other words, he wasn't really cut out for Hollywood. Despite his charismatic public diplomacy and his democratic inclusiveness, it's not surprising Welles never found the enduring mass American audience that would have economically sustained his experimental work in film. Nevertheless, he continued angling for such success until the end of his life.

Meanwhile Welles's filmmaking proved less and less compatible with the expectations of the international film business, even as new funding opportunities appeared in the 1960s and 1970s. In later years he avoided binding contracts and traditional accounting. He always worked with astonishing energy, but his process of low-budget filming and intricate editing was drastically prolonged, particularly as he took on multiple projects. Welles seems to have responded to the situation in one of two ways, depending on the malleability of his production partners of the moment: either by trying to reconcile the differences, or else by pretending to conform to expectations of commercial practice while continuing to work in his own way. His game-playing didn't always pay off. From this perspective, each completed Welles film must be considered the triumph of a maverick's doggedness against varied oppositions.

His uncompleted projects have often been assessed as evidence of failure rather than important (if fragmentary) parts of his oeuvre in their own right. Archival research of his many unfinished or unmade projects only reveals that each was subject to unique circumstances that made it impossible to realise within the realities of the international film industry.

4.

With such an unusual career, and with the steady appearance of archival discoveries and alternative editions since his death, how is it possible to establish an Orson Welles canon? This is not a new dilemma. James Naremore, one of Welles's most insightful critics, acknowledges the provisional nature of most of Welles's work and that "his reputation will always depend to some degree on fragments and traces".[18] To Rosenbaum, the "Wellesian oeuvre [is] in a perpetual state of becoming, where each new work or fragment thereof transforms our understanding of the rest".[19]

As only about half of the films released during Welles's lifetime represent his final artistic intentions, it doesn't make sense to disregard a posthumously discovered segment such as 'New Wien', which was essentially completed by the director without interference (like most of *Orson's Bag*), even if not quite to the technical standards of broadcast television.

Therefore, this study goes beyond Welles's thirteen commercially released feature films to consider the oeuvre lurking in the shadows. It attempts, as much as possible with surviving and available evidence, to critically assess the more Wellesian pre-release versions of films, before they were altered by the studios. It also opens up the field of study to the numerous unfinished fragments and works-in-progress Welles left behind. I approach these materials with caution but in a spirit of inclusiveness appropriate to Welles's unique work and difficult career. Of course, the study of unfinished work requires its own flexible methods of criticism. This is especially true in the case of unproduced treatments and scripts. Rosenbaum, in his study of Welles's unproduced *Heart of Darkness* screenplay, acknowledges that "scripts are blueprints, not finished works, and even to discuss one that was never filmed is to give it an identity of its own that was never intended".[20] I have tried to always appreciate the role such provisional pre-texts played in Welles's creative process. Comparison of his shooting scripts with the resulting films shows how ceaselessly he embraced contingencies during shooting and editing. He said:

> If you have a masterplan for what you're going to do, exactly where the camera's going to be, exactly where the scene is supposed to start, if you are locked into that you are depriving yourself of the divine accidents of movie making because everywhere there are beautiful accidents.[21]

By necessity, this book is built on a foundation of previous scholarly research into Welles's career, particularly regarding the unfinished works. It is also based on my archival research of primary documents and film materials at the University of Michigan, the Lilly Library at Indiana University, and the Filmmuseum München.

***

This book is structured thematically rather than by strict chronology. There are also interludes which contextualise Welles's changing position in Hollywood and the international film industry, and his evolving methods of production.

Although distinct in mood, Welles's first two features, *Citizen Kane* and *The Magnificent Ambersons* (1942), are both ambitious efforts to mythologise American urban political and material developments in the long period following the American Civil War. The contexts of *Kane* and *Ambersons* are the industrialisation of the Midwest and the rise of the automobile; the battle between Wall Street capitalism and progressive reform; the birth of the US empire in the Spanish–American War; and the development of the mass media. In both of these films the American city is the site of the struggle for personal and political power.

Part I examines these two films in relation to the documented histories of New York and Indianapolis, and explores how their weaknesses as history illuminate the tensions between Welles the political activist and Welles the poetic myth-maker.

Part II examines a series of films with contemporary Pan-American settings Welles attempted to make from the late 1930s through the 1940s and sporadically thereafter. Not one of these projects was completed to Welles's satisfaction, and most never reached production. *It's All True* was an unfinished anthology project incorporated into the United States' Good Neighbor Policy during World War II. Most of Welles's other explorations of contemporary Pan-America were conducted within the thriller genre – what would later be classified as film noir – and concerned fascism. As Welles was squeezed out of his role of political insider after the war, symptomatic of the widespread sidelining of progressives, both his understanding of fascism and his transformation of found locations became more sophisticated. More and more he reimagined the cities of the United States and Latin America in ways that illustrated the operation of power.

Part III looks at how Welles's cosmopolitan sensibility and political concerns found expression in the contemporary films of his postwar European self-exile, *Mr. Arkadin* and *The Trial*. The cities in these films frequently reveal traces of a vanished, older Europe, and make a mockery of the political fictions of Cold War nationalism.

Part IV explores Welles's cinematic cities of a more distant and mythical Europe, his romantic nostalgia for the values and rituals of the past, and his long-term exploration of Spain. In the tales of the Danish writer Isak Dinesen he found static nineteenth-century settings for old-fashioned storytelling outside the trappings of the contemporary world. He found more profound resonance when he depicted the obliteration of the values of one era by another. He often used contrasting models of urban spaces to emphasize this transition. Welles called himself "a man of the Middle Ages",[22] and his tender view of the passing of that epoch appears in his adaptations of Falstaff and *Don Quixote*.

Despite his lifelong romantic celebration of Spanish traditions, Welles became critical of twentieth-century Americans in Spain, particularly the macho enthusiasms of his sometime friend Ernest Hemingway. Until his death in 1985, he continued to plan films set in either a nostalgic Spanish past or a political Spanish present. This work is capped by his unproduced script for *The Big Brass Ring*, the tender and strange adventure of two desperate men in a memory-haunted modern-day Madrid.

NOTES

1. Welles quoted in Simon Callow, *Orson Welles: Hello Americans* (London: Vintage, 2007), 63.
2. Krohn quoted in Jonathan Rosenbaum, *Discovering Orson Welles* (Berkeley: University of California Press, 2007), 217.
3. This part of the narration didn't make the surviving cut but can be found in draft pages of the script, which uses the working title 'New Wien'. In *Orson's Bag* (1968–70) (subseries), Draft pages (various scenes) (typescript, carbon, and photocopy, annotated), 10 April – 11 September 1969 (folder 2). Box 17, Orson Welles–Oja Kodar Papers, Special Collections Library, University of Michigan.
4. Welles quoted in 1967 in Kenneth Tynan, '*Playboy* Interview: Orson Welles', reprinted in Mark W. Estrin (ed.), *Orson Welles: Interviews* (Jackson: University Press of Mississippi, 2002), 131.
5. *Orson Welles's Sketchbook* (Orson Welles, 1955). Episode 4, 14 May (UK: BBC TV).
6. This scripted narration was slightly edited for the surviving cut.
7. Welles quoted in Orson Welles and Peter Bogdanovich, *This Is Orson Welles*, ed. Jonathan Rosenbaum (London: Harper Collins, 1993 [1992]), 100.
8. Surviving script pages and production notes at the University of Michigan note the Zagreb location and filming dates in early November 1969. Welles's fully edited and partly mixed workprint of 'New Wien' survived; the Munich Film Museum restored it under the title *Orson Welles' Vienna* in 1999. Viewed 17 June 2013 at the Filmmuseum München, Germany. The museum has also restored other parts of *Orson's Bag/One-Man Band* in varying states of completeness.
9. Welles interviewed by Huy Wheldon on *Monitor* (UK: BBC TV, 1962). Transcript reprinted

at http://www.wellesnet.com/trial bbc interview.htm (accessed 16 August 2015).
10. Welles quoted in 1958 in André Bazin, Charles Bitsch, and Jean Domarchi, 'Interview with Orson Welles (II)', reprinted in Estrin (ed.), *Orson Welles: Interviews*, 63.
11. Mike Davis, 'Bunker Hill: Hollywood's Dark Shadow', in Mark Shiel and Tony Fitzmaurice (eds), *Cinema and the City: Film and Urban Societies in a Global Context* (Oxford: Blackwell, 2001), 33–4.
12. The *Too Much Johnson* film material was ultimately not used for the stage production, and was long considered lost. A partially edited workprint was found in Italy and restored by George Eastman House and the National Film Preservation Foundation in 2014. See Scott Simmon, '*Too Much Johnson*: The Films Reimagined', *National Film Preservation Foundation*, at http://www.filmpreservation.org/userfiles/image/preserved-films/TMJ-press-photos/TMJ-reimagined-essay.pdf (accessed 17 August 2015). See also Joseph McBride, '*Too Much Johnson*: Recovering Orson Welles's Dream of Early Cinema', *Bright Lights Film Journal*, 24 August 2014, at http://brightlightsfilm.com/too-much-johnson-orson-welles-film-recovering-orson-welless-dream-of-early-cinema (accessed 7 June 2015).
13. *Filming 'Othello'* (Orson Welles, 1978).
14. Mark Shiel, 'Cinema and the City in History and Theory', in Shiel and Fitzmaurice (eds), *Cinema and the City: Film and Urban Societies in a Global Context*, 5–6.
15. Rosenbaum, *Discovering Orson Welles*, 269.
16. Orson Welles, 'Twilight in the Smog', *Esquire*, March 1959, reprinted at http://www.wellesnet.com/twilight-in-the-smog-by-orson-welles-esquire-march-1959 (accessed 11 May 2015).
17. Welles quoted in Bazin, Bitsch, and Domarchi, 'Interview with Orson Welles (II)', 63.
18. James Naremore, *The Magic World of Orson Welles* (Dallas: Southern Methodist University Press, 1989), 263–4.
19. Rosenbaum, *Discovering Orson Welles*, 225.
20. Rosenbaum, *Discovering Orson Welles*, 38.
21. *Filming 'Othello'*.
22. Welles quoted in Bazin, Bitsch, and Domarchi, 'Interview with Orson Welles (II)', 71.

PRELUDE

A NUISANCE IN A FACTORY

Hollywood: 1939–48, 1956–57

For several spells in his long career, Orson Welles tried to accommodate his filmmaking to the industrial model that had dominated the international movie business since the 1920s. Working without interference on *Citizen Kane* at RKO, he quickly mastered existing Hollywood studio techniques and, demanding perfection, pushed his studio collaborators into major innovations. But in 1959, freshly wounded from another lost battle over artistic control, Welles dismissed the maverick in Hollywood as "an outright nuisance in a factory".[1] Years later he would lament "how many great people that town ha[d] destroyed since its earliest beginnings".[2]

How did he wind up in Hollywood? It was another temporary stop on this vagabond's colourful world journey. In Welles's telling, he came from an aristocratic and eccentrically bohemian background. He was a Midwesterner, born 1915 in Kenosha, Wisconsin, home to automobile manufacturers such as Nash Motors and Thomas B. Jeffery. Welles later suggested his father, Richard Head Welles, the inventor of a bicycle lamp adopted by the automobile industry, had been the inspiration for Eugene Morgan in Booth Tarkington's novel *The Magnificent Ambersons* (1918).[3] Father and son travelled the world together. His mother, Beatrice Ives Welles, had been a radical suffragette and a pianist. Her son, supposedly a musical prodigy, claimed he never played the piano again after she died in 1924. Welles's father died a lonely alcoholic death just after Christmas in 1930. His orphaned son was fifteen, wracked with guilt, and left in the care of his reliable guardian, Dr Maurice Bernstein.

The Todd School for Boys in rural Illinois offered a serious education alongside sailing, flight instruction, travel, and dramatics. Welles, who had enrolled at the age of eleven, found another surrogate father and lifelong friend in headmaster Roger 'Skipper' Hill. With the Todd Troupers, Welles staged a number of productions, including his Shakespeare extravaganza *The Winter of Our Discontent* (1930), based on *Henry VI* and *Richard III*. This was a preliminary second part of Welles's epic *Five Kings*; the first part, focusing on the character of Falstaff, would be produced on stage in 1939, again in 1960, and eventually as Welles's classic film *Chimes at Midnight*.

Welles briefly studied at the Art Institute of Chicago and then bargained with 'Dadda' Bernstein for a solo painting tour of Ireland. Here is the myth, frequently told by Welles: turning up impoverished at the Dublin Gate Theatre in September 1931, he persuaded director Hilton Edwards that he was already a star of the New York stage. He was immediately offered the part of Duke Karl Alexander in Leon Feuchtwanger's *Jew Süss*. Now he really was a theatrical star. "I've been working my way down ever since," Welles would later quip.[4] He continued in numerous productions at the Gate into 1932.[5] Meanwhile, back in the United States, 'Skipper' Hill was promoting Welles to Cornell College:

> Nearly everyone connected with the arts, the opera, or the stage in Chicago knows him and they have all done their best to spoil him, but I think he is very sound and very sensible, although he is definitely talented to the point of genius.[6]

But by then Welles was already off and running, hardly tameable by institutions of any kind.

His theatrical stardom in Ireland was not immediately matched in the United States. He returned to Todd in 1933 to stage *Twelfth Night* with the current generation of students. It was that year he went to live for a short period in Triana, then still the Gypsy barrio of Seville. Welles claimed to have prospered on the proceeds of pseudonymous science fiction or detective stories written for American pulp magazines and to have trained as a *torero*, albeit only by buying his own bulls.[7] Ernest Hemingway's bullfighting study *Death in the Afternoon* had been published a year earlier and *The Sun Also Rises* (1926), which cast Spain's traditional culture as a virtuous remedy to the spiritual emptiness after the Great War, had initialized a new American school of *españolada*. Spain, its myths and traditions, was to become a central preoccupation in Welles's life and art.

Returning to the US, he began to act in repertory theatre. His series of *Everybody's Shakespeare*, a collaboration with 'Skipper' Hill, began publication in 1934. Around the same time he made a lark of a short film, *Hearts of Age*, in one afternoon with a friend and he began to perform small parts on radio.

Welles acquired American fame with a series of controversial projects and a flair for publicity. He made his place in the culture at a fortuitous moment. As the Depression endured, the Roosevelt administration initiated the Federal Theatre Project as part of the Works Progress Administration (WPA). One unit was the Negro Theatre Project, headed by John Houseman in Harlem. In 1936, Houseman gave Welles the opportunity to direct an all-black cast in *Macbeth*, substituting a nineteenth-century Haiti-like setting for medieval Scotland, witch doctors for witches. It proved a sensation. Welles and Houseman subsequently formed their own unit within the Federal Theatre, for which Welles directed *Horse Eats Hat* (1936, an adaptation of Eugène Labiche's *Italian Straw Hat*) and Christopher Marlowe's *Doctor Faustus* (1937). Welles began to play the nationally popular role of 'The Shadow' (in the radio drama of the same name) for the Mutual Broadcasting Company and narrated Archibald McLeish's radio play *The Fall of the City*, which personified fascism as a machine-like dictator "in the end of the street in the shadow".

With the onset of the Spanish Civil War, Welles campaigned against fascism and associated with leading radical artists of the Popular Front. In the summer of 1937 he directed Marc Blitzstein's Marxist opera *The Cradle Will Rock*, which creatively escaped forced closure by its sponsoring organisation, the Federal Theatre Project. Welles was additionally busy adapting and directing a seven-part radio version of *Les Misérables*.

Welles and Houseman founded the Mercury Theatre in 1937. Their first production was a modern-dress *Julius Caesar* meant to evoke Mussolini's Italy. In 1938 the Mercury produced *The Shoemaker's Holiday* and a revived *Cradle Will Rock*. That year Welles made the cover of *Time* magazine as the star and director of George Bernard Shaw's *Heartbreak House*.

In the summer of 1938 Welles moved more seriously towards moviemaking. He shot ambitious silent film sequences intended, but not used, for projection during the Mercury stage production of William Gillette's *Too Much Johnson*. Around the same time Welles and the Mercury were invited to create a weekly series of CBS radio dramas named successively *First Person Singular*, *The Mercury Theatre on the Air*, and *The Campbell Playhouse*. At twenty-three

Welles already possessed one of the century's most distinctive voices. He used that voice (as narrator and actor) to tie together adaptations of mostly classic and contemporary plays and novels. The source texts were varied and indicative of Welles's high- and middle-brow tastes. The adaptations were written by Welles or by Houseman, Howard Koch, Howard Teichmann, or Herman J. Mankiewicz. *War of the Worlds* gained Welles global notoriety on 30 October 1938. At the same time Welles's theatrical productions continued: *Danton's Death* (1938), the first part of *Five Kings*, and *The Green Goddess* (1939).

Precociously famous for his attention-grabbing innovations in theatre and radio, Welles was invited to make movies in Hollywood. He later claimed a reluctance to move into cinema; to scare away the studios, he demanded impossible conditions of artistic autonomy that, to his surprise, were met by RKO studio chief George Schaefer. Welles signed a two-picture contract in 1939. He later called the contract "a kind of a defiance of everything that was established in the Hollywood industrial system".[8]

Welles first scripted an anti-fascist adaptation of Joseph Conrad's *Heart of Darkness* (1899) moved to the contemporary world. For the production he planned a subjective camera technique: nearly every shot would present the eyes of its narrator. That film was never made. Throughout his long period of project development in 1939–40, Welles remained active in radio and in theatre, for which he directed Richard Wright's *Native Son*.

Welles finally moved forward in Hollywood with *Citizen Kane*, a fragmentary portrait of a news mogul who resembled William Randolph Hearst. It was scripted in collaboration with Herman J. Mankiewicz. The Mercury Theatre company provided actors without prior experience in films including Joseph Cotten, Agnes Moorehead, Ruth Warwick, and Everett Sloan. Welles also brought CBS radio composer Bernard Herrmann to the West Coast to work on the film and revolutionise film music.

With *Kane*, Welles made the most auspicious debut of any American filmmaker. It is still widely considered the pinnacle of American filmmaking for its structural and technical innovations, and the brilliance of its collaborators on and off screen. And somehow *Kane*'s sum is even greater than its numerous brilliant components.

Conditions did not endure to allow Welles to repeat that miraculous first effort, although he came close to scraping through with *The Magnificent Ambersons*. The two movies engaged with the same period in American history. Each was audacious and difficult for its time. In 1941 Hearst's press empire attempted to suppress *Citizen Kane* and slander Welles's reputation. The following year RKO assumed complete authority over the final cut of *Ambersons* while Welles was serving as a Good Will Ambassador in South America and filming the semi-documentary anthology project *It's All True*.

After his falling out with RKO, which also resulted in the cancellation of *It's All True*, Welles continued his work in American radio and focused more intently on progressive politics. He also produced an ambitious and costly production of *Around the World in Eighty Days* for the stage in 1946.

His next films for Hollywood turned out to be a trilogy of unsatisfactory compromise, each made for a different production company or studio – respectively International Pictures, Columbia, and Republic. From the outset Welles tried to work creatively within circumscribed limits to his authority; in each case he was unable to see the film finally released in his preferred version. His screenplay for the thriller *The Stranger*, which had been originally co-written by Anthony Veiller and John Huston, suffered studio cuts before shooting even commenced. The prologue in a fictional South American city was shortened, and then the sequence was cut further during editing. *The Lady from Shanghai*'s making proved a torturous process of negotiation with studio boss Harry Cohn, who demanded substantial cuts, retakes, close-ups, a musical number by Rita Hayworth, and a score dominated by the melody of that theme song. *Macbeth* was made with a brisk shooting schedule and small budget. Welles was able to prepare a 107-minute edit to his satisfaction, which premiered in 1948, but it was withdrawn and rereleased in 1950 in a shorter, redubbed cut. In this case Welles was able to prepare the 86-minute edit himself, and both versions have survived.

In 1947, as opportunities opened up in the Italian film industry, Welles left Hollywood. He briefly returned to the United States in late 1955 for a period of about two years. In addition to acting in film and theatre, he worked on several television projects in Hollywood. *The Fountain of Youth* was an innovative pilot financed by Desilu Productions in 1956 and broadcast in 1958, but it was never picked up. He also produced a never-broadcast and now-lost pilot based on the life of Alexandre Dumas called *Camille, the Naked Lady and the Musketeers*. Frank Sinatra provided financing for a television *Don Quixote*, which Welles began to film in Mexico. It evolved from the television format into a long-term, privately financed project, a permanent work-in-progress.

A fortunate set of circumstances led to Welles's promotion from supporting actor to writer, director, and star of *Touch of Evil* at Universal. By that time he seems to have been almost forgotten as a director by Hollywood. Even that studio deal deteriorated during editing and the film came out partially reshot, restructured and significantly truncated.

Welles continued to work as an actor in Hollywood films and television when in the United States, but apart from some screenplay commissions in the early 1970s, he was never again hired in a creative capacity by mainstream Hollywood.

NOTES

For this section, I have drawn on Jonathan Rosenbaum's chronology of Welles's career in Welles and Bogdanovich, *This Is Orson Welles*, 323–453; and Jean-Pierre Berthome and François Thomas, *Orson Welles at Work* (London: Phaidon, 2008).

1. Orson Welles, 'Twilight in the Smog'.
2. Welles interviewed on *Parkinson* (UK: BBC TV, 1974). Available at https://www.youtube.com/watch?v=6dAGcorF1Vo (accessed 19 May 2015).
3. Orson Welles, 'My Father Wore Black Spats', *Vogue* (Paris), December 1982 – January 1983, reprinted at http://www.wellesnet.com/orson-welles-on-his-childhood-my-father-wore-black-spats-and-a-brief-career-as-a-musical-prodigy (accessed 19 May 2015).
4. *F for Fake* (Orson Welles, 1974).
5. Joseph McBride argues that Welles was influenced by German Expressionism indirectly through Hilton Edward's direction at the Gate. See McBride, '*Too Much Johnson*: Recovering Orson Welles's Dream of Early Cinema'.
6. Todd Tarbox (ed.), *Orson Welles and Roger Hill: A Friendship in Three Acts* (BearManor Media, 2013), 12.
7. *Parkinson*.
8. Undated, uncredited interview (late 1970s). Available at https://vimeo.com/127736401 (accessed 19 May 2015).

WELLES'S U.S.A.

CHAPTER ONE

THE DECLINE AND FALL OF THE LINCOLN REPUBLIC

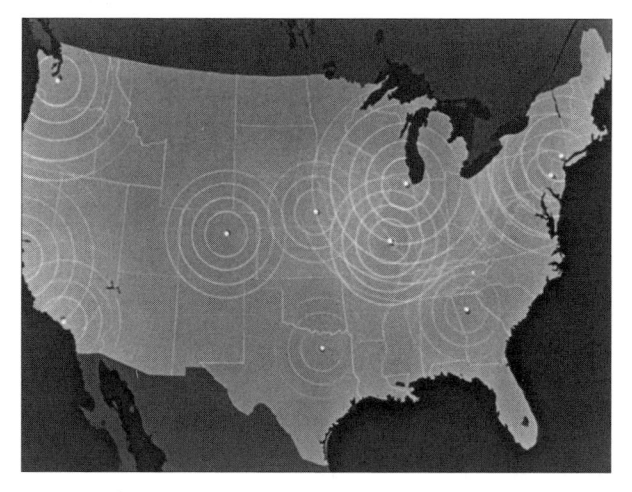

Charles Foster Kane's "empire upon an empire"

Citizen Kane and *The Magnificent Ambersons* were not conceived as sister projects. They were only two of several features developed for production while Orson Welles was under contract to RKO Studios between 1939 and 1942. Nevertheless, while widely divergent in their stylistic approaches, Welles's first two released films reimagine much of the same sweep of American history. Both are mythical narratives of national decay in the half-century following the Civil War.

The settings are American cities. *Kane*'s Gilded Age New York is one theatre of the ideological war between unchecked capitalism and progressive reform. The battlefield of the city's slums and infrastructure is clouded by the interference of a megalomaniac newspaper tycoon who tries to become a politician. In *Ambersons*, the rise of the automobile at the turn of the century is the catalyst for a shift of wealth and social power from a genteel urban aristocracy to a suburban entrepreneurial class. The Ambersons of Indianapolis humanise the transformation of the near-pastoral 'midland' into the grim industrial Midwest. In these films Welles creates American cities in the flux of transformation, cities that situate the characters' struggles for personal and political power.

Most of Welles's subsequent cinematic cities were shot on location, as had been the historical New York of *Too Much Johnson*. This makes the cities of *Kane* and *Ambersons* unique within the Welles oeuvre: they were almost totally created at RKO's facilities in Hollywood, with full access to studio resources, including a brilliant special effects department. They are also the only two feature films Welles was able to make about the history of the United States.

***

The title of this section is intended to draw comparison to John Dos Passos's trilogy of novels – *The 42nd Parallel* (1930), *1919* (1932), and *The Big Money* (1936) – republished together as *U.S.A.* in 1938. The author's *Manhattan Transfer* (1925) had sought an encompassing view of New York City in the early decades of the twentieth century: its diversity of personalities, sensations, energy, and human subjectivities. *U.S.A.*'s ambition expanded to chronicle the nation's growth in the same period.

When *Cahiers du cinéma* asked Welles in 1958 about Dos Passos's influence on *Kane*, he claimed that he had never read the author's fiction.[1] There's no reason to doubt his word, but in *Kane* and *Ambersons* Welles attempted an artistic-historical project that shared *U.S.A.*'s historical breadth, albeit without its vast extended form.[2] What's more, the two figures were active in the liberal artistic wing of the Popular Front. In 1934 the Soviet Comintern had altered their aggressive policy attacking international socialists and liberals and instead favoured alliances across the left to oppose the fascism that was conquering Europe and spreading throughout the world. The Popular Front found sympathy across the Depression-stricken United States.[3]

Nevertheless, with the simultaneous official ascendancy of Socialist Realism in the USSR, Dos Passos was already an ideological outcast among the

Stalinists. In 1934 he had been denounced by the Soviet Writers' Congress as a follower of James Joyce, that creator (so they insisted) of "a dunghill swarming with worms seen through a microscope held upside down".[4] Like Welles, Dos Passos lamented an idealised American past. The regressive historical arc he sketched in his work registered poorly with the dogmatic left; John P. Diggins notes that "underlying the eloquent rage and protest of *U.S.A.* is a conservative desire to restore what contemporary radicals wanted to transcend".[5]

Dos Passos's break from the Popular Front came in 1937 when he was working in Spain as a writer on Joris Ivens's *The Spanish Earth*. His friend José Robles had just been mysteriously executed, possibly under false charges of spying for Franco. For demanding an explanation, Dos Passos was mocked by such ideological tourists as Ernest Hemingway, who had essentially supplanted him as the writer of *The Spanish Earth*. Dos Passos soon went public in revolt against the Stalinist influence in Spain.[6]

Welles was never so sidelined by the Popular Front, although he was also excluded from contributing to the final cut of *The Spanish Earth* in the marginally less tense atmosphere of a New York recording studio. In Welles's version of the story, the circumstances were not tragic but farcical: Hemingway's baseless homophobic contempt for the young Welles led to a provocation and a fist fight, and Hemingway subsequently replaced Welles's narration with his own voice.[7] Following Welles's brave standoff with the Federal Theatre over the attempted censorship of Blitzstein's *Cradle Will Rock*, he created several overtly anti-fascist projects. Welles's theatrical audacity helped make him a celebrity, although the Mercury Theatre did not win over all left-wing critics. The *Partisan Review* viewed Welles's aesthetics as middlebrow kitsch, which they deemed representative of the Popular Front.[8]

Welles is probably best considered a committed progressive of conflicting allegiances. Prone to dogma in his political speeches, his film, radio, and theatre works betray a higher calling than any sort of ideological obedience, even when ostensibly anti-fascist in conception.

* * *

For *Kane*'s audacity in reimagining the life of proto-fascist William Randolph Hearst, the Hearst empire declared war on the film even before its release. There was an attempt, in the name of rival studio executive Louis B. Mayer, to buy the negative from RKO in order to destroy it. George Schaefer at RKO persisted with *Kane*. Hearst newspapers refused to advertise the film and some cinema chains were too intimidated to book it.

A month before *Kane*'s premiere, editorials smeared Welles's patriotic radio play *His Honor, the Mayor* as pro-communist. In this atmosphere, and possibly through the influence of Hearst, the FBI began investigating Welles for his communist associations and ridiculously deemed *Kane* "nothing more than an extension of the Communist Party's campaign to smear one of its most effective and consistent opponents in the United States".[9] Welles was not a communist, but the League of American Writers, an organ of the Communist Party, campaigned for the film's release.[10] The film failed to make a profit.[11]

J. E. Smyth has persuasively argued that the effort to downplay the Hearst biographical connection, as well as *Kane*'s innovations in cinematography, have distracted from the film's serious critical engagement with post-Civil War history and how that history had been depicted on screen.[12] *Kane* is indeed a serious historical fiction, although Welles's critical reimagining of America's past is neither scrupulous nor warped by ideology: it is personal and mythical.

The Magnificent Ambersons is difficult to read as any sort of politically radical film. In his adaptation, Welles acquiesces to Booth Tarkington's middle-class lament over the decline of a short-lived Midwestern aristocracy, albeit with a little more affectionate irony and some judicious cuts. By almost any standards the Ambersons are a parasitic, socially worthless bunch – lacking creative energy and imagination, condescending and shallow in their judgments of the other townsfolk, and oblivious to change – but their passing into death, poverty, and obscurity is the film's melodramatic tragedy, an inevitable but lamentable shame. Welles pulls it off by his tender evocation of the vanished, purer American culture the Ambersons represented at their peak of influence.

Fascism was the era's present danger, and most of Welles's ideologically driven anti-fascist projects were set in the contemporary Americas. The past, by contrast, was Welles's playground, the irresistible opportunity to create a mythical 'Merrie England' out of the America as it existed before his birth, and in doing so he focused mainly on the upper middle class and aristocratic milieu of his own family. Welles later said that he had deep sympathy for *Kane*'s Jedediah Leland, the impoverished, drunken southern aristocrat whose sense of honour and *noblesse oblige* leads him to break with Charles

Foster Kane.[13] The only significant working-class character in either film is the salesgirl Susan Alexander, who becomes the second Mrs Kane – and perhaps Kane's parents in rural Little Salem, Colorado. In *Kane* the working masses are mostly invisible. The newsreel includes some stock footage of a workers' rally in San Francisco, which is combined with an original shot of a rabble-rouser denouncing Kane as a fascist. On the other hand, the crowds in Kane's Madison Square Garden political rally are matte art and inevitably appear as an abstraction, even when given some clever animation by the use of lights flickering through pinholes in the painting.[14]

There are other factors which limit the political radicalism of Welles's early historical films. Firstly, there is Welles's consistently humanist enactment of his villainous characters, often those whose politics he most despised. In the 1930s he evoked *Uncle Tom's Cabin* when disdaining "the error of left-wing melodrama, wherein the villains are cardboard Simon Legrees".[15] He also remarked later that "an actor is not a devil's advocate: he is a lover".[16]

There is also Welles's status as an adaptor, his formidable skill as a writer. He did not create the scripts of *Kane* and *Ambersons* from scratch. Welles's priorities were to transform source texts into innovatively cinematic material as well as to elevate melodrama into moving human drama. Herman J. Mankiewicz's early muckraking drafts of *Kane* were commissioned as raw material for Welles's extensive rewrites, so there was never a question of faithfulness to a source text.[17] For *Ambersons*, a popular Pulitzer Prize-winning novel, Welles liberally reworked the material but, apart from some specific departures and omissions, remained essentially faithful to the author's worldview. In fact, if Welles had shed Tarkington's conservative historical myth of decline, the story would have lost its *raison d'être*.

James Naremore identifies Tarkington's *Ambersons* as "less interesting as a recreation of historical truth than as a projection of political and psychological attitudes back upon an imaginary past".[18] In adapting the book, Welles takes on board the author's political and psychological history without the imposition of too much historiographic criticism.

***

The jigsaw-puzzle structure of *Citizen Kane*, while extending in historical scope from 1871 to 1941, focuses most of its many flashbacks on two key periods: 1893–1900, the tail end of the 'Gilded Age', and 1916–1919. The bulk of the chronologically structured *Ambersons* slots into 1904–1912, an era mostly skipped over by *Kane*.

Chronologically tabling the main events of each film illustrates their historical comprehensiveness, the way they complement each other as narratives of the post-Civil War era.

Year	*The Magnificent Ambersons* (131 minute version)[19]	*Citizen Kane*[20]	American History
1864/5		Charles Foster Kane born.	End of Civil War.
1868		Colorado Lode deeded to Mrs. Kane.	
1871		Kane leaves Colorado with Walter P. Thatcher.	
1873	Major Amberson's fortune and the beginning of "the magnificence of the Ambersons".		The Great Panic.
1885	Eugene Morgan's botched serenade. Isabel Amberson marries Wilbur Minafer. George Amberson Minafer born soon after.		
circa 1890		Kane takes over *NY Inquirer* and publishes his 'Declaration of Principles'. Fights traction trusts, copper swindles, slum lords (to 1898).	
1895	George (ten) fights with other boy in street.		
1898		Kane propagandises for war with Spain and wins circulation war. Goes to Europe and romances Emily Norton.	Spanish-American War.
1900		Marries Emily on White House lawn.	
1901		Breakfast with Emily (1).	
1902	George (seventeen) home from school.	Breakfast with Emily (2).	

1904	Ball in honour of George. The Ambersons and Morgans drive through snow. Wilbur dies.	Breakfast with Emily (3).	
1905	Excavations for subdivision on the Amberson property. George insults Eugene. Isabel spurns Eugene's proposal on George's insistence. George and Isabel abroad.	Breakfast with Emily (4).	
1906		Breakfast with Emily (5).	
1909		Breakfast with Emily (6).	
1910	Isabel returns to Indianapolis and dies; Major Amberson dies. The family finances in disarray.		
1911	Jack Amberson leaves Indianapolis. George and Aunt Fanny leave the mansion. George begins work with explosives.		
1912	George's accident. Eugene visits Fanny in the boarding house. [END]		
1915		Kane meets Susan Alexander.	
1916		Kane's failed political campaign for NY state governor.	
1917		Divorces Emily, marries Susan.	US enters WWI.
1918		Death of Emily and their son, Charles Jr.	
1919		Susan's opera debut in Chicago and tour.	
1920		Susan's suicide attempt.	
1929			Market crash.
1932		Kane loses control of his empire to Thatcher. Susan leaves Kane.	
1941		Kane dies. The quest for Rosebud. [END]	

In *Kane* and *Ambersons*, American history in the fifty years after the Civil War, at least in the Midwest and on the East Coast, is represented by wealthy and influential people. The lives of Charles Forster Kane, Walter Parks Thatcher, the Amberson family, and Eugene Morgan are entangled with what contemporary audiences would have seen as moments of irrevocable urban transformation. Kane's success in yellow journalism is specific to the conditions of *fin-de-siècle* New York City: a large and dense urban population, mass literacy, and the technologies of newspaper production. *Ambersons* is more explicitly technologically determinist. Indianapolis's economy, its social hierarchy, its whimsical customs, and its very material form are permanently altered by a revolution in transportation. While technology is driven by the entrepreneurial spirit of innovators, once set in motion it is unstoppable.

The old order – for all its corruption, backwardness, and social unfairness – does not vanish without tender lament. Remembrance of things past furnishes Welles's characters with emotional logic. In fact, the agitators for change tend to wind up the most regretful. Kane, who more successfully than anybody disrespects tradition and imposes his personality on American society via the technology of the news business, aches for his interrupted childhood. Automobile entrepreneur Eugene Morgan is ambivalent about automobiles, conceding that "with all their speed forward they may be a step backward in civilization".

Both films locate their Merrie England in the decades immediately following the Civil War: pastorals to contrast with the dirty cities of the twentieth century. In *Kane* it is the wintry Colorado of 1871. In *Ambersons* it is Indianapolis as the "midland town" of the 1880s, with its quaint bygone fashions, unhurried horse-drawn street cars, and moonlit serenades. Those customs barely linger on into the new century. Around Christmas 1904, we witness a spectacular "pageant of the tenantry" in honour of spoilt brat George Amberson Minafer. It is "the last of the great, long-remembered dances that everybody talked about"; the following day George topples his horse-drawn sleigh and Eugene's primitive horseless buggy comes to the rescue. The characters observe that the town is getting dirtier, more industrial. The Ambersons and the Morgans chug through the snow singing 'The Man Who Broke the Bank at Monte Carlo'. The final shot of this sequence does not fade to black but is masked out by an iris, another of Welles's quotes from the language of silent film to roughly, if anachronistically, suggest old times.[21] The sequence signifies not only the town's inescapable descent into modernity, but also the last moment of harmony between the two families.

Here and elsewhere Welles puts a personal spin on winter as the age-old symbol of death. In *Kane*, snow is associated with childhood from the vantage of old age. It works as a Proustian memory trigger: flakes swirling through a snow globe twice prompt the tycoon to mutter "Rosebud", the name of his old snow sled – the last utterance on his deathbed.[22] In Welles's later films *Mr. Arkadin* and *Chimes at Midnight*, snow coincides respectively with dying Jakob Zouk's nostalgic desire for a Christmas goose liver and Master Shallow's happy reflection on "the days that we have seen!"

The western had mythically reimagined the country's violent post-Civil War frontier history for modern American audiences, usually as a triumphalist narrative. *Kane* is only a western for a few minutes, but the vanished frontier seems central to the character's sense of self. Kane is suddenly ejected from his childhood in Colorado and, as heir to a fortune, sent east to be educated. The purely accidental beneficiary of a gold mine, he is thereafter geographically isolated from the engine of his wealth, the fortune wrestled from the frontier. Upon assuming his inheritance, Kane tells Thatcher, "I'm not interested in gold mines, oil wells, shipping, or real estate." Sixty years later, still in rebellion against his former banker-guardian, he reflects: "If I hadn't been very rich, I might have been a really great man." A few years later he dies thinking of Rosebud.

Frederick Jackson Turner's 'The Significance of the Frontier in American History' (1893) had argued that in the process of westward expansion the United States had founded its uniquely democratic institutions and way of life, but by then the frontier had been finally conquered. In 1898 Kane, the frontier exile, champions the Spanish-American War as a patriotic cause through ludicrous fabricated news stories. This aspect of Kane's history is faithfully based

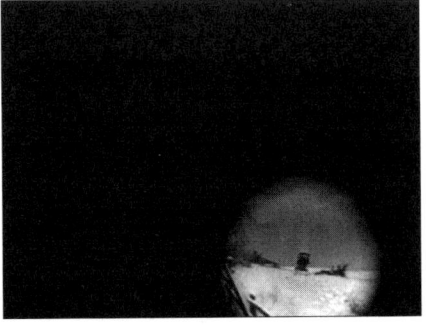

Kane in Colorado, 1871; the Ambersons and the Morgans in Indianapolis, 1904

on Hearst's press campaign.[23] Smyth argues that this shift from American expansionism to empire seems to represent the beginning of "national decay, a betrayal of [Kane's] western frontier 'childhood' and the Lincoln Republic".[24]

NOTES

1. Welles quoted in Bazin, Bitsch, and Domarchi, 'Interview with Orson Welles (II)', 64.
2. Michael Denning makes a similar connection between the Welles and Dos Passos projects; he considers the postwar thriller *The Stranger* the third volume in Welles's 'USA trilogy', although he admits only *Kane* "succeeds in uniting social content with formal experimentation". Denning, 'The Politics of Magic: Orson Welles's Allegories of Anti-Fascism', in James Naremore (ed.), *Orson Welles's Citizen Kane: A Casebook* (New York: Oxford University Press, 2004), 201–2.
3. Michael Denning, *The Cultural Front: The Laboring of American Culture in the Twentieth Century* (New York: Verso, 1998), 4–5. My chapter title is indebted to Denning's groundbreaking study.
4. Karl Radek quoted in David Caute, *Politics and the Novel During the Cold War* (New Brunswick: Transaction, 2010), 34.
5. John P. Diggins, 'Visions of Chaos and Visions of Order: Dos Passos as Historian', *American Literature*, Vol. 46, No. 3, November 1974, 331.
6. George Packer, 'The Spanish Prisoner', *New Yorker*, 31 October 2005, at http://www.newyorker.com/magazine/2005/10/31/the-spanish-prisoner (accessed 6 June 2015).
7. Parkinson.
8. Denning, 'The Politics of Magic: Orson Welles's Allegories of Anti-Fascism', 209.
9. FBI report quoted in Joseph McBride, *Whatever Happened to Orson Welles? A Portrait of an Independent Career* (Lexington: University Press of Kentucky, 2006), 45; Louis Pizzitola, *Hearst over Hollywood: Power, Passion, and Propaganda in the Movies* (New York: Columbia University Press, 2002), 370. Also see James Naremore, 'The Trial: The FBI vs. Orson Welles', *Film Comment*, Vol. 27, No. 1, January–February 1991, 22–7.
10. Denning, 'The Politics of Magic: Orson Welles's Allegories of Anti-Fascism', 199.
11. Robert L. Carringer, *The Making of Citizen Kane* (Berkeley: University of California Press, 1996), 111–7.
12. J. E. Smyth, *Reconstructing American Historical Cinema: From Cimarron to Citizen Kane* (Lexington: University Press of Kentucky, 2006), 325–6.
13. Welles and Bogdanovich, *This Is Orson Welles*, 84.
14. Carringer, *The Making of Citizen Kane*, 87–8.
15. Welles quoted in Denning, 'The Politics of Magic: Orson Welles's Allegories of Anti-

Fascism', 188.

16 Welles quoted in Catherine L. Benamou, *It's All True: Orson Welles's Pan-American Odyssey* (Berkeley: University of California Press, 2007), 186.
17 Robert Carringer, 'The Scripts of *Citizen Kane*', in Naremore (ed.), *Orson Welles's Citizen Kane: A Casebook*, 117.
18 Naremore, *The Magic World of Orson Welles*, 90.
19 The timeline is adapted from Robert L. Carringer, *The Magnificent Ambersons: A Reconstruction* (Berkeley: University of California Press, 1993), 39–41.
20 The source is the shooting script except where the film departs. Orson Welles and Herman J. Mankiewicz, *Citizen Kane* '3rd Revised Final' (16 July 1941). Orson Welles Manuscripts, Manuscripts Department, Lilly Library, Indiana University, Bloomington, Indiana (henceforth Lilly Library).
21 For an examination of the anachronistic iris shot, see David Bordwell, 'The Magnificent Ambersons: A Usable Past', www.davidbordwell.net, 30 May 2014, at http://www.davidbordwell.net/blog/2014/05/30/the-magnificent-ambersons-a-usable-past (accessed 7 June 2015).
22 Welles always gave Mankiewicz credit for the 'Rosebud' plot device, which he thought gimmicky. The snow globe as memory trigger was also possibly a Mankiewicz invention, as it occurs in the first draft, written by Mankiewicz with Houseman. See Carringer, 'The Scripts of *Citizen Kane*', 82.
23 Ben Proctor, *William Randolph Hearst: The Early Years, 1863–1910* (New York: Oxford University Press, 1998), 95–103.
24 Smyth, *Reconstructing American Historical Cinema*, 333–4.

CHAPTER 2

AN EMPIRE UPON AN EMPIRE
Citizen Kane (1941)

Citizen Kane retells the life of Charles Foster Kane (Orson Welles), one of America's wealthiest businessmen, in the format of a newsreel and as it can be gleaned from the stories of five witnesses. These are, in order of appearance, Kane's bank manager and guardian, Walter Parks Thatcher (George Coulouris), his second wife, Susan Alexander Kane (Dorothy Comingore), his general manager, Mr Bernstein (Everett Sloane), his friend Jedediah Leland (Joseph Cotten), and his valet, Raymond (Paul Stewart).

The film begins one night in 1941 at Xanadu, Kane's sprawling, unfinished estate on the Florida Gulf Coast. Kane mutters "Rosebud", drops a snow globe, and dies. We then see a rough cut of a newsreel obituary. Reporter Thompson (William Alland) is sent to interview Kane's former associates in the hope that solving the mystery of that final word will provide a personal insight the newsreel lacks.

Thompson approaches Susan at the El Rancho nightclub in Atlantic City, where she has been performing. Drunk, she refuses to talk, but the headwaiter (Gus Shilling) confides Susan does not know the meaning of "Rosebud".

An unpublished memoir by Thatcher lies in his grand memorial library in Philadelphia. In it, Thatcher recalls removing the boy Kane from his parents in 1871. Having come unexpectedly into great wealth from the proceeds of a gold mine, Mrs Kane's wish is that her son be educated privately and removed from the violence of his father. The boy dislikes Thatcher on sight and butts him with his snow sled.

Thatcher's narrative skips to about 1890, when Kane is twenty-five and now in possession of his inheritance. Kane decides to take over the day-to-day running of a minor asset, the *New York Inquirer*. Thatcher is soon appalled by Kane's muckraking attacks on copper barons, slum lords, and urban transit monopolies (the 'Traction Trust', in which Kane, ironically, has a large stake). Kane is also stoking war by falsely reporting "GALLEONS OF SPAIN OFF JERSEY COAST!" Confronted at the *Inquirer* offices by Thatcher in 1898, Kane declares his self-appointed "duty and privilege" as protector of the people, and his indifference to the newspaper's considerable financial losses.

Years pass, and during the Depression Kane has to give up control of his business to Thatcher. Thompson moves on to New York City. The elderly Mr Bernstein recalls Kane taking over the *Inquirer* in the 1890s and remaking its journalistic policies. Early on Kane prints a 'Declaration of Principles' which promises to defend the rights of the common people. By 1898 he has raised circulation of the *Inquirer* to beat its biggest competitor, the *Chronicle*, mainly by poaching its staff. In 1900 Kane marries Emily Norton, niece of the President.

The next interview subject is Jedediah Leland, Kane's bitter former best friend and a one-time 'dramatic critic' for Kane newspapers in New York and Chicago. Leland recalls Kane's first marriage to Emily. A montage of breakfasts between the years 1901 and 1909 shows the fading of affection and interest. Leland recalls how Kane met the twenty-two-year-old Susan Alexander in West Manhattan on a wet evening in 1915. Kane was on his way to explore his late mother's belongings in warehouse storage.

In 1916 Kane runs for state governor of New York against 'Boss' Jim Gettys (Ray Collins). Kane addresses a rally at Madison Square Garden and his chances seem strong. However, Gettys has discovered Kane's affair with Susan, makes Emily aware of it, and now attempts to blackmail Kane into pulling out of the race. Kane refuses. The affair is exposed in the *Chronicle* and Kane loses the election. Leland, critical of Kane's megalomania, asks to be reassigned to Chicago.

Kane divorces Emily, marries Susan in 1917, and by 1919 has built the Chicago Municipal Opera House to stage Susan's debut performance. Leland, as the *Chicago Inquirer*'s dramatic critic, begins to write a damning notice of her debut but passes out drunk. Kane finishes the review as Leland intended and then fires him.

Susan is now prepared to speak to Thompson. We see the dreariness of her enforced singing training, another view of her disastrous debut, her hysterical reaction to Leland's bad review, and her gruelling tour promoted by Kane's national network of metropolitan *Inquirer*s. Her opera career ends only with her suicide attempt. Thereafter she lives a bored life mostly assembling jigsaw puzzles at Xanadu. She finally walks out on Kane in 1932 because of his narcissism and inability to love.

Thompson's next interview is with Raymond at Xanadu, who remembers Kane destroying Susan's room after she leaves him. Her snow globe prompts him to mutter "Rosebud." Almost ten years later, in isolation in Xanadu, Kane dies after mysteriously muttering the word again.

Thompson fails in his quest to discover the meaning of the word. He speculates that "maybe Rosebud was something he couldn't get or something he lost, but it wouldn't have explained anything. I don't think any word explains a man's life."

The final shots show Kane's numerous possessions being catalogued or consigned to an incinerator. The sled from Colorado is thrown into the fire, and as it burns up we see the decal in close-up: "Rosebud".

* * *

The short film sequences intended as prologue and interludes for the stage production of *Too Much Johnson* constitute Welles's first, albeit unfinished, attempt to invent a cinematic city, in this case a stylised historical Manhattan. Film preservation scholar Scott Simmon notes how references in the playscript drafts and the "traffic mix of automobiles with horse-drawn carriages" in the film sequences fix the period setting at about 1910[1] – a transitional moment of urban history that Welles would properly explore a little over three years later in *The Magnificent Ambersons*.

Welles rewrote Gillette's 1894 sex farce by screwballising the dialogue. The silent film sequences were designed in tribute to vintage slapstick.[2] Welles and crew prepared by watching films by Mack Sennett, Charlie Chaplin, and Harold Lloyd. He later told one biographer that Lloyd's *Safety Last* (1923) had been a key reference.[3]

The prologue was meant to be a long chase sequence taken to comically absurd lengths: the characters run, crawl, and leap across the roofs and through *ad hoc* passageways in the industrial cityscape. One sequence was filmed in the now-vanished Little Syria section of the Lower West Side.[4] Working with cinematographer Harry Dunham, Welles obtained a variety of unusual shots to emphasise the dangers to Billings (Joseph Cotten) as he escapes the husband he has a cuckolded (Edgar Barrier).

Too Much Johnson (Unfinished, 1938)

Welles never finished editing the material, so it is difficult to come to definitive conclusions about the urban spatiality of his first cinematic city, and whether he would have remade geography as cavalierly as he did in later years. Nevertheless, the surviving workprint proves that before his Hollywood stint Welles had already explored the possibilities of location shooting, and did so while working completely outside Hollywood's industrial norms, apparently filming without a script.[5]

When Welles came to recreate historical New York again for *Citizen Kane* – this time the 1890s and the late 1910s – he did so with the full technical resources of a Hollywood studio and with contractually assured independence from executive oversight. Historical stock footage was used in a number of parts of the newsreel, but otherwise urban spaces were created in the studio. Urban exteriors are rare; in fact, usually limited to doorways and glimpses through windows. Some settings, including the Manhattan street where Kane first meets Susan, are conventional and slightly artificial backlot constructions, even though Welles films the set in unconventional long takes.

Welles's key creative collaborators in the production of *Kane* were cinematographer Gregg Toland and art director Perry Ferguson. Robert L. Carringer calls the trio the "creative nucleus of the production".⁶ Toland was not an RKO staff cinematographer. His contract with Samuel Goldwyn allowed him to shoot projects at other studios. He had worked for John Ford on *The Grapes of Wrath* and *The Long Voyage Home* (both 1940), and had won an Academy Award for William Wyler's *Wuthering Heights* (1939). He was a bold innovator and quietly instructed Welles in the fundamentals of cinematography. He'd seen Welles's stage version of *Julius Caesar* and was eager to experiment for *Citizen Kane*.⁷ Welles later lauded Toland at every opportunity.

Welles and Toland's visual scheme for *Kane* was dominated by high-contrast, deep-focus cinematography. The distortion produced by the very wide-angle lenses made close-ups tricky. Welles hardly used them, favouring long takes of carefully choreographed camera movement and blocking. Toland used extra-sensitive black-and-white film stock and arc lamps to light the various spatial planes of the deep image.⁸ Sharp from forefront to the far distance, the images were more in line with the tradition of German Expressionism than contemporary Hollywood conventions.⁹

Deep focus in *Citizen Kane:* the *Inquirer* newsroom (1916)

Carefully planned long takes ensured that only the essential fragments of the numerous sets required by the script needed to be built. Perry Ferguson, an RKO staff art director, marshalled a team of illustrators and draftsmen. Under Ferguson, the sets for *Kane* were built with exceptional economy – less than seven per cent of the overall cost of the film.¹⁰

A great deal of the world of *Kane* was created through special effects, including optical printing. Miniatures and matte paintings by Mario Larrinaga were sometimes used to complete fragmentary sets. Several shots of the exterior of the *New York Inquirer* building, for example, were a composite of built structures and matte painting.¹¹

* * *

Welles's collaborator on the *Kane* screenplay was Herman J. Mankiewicz, who had written scripts for the Campbell Playhouse and had worked on many Hollywood screenplays, often without screen credit. Robert Carringer's

The *Inquirer* exterior: sets and matte paintings

extensive archival study of the *Kane* drafts conclusively establishes that Welles contributed at least as substantially as Mankiewicz to what became the final shooting script – contrary to claims made by *New Yorker* critic Pauline Kael which attempted to elevate Mankiewicz to the status of sole author.[12] Mankiewicz's role had actually been to develop a rough draft. With help from John Houseman, Mankiewicz wrote the first two drafts of the screenplay in Victorville, California, in the spring of 1940. Carringer suggests Mankiewicz's first draft was heavily indebted to two published Hearst biographies, and that a "de-Hearstification of the material" would have been necessary for legal reasons alone. Welles's extensive rewrites fictionalised the characterisation of Kane, eliminating Mankiewicz's "*à clef* plotting". Nevertheless, the released version of the film was later subject to a plagiarism lawsuit by Ferdinand Lundberg, author of *Imperial Hearst* (1936), which was settled out of court.[13]

Surely with the intention of warding off the identification of Kane-as-Hearst, Welles elaborated his process of developing the character in a contemporary statement. Only published in full after his death, the statement is a typically diplomatic piece of game-playing, and Welles never mentions the tycoon by name.

Ignoring Mankiewicz's role in the early writing process, Welles wrote that his impulse had been to depict on film the "failure story" of a character who had in a long life exercised great power in American democracy – "a man imposing his will upon the will of his fellow countrymen" – and to show the "back stairs" aspect of that story. Not interested in pursuing the subject of a fictional president, Welles had to choose an individual with access to "some important channel of communication". Radio was too recent a technological invention; he therefore was forced to create a newspaper tycoon. And if this character resembled certain real-life yellow journalists at key moments in

American history, so be it: "I declined to fabricate an impossible or psychologically untrue reaction to American historical events." In fact, "[Kane's] dealings with [these historical] events were determined by dramaturgical and psychological laws which I recognize to be absolute. They were not colored by the facts in history. The facts in history were actually determined by the same laws which I employed as a dramatist." And on the matter of Kane as an impulsive collector of objects – Hearst shared this characteristic – Welles explains it as a necessary gimmick to explain the survival of Rosebud for seventy years.[14]

Hearst looms over *Citizen Kane*, first as the key biographical inspiration (despite early protests to the contrary) and eventually as its attempted censor. But what was widely perceived on release as a muckraking exposé of the private life of the tycoon is complicated and enriched by Welles's fictionalisation of the material.

George Hearst, born to a well-off slave-holding Missouri farming family in 1820, had built enormous wealth through mining investments in Nevada, Utah, Montana, and South Dakota. His son, William Randolph Hearst, was born in 1863. Expelled from Harvard, the younger Hearst took over his father's neglected *San Francisco Examiner* in 1887. He triumphantly boosted circulation by a combination of exploitative human interest stories, prize draws and giveaways, and crusades for populist causes such as better school systems and improved sewage and road infrastructure. He also campaigned against the Southern Pacific Railway.

Already a success in the newspaper business, Hearst entered the New York news market with the purchase of the failing *Morning Herald* in 1895, financed by the sale of the Hearst shares in Anaconda Copper. He repeated the process he had used so successfully in San Francisco to boost circulation. Deep-pocketed Hearst, heir to the family millions, poached top editorial staff from his main rival, Joseph Pulitzer's *Sunday World*, including the cartoonist Richard F. Outcault, creator of *The Yellow Kid*, which gave its name to the genre of 'yellow journalism'.

Hearst began to print totally false stories, especially about events in Cuba, in his campaign for the American government to launch what would become the Spanish-American War. By the late 1890s Hearst had moved away from direct day-to-day management of his papers and into the political arena as a campaigner and eventual Democratic candidate himself.[15]

In *Kane*, Thompson investigates the inner life of Charles Forster Kane. The rough cut of the newsreel is restricted to a summary of the publicly known facts about Charles Forster Kane, which are ambivalent. Who was Kane? What were his politics – communist, fascist, or merely "American"?

As J. E. Smyth has argued, *Kane* is a film about American historiography and the limits of contemporary forms of news reporting. "Rosebud" is thought to be the key that might unlock the real story of Charles Forster Kane. Welles's film of Thompson's quest becomes that real story. In this way the film is both historical fiction and a critique of historiography.[16]

A historiographical reading of *Kane* itself reveals the film's limits as a thinly disguised biography of Hearst – and, by extension, as American economic and industrial history. Kane's greatest crimes in the public sphere are irresponsible journalism, support for American imperialism, and links to European fascists; on a personal level he is a lonely man whose narcissistic need to be loved is not matched by a capacity to return it. It is a critical yet sympathetic portrait, not the radical film one might have expected from a prominent anti-fascist.

Naremore reflects that Kane may give us "the definitive satire of a certain American type" but he is presented "with a fascinating ambivalence, using Freud as much as Marx in order to understand him".[17] The newsreel tells of Kane's "empire upon an empire", ultimately encompassing many and varied industries. It was "an empire through which for fifty years flowed, in an unending stream, the wealth of the earth's third richest goldmine". But after Kane seizes on the *Inquirer* as his vocation, we do not hear again of the western source of the capital that drives his urban newspaper business, initially at a loss of a million dollars a year.

Hearst was similarly obsessed with the newspaper business at an early age and rejected his father's proposals that he assume managing ownership of the family ranches in Mexico and California, the Anaconda copper mine in Montana, or the Homestake gold mine in South Dakota.[18] Before World War I, Hearst papers had at least publicly supported unions and progressive reforms. In later years, particularly during the administration of Franklin D. Roosevelt, his newspapers openly took the side of big business over organised labour.[19] Ferdinand Lundberg's muckraking biography, supposedly one of Mankiewicz's key sources, argued that all along Hearst had been anti-labour in his business practices. Hearst had connections to union-baiting Chicago gangsters and exploited his workers at the Homestake mine in South Dakota. With his army of newsboys, Hearst was "the biggest employer of child labor in the United States, and one of the biggest foes of a Child Labor Amendment to the Constitution." Lundberg claimed that hired thugs beat striking newsboys at Hearst's instigation.[20]

Even worse were the conditions in the Cerro de Pasco copper mine in Peru, partly owned by Hearst along with various New York banking interests (including J. P. Morgan), where miners worked in conditions of near-slavery.[21]

The earliest Mankiewicz drafts depict a more violent milieu. Kane appears to be responsible for the murder of one of Susan's would-be lovers, a sequence based on Hearst's connection to the mysterious death of the film director Thomas H. Ince. Kane's son dies not in an automobile accident with his mother but as a member of a fascist militia.[22] But the final version of *Kane* focuses on the fictional tycoon's relationship with Susan Alexander, which Naremore reads as a symbol for Kane's treatment of society as a whole.[23] Welles's revisions and also his performance create a more sympathetic portrait of the powerful tycoon, a man capable of tender moments, even if they are usually self-pitying and narcissistic.

* * *

Attempting to identify the *Morning Herald* with the interests of the people of New York City, Hearst campaigned for municipal ownership of essential utilities from the 1890s. In February 1899 he presented a plan for 'An American Internal Policy' that included the "destruction of criminal trusts" in oil, steel, copper, beef, timber, and railroads, and advocated for the "public ownership of public franchises" including water, gas, and rapid transit. Other causes included improvement of public schools and "expansionism without imperialism". That year the paper successfully attacked the Amsterdam Light & Gas Company and drove down the price of gas in New York City. It fought and defeated the predatory Ramapo Water Trust in its attempt to secure a twenty-year contract to supply water to the city. The next year Hearst papers exposed Mayor Van Wyck's corrupt involvement with the American Ice Company – the Ice Trust.[24]

Hearst's campaigns for public control of urban infrastructure went on for decades. In 1917 he managed to launch a stooge, John F. Hylan, into the mayor's office of New York City. When in office, Mayor Hylan fought the Interborough Rapid Transit and Brooklyn Rapid Transit companies over fare increases.[25]

Elements of Hearst's historical involvement in New York's urban development survive intact in *Citizen Kane*, which depicts the *Inquirer* campaigning for municipal ownership of transit and essential utilities, and against slum lords in the 1890s. We never see the masses who will benefit from Kane's campaigns. The fight is seen via a montage from the perspective of one of the paper's "most devoted readers", Walter P. Thatcher. His infuriation grows as he reads a succession of *Inquirer* headlines. In 1925 Thatcher will label Kane a communist for such activities to a congressional investigation committee (the shooting script calls the scene a "reproduction of existing J. P. Morgan newsreel"[26]).

By identifying with the interests of the impoverished urban working class – even, as he acknowledges, against his own financial interests – Charles Foster Kane angles for saviour status. He explains to Thatcher: "I have money and property. If I don't defend the interests of the underprivileged, somebody else will – maybe somebody *without* any money or any property – and that would be too bad."

Thatcher is also outraged by Kane's baseless provocations to encourage war with Spain over Cuba. Kane's directive to his bemused Cuban correspondent – "you provide the prose poems, I'll provide the war" – may be an apocryphal Hearst paraphrase but it is an accurate indication of Hearst's *modus operandi*.

Kane winds up central to shaping the dawning American empire. After his death, Mr Bernstein shrugs off Kane's war-mongering and looks at the legacy; he wonders "do you think if it hadn't been for [the Spanish-American] war, we'd have the Panama Canal?"

* * *

The 'News on the March' rough cut credits Kane at his peak with "thirty-seven newspapers, two syndicates, a radio network – an empire upon an empire". The empire is presented by an animated map with pulsing beacons to signify urban centres of Kane's newspaper and radio production. This is a simpler and more effective version of the animation described in the shooting script: "Starting from New York, miniature newsboys speed madly to Chicago, Detroit, St Louis, Los Angeles, San Francisco, Washington, Atlanta, El Paso, etc."[27] A reverse of that animation occurs when the Depression starts to choke the Kane empire.

The synoptic impression in this early part of the film efficiently conveys Kane's reach. We see representative images of the various Kane businesses – "grocery stores, paper mills, apartment buildings, factories, forests, ocean liners". But as Kane tells Thatcher, he is interested in newspapers.

In an editorial published in the *New York Journal* on the last day of 1899, Hearst declared that the newspaper's democratic role was not to be limited to mere Fourth Estate oversight of the powerful. He advocated something more startling and radical: "Government by newspaper". He argued that dominant newspaper circulation was synonymous with a mandate for political leadership – that citizens voted their support for or opposition to the paper's editorial line on a daily basis by purchasing the paper, a kind of daily referendum, a far more sensitive register of the public will than the electoral process. Hearst predicted that with this revolution in the twentieth century "we shall see the press fulfill its noble calling, and as the mouthpiece of the people, rule, regulate, and reform the world". It was an alarming conflation of the market appeal of his scandal sheet with the democratic process.

Hearst regularly took over what would normally have been municipal responsibilities, often with great generosity but always waving the banner of his newspapers, asserting their central position in urban life. Hearst papers had organised and paid for the inauguration celebrating the 1897 Greater New York City charter, which incorporated the four outer boroughs with Manhattan, making New York the second-largest metropolis on earth; his charitable works included disaster relief – particularly in the wake of the 1906 San Francisco earthquake and fire – and clothing, housing, coal, and meals for the poor during New York's worst winters.[28]

Charles Foster Kane pursues an equally megalomaniacal equation of the *Inquirer*'s editorial line with the interests of "the people". In the early 1890s, still dissatisfied with his renovations to the format of the *Inquirer*, Kane tells Bernstein and Leland, "There's something I've got to get into this paper besides pictures and print. I've got to make the *New York Inquirer* as important to New York as the gas [fuelling the light in my office]."

Stepping out of the editorial shadows, Kane composes a front-page 'Declaration of Principles'. He asserts his commitment to honest reporting and to championing the rights of his readers "as citizens and as human beings". Kane, as the film will illustrate, is the sole decider of what constitutes honesty as well as the rights of the masses, and he expects a wave of love from the people in return. Years later, when Kane loses the election and wallows in self-pity, Leland upbraids him:

> You talk about the people as though you own them. As though they belong to you. As long as I can remember you've talked about giving the people their rights, as if you could make them a present of liberty, as a reward for services rendered.

Leland knows organised labour is growing in power, and Kane is psychologically ill-equipped to accept anything but a paternal role in relation to the "working man".

The life cycle of newspapers

AN EMPIRE UPON AN EMPIRE

Kane's choice of gaslight as a model for the newspaper is visionary. It departs from Hearst's cynical, self-interested reinvention of democracy as 'government by newspaper'. Kane's comparison with gaslight implies a reimagining of the newspaper as an essential utility within the public infrastructure. Various shots, scattered across the film and taken from different periods of the city's history, disjointedly depict the stages of newspaper production and distribution through the built urban spaces of New York City. The commodity is news, but the material commodity is paper: we see giant rolls in Kane's paper mills, the work of typesetters and compositors, the printing presses, bound stacks of finished papers, a newsboy on a corner,[29] readers in public spaces, and finally discarded pages in the dirty streets. Welles several times incorporates paper detritus into his *mise-en-scène*, including the crushed campaign streamers after Kane's electoral defeat in 1916 (paper detritus is a symbolic element in several subsequent films, notably *Touch of Evil*). Under Kane's control, newspapers are flushed through the city as daily vehicles for his megalomania.

* * *

Hearst was elected to Congress for a single term as representative of New York's 11th District in 1903. After that he campaigned for sympathetic figures such as Mayor Hylan.[30] Kane's political campaign for state governor in 1916 backfires with the exposure of his love affair with Susan Alexander. Through with the democratic political process, awash in self-pity after his abandonment by the

The Chicago Municipal Opera House in *Citizen Kane*

people, he attempts to remake the urban landscape in the image of his own vanity. His first step is to construct the $3 million Chicago Municipal Opera House as a venue for Susan's disastrous opera debut. Welles makes an economical choice: the only exterior glimpse is an architectural drawing in the style of the working drawings Perry Ferguson's department had created.

Ultimately Kane retreats from the city to the Florida Gulf Coast, where he constructs his never-finished estate, Xanadu: as Leland says, "He was disappointed in the world so he built one of his own, an absolute monarchy. Something bigger than an opera house, anyway."

NOTES

1. Scott Simmon, 'Too Much Johnson in Context', National Film Preservation Foundation, 2014, 2, at http://www.filmpreservation.org/userfiles/image/preserved-films/TMJ-press-photos/TMJ-workprint-essay.pdf (accessed 7 June 2015).
2. Simmons, 'Too Much Johnson in Context', 2.
3. Frank Brady, Citizen Welles: A Biography of Orson Welles (New York: Scribner's, 1989), 147.
4. McBride, 'Too Much Johnson: Recovering Orson Welles's Dream of Early Cinema'.
5. The Too Much Johnson sequences never graduated beyond the editing room. They were not screened even during the initial theatrical production in 1938, and the workprint was thought destroyed in a fire at Welles's house outside Madrid in August 1970. In one of the miracles of film archaeology, Welles's nitrate workprint was rediscovered in an Italian warehouse, identified definitively in 2012, and restored and screened to acclaim in 2013. See Simmons, 'Too Much Johnson in Context', 1.
6. Carringer, The Making of Citizen Kane, 40.
7. Carringer, The Making of Citizen Kane, 66–72.
8. Berthome and Thomas, Orson Welles at Work, 51.
9. James Naremore, 'Style and Meaning in Citizen Kane', in Naremore (ed.), Orson Welles's Citizen Kane: A Casebook, 132.
10. Carringer, The Making of Citizen Kane, 65.
11. Carringer, The Making of Citizen Kane, 87–99.
12. See Pauline Kael, 'Raising Kane', introduction to The Citizen Kane Book (Boston: Little, Brown, 1971).
13. Carringer, The Making of Citizen Kane, 81, 98, 117, 155n12.
14. Orson Welles, 'Orson Welles on His Purpose in Making Citizen Kane', in Ronald Gottesman

(ed.), *Perspectives on Citizen Kane* (New York: G. K. Hall, 1996), 23–5.
15 Proctor, *William Randolph Hearst: The Early Years*, 4–7, 49, 76, 77, 138, 142.
16 Smyth, *Reconstructing American Historical Cinema*, 329, 335.
17 James Naremore, 'Introduction', in Naremore (ed.), *Orson Welles's Citizen Kane: A Casebook*, 9.
18 Proctor, *William Randolph Hearst: The Early Years*, 43.
19 Ben Proctor, *William Randolph Hearst: The Later Years, 1911–1951* (New York: Oxford University Press, 2007), 247–8.
20 Ferdinand Lundberg, *Imperial Hearst: A Social Biography* (New York: Modern Library, 1936), 196.
21 See Naremore, 'Introduction', in Naremore (ed.), *Orson Welles's Citizen Kane: A Casebook*, 9–11; and Lundberg, *Imperial Hearst*, 174–80.
22 Carringer, 'The Scripts of *Citizen Kane*', 88–9.
23 Naremore, 'Style and Meaning in *Citizen Kane*', 153–4.
24 Proctor, *William Randolph Hearst: The Early Years*, 146–8, 154.
25 Zachary M. Schrag suggests in both Hearst and Hylan "a sincere and progressive hostility towards monopolies with a demagogic willingness to oversimplify economics for the sake of getting votes". See Schrag, '"The Bus Is Young and Honest": Transportation Politics, Technical Choice, and the Motorization of Manhattan Surface Transit, 1919–1936', *Technology and Culture*, Vol. 41, No. 1, January 2000, 51–79.
26 Welles and Mankiewicz, *Citizen Kane* '3rd Revised Final', 10.
27 Welles and Mankiewicz, *Citizen Kane* '3rd Revised Final', 9.
28 Proctor, *William Randolph Hearst: The Early Years*, 112, 137, 148.
29 Admittedly the only shot of a newsboy in *Citizen Kane* is of one selling the rival *Chronicle*.
30 Proctor, *William Randolph Hearst: The Later Years*, 62.

CHAPTER 3

THE DARKENING MIDLAND
The Magnificent Ambersons (1942)

> It lives on as the truest, cruelest picture of the growth of the Middle West and the liveliest portrait left to us of the people who made it grow. It's better than a good book.
>
> – Orson Welles[1]

None other of Orson Welles's films so explicitly concerns the transformation of a city as *The Magnificent Ambersons*. For his second feature production, Welles was again able to exploit RKO's studio resources to reimagine American urban history on screen. This time a much larger percentage of the budget was devoted to the construction of elaborate and spatially comprehensive sets.[2] He worked with a new art director and cinematographer, respectively Mark-Lee Kirk and Stanley Cortez, and although the results were spectacular, the collaboration proved a less happy experience for Welles than the *Kane* collaboration with Ferguson and Toland. He eventually fired Cortez, supposedly for slowness, and the film went substantially over budget.[3]

Welles had typically loaded himself with projects following the May 1941 release of *Citizen Kane*. He'd already adapted Arthur Calder-Marshall's recent thriller *The Way to Santiago*, and had commissioned draft scripts for segments of his gestating anthology film *It's All True*. In the summer, at RKO's request, Welles and Joseph Cotten co-wrote an adaptation of Eric Ambler's thriller *Journey into Fear*. Welles later denied he was ever going to direct that film, but it seems to have been his original plan.[4] He was also developing a script based on the case of the French serial wife-murderer Henri Désiré Landru that later became Charlie Chaplin's *Monsieur Verdoux* (1947). In September 'My Friend Bonito', an episode of *It's All True*, began production in Mexico under the supervisory direction of Norman Forster. Welles had visited Mexico briefly that month before the shoot and intended to share a co-directing credit with Foster.[5] From 15 September he produced, directed, and starred in *The Orson Welles Show*, a weekly CBS radio variety programme.

Welles had already adapted Booth Tarkington's novel *The Magnificent Ambersons* (1918) for a 1939 *Campbell Playhouse* radio broadcast. Welles's final script for the film adaptation was dated 7 October 1941, three weeks before the commencement of production. The Japanese attack on Pearl Harbor on 7 December changed Welles's priorities and forced him to re-evaluate his current film commitments. Nelson Rockefeller, who headed the Office of the Coordinator of Inter-American Affairs (OCIAA) under President Roosevelt, asked Welles to travel to South America in early February as a Good Will Ambassador for the Good Neighbor Policy. Rockefeller was also a stockholder on the RKO board of directors. In response to a request from the Brazilian government, the OCIAA invited Welles to film Rio de Janeiro's 1942 Carnaval. Welles decided to incorporate this mooted Carnaval documentary into his evolving *It's All True*, which now obtained United States government co-sponsorship, with the OCIAA guaranteeing $300,000 against any RKO losses. Welles would work in South America without a salary, although his expenses would be paid. The idea was to strengthen Pan-American unity against fascism.[6]

Rio's Carnaval would start on 8 February, so Welles had to finish his Hollywood work ahead of schedule. Norman Foster was brought back to the United States just before Christmas, which forever postponed completion of 'My Friend Bonito'. He was assigned to direct *Journey into Fear* starting 6 January. Welles performed his supporting role as Colonel Haki at night while continuing to film on *The Magnificent Ambersons* by day.

Principal photography of *Ambersons* wrapped on 22 January, with a few additional shots made in the days before Welles left Hollywood on 2 February. For three days in Miami, with the clock ticking down to his departure to Brazil, he worked on post-production with editor Robert Wise. The studio agreed to send Wise to Brazil to work on the film with Welles, but this proved impossible during wartime.[7]

On 11 March Wise sent a 131-minute print of *Ambersons* to Rio de Janeiro.[8] A typed cutting continuity of this lost version – a shot-by-shot transcription of the editing – was made at RKO on 12 March.[9] The continuity has survived as the most detailed record of the longest version of the film before it was altered, partially reshot, and progressively shortened by RKO.

Whereas *Kane* uses a multiple flashback structure to dance across its seventy years of history, the action of *The Magnificent Ambersons* progresses chronologically from 1885 to 1912, with a narrator – Welles himself – looking back from the vantage of a modernity positioned somewhere between 1918 and 1942. Like Tarkington's, Welles's narrator makes a direct identification with the audience.

The 131-minute version begins in 1884 when Eugene Morgan (Joseph Cotten), experimenter in automobiles, embarrasses himself attempting to woo Isabel Amberson (Dolores Costello) with a serenade: he falls drunkenly through his bass viol under her window. Isabel's fragile sense of propriety is offended and she marries instead the dull Wilbur Minafer (Don Dillaway). The town gossip predicts the offspring of this loveless marriage will be the "worst spoiled lot of children this town will ever see". As it turns out, there is only one child, a "princely terror" named George Amberson Minafer. George's childhood fights with the townsfolk are gently tolerated by his weak parents. In 1902 George (Tim Holt) returns from school and demonstrates his bullying arrogance in retaking leadership of the 'Friends of the Ace' society.

Two years later the Ambersons host a Christmastide ball in honour of George, home from his sophomore year at college. At the ball Isabel is reunited with Eugene, by now a successful businessman in the emerging automobile industry. A widower, he introduces his pretty daughter, Lucy (Anne Baxter). Eugene and Isabel are chastely entranced with one another, and George in turn attempts to court Lucy, all the while condescending to her father and his involvement in automobiles.

Wilbur dies shortly after Christmas. His spinster sister Fanny (Agnes Moorehead), who lives with the Ambersons, mourns both her brother and her lost chance with Eugene now that Isabel is free. The next year Fanny is dismayed by Isabel's closeness with Eugene. George and Isabel's brother Jack (Ray Collins) tease that Eugene is really scheming for Fanny's hand and drive her to tears. Meanwhile, the patriarch, Major Amberson (Richard Bennett), has begun to subdivide the grounds of his estate, to his grandson George's horror and bewilderment.

Lucy refuses to accept George's proposal of marriage because of his disdain for work and lack of ambition. George interprets this as the imposition of her father's values, and later fantasises that Lucy grovels in apology to him and renounces her father. During a dinner, George insults Eugene indirectly by dismissing the very invention of the automobile. Eugene is unruffled, ambivalent himself about the technology's effects on civilisation.

Fanny approves of George's attack on Eugene; she chooses to interpret it as a defence of his mother's reputation against unseemly town gossip. The self-obsessed George has been ignorant of talk that the romance between Isabel and Eugene preceded Wilbur's death – ignorant, it turns out, of any romance at all. Absurdly over-sensitive about his family's reputation, George attacks Mrs Johnson, the town gossip, and is resolutely against his mother's marriage to Eugene. He bars Eugene from visiting Isabel and demands she renounce her true love. Uncle Jack cannot persuade George to butt out. Isabel agrees to depart with her son for a long period abroad. When George farewells Lucy, she feigns cheerful ignorance of George's manoeuvers.

In 1910 Jack Amberson relays the news to Eugene and Lucy that Isabel has fallen ill during her long absence. When Isabel returns to Indianapolis that year, she is close to death. George once again prevents Eugene from seeing her. She dies, followed shortly by her elderly father.

The Amberson finances are in disarray. Major Amberson died without having deeded the mansion to his children, and Jack and Aunt Fanny have each lost their own money investing in a headlamp company. In 1911 the remaining three must vacate the mansion. Jack departs by train to Washington to find a consulship that will see out his remaining days. As George walks home from the station, he is shocked by the ugly, empty, alien city. In the lonely mansion he begs forgiveness of his dead mother. Then Fanny hysterically reveals she is broke. In order to support Fanny's upkeep at her preferred boarding house, George abandons a low-paid but respectable job at a law office to take an immediately lucrative job dealing with dangerous chemicals.

Meanwhile, Lucy has renounced romance and decided to live with her father. In 1912, George is hit by a car and laid up in hospital. Eugene hears the news while in his factory. We see him enter and leave the hospital, then proceed to Fanny's boarding house. Eugene tells Fanny that George has asked for forgiveness. It also seems Lucy and George will now be married after all. Fanny is listless and disinterested. Eugene leaves the boarding house alone.[10]

* * *

This lost and longest version of *The Magnificent Ambersons*, which has become the Holy Grail for film lovers, can only be considered a provisional cut based on Welles's instructions as of early March. In fact, before Welles had received his copy of this print, on which he intended to base his editorial responses, he had already requested the deletion of the long section spanning the years 1905 to 1911, probably in response to the studio's complaints about the film's length. The exile of George and Isabel would be replaced by a short new bridging scene to be directed by Wise: Isabel would die suddenly in 1905 after George's refusal to give his blessing to her marriage. Welles obtained a print of Wise's new scene before 25 March, when he wrote to his business manager, Jack Moss, to criticise its quality. He asked for Norman Foster to reshoot the scene.

Meanwhile, a different version running 110 minutes – three scenes had been removed at the request of George Schaefer – was prepared for a 17 March preview in Pomona, California. The film was presented as part of a double bill with a patriotic musical, *The Fleet's In*, and a concluding in-person appearance by actor James Cagney. The audience's comment cards in response to the *Ambersons* preview were mixed, although the negative comments and the general atmosphere discouraged RKO's executives.[11]

A second preview in Pasadena on 20 March seems to have reverted to the 131-minute version. Despite the more enthusiastic audience reception, RKO maintained that the film needed substantial revision before release. Ultimately RKO, in the middle of an executive power struggle, relied upon Wise, Cotten, Moss, and first assistant director Freddie Fleck – all Welles associates now working independently and counter to his instructions – to write and direct eleven minutes of replacement scenes. From afar Welles tried to retain authority, but RKO mostly ignored him. The final cut of the film – the only one to have survived – is a mere 88 minutes. Many of Welles's surviving scenes were altered, shortened, or moved to different places within the film's structure. Inferior new music by Roy Webb supplemented what remained of Bernard Herrmann's score; the loyal and uncompromising Herrmann insisted his name be removed from the credits. The non-Welles elements only diminish the film's dramatic power, coherence, and continuity. The film was approved for release and premiered in Welles's absence on 10 July 1942, on a double bill with the slightly less ambitious *Mexican Spitfire Sees a Ghost*. By then Shaefer had been ousted from his position as studio head.[12] His successor, Charles Koerner, ordered the destruction of *Amberson*'s outtakes later that year.[13] The

131-minute print sent to Welles was left behind in Rio and languished for a time at Cinédia Studios. It was probably destroyed in line with RKO's instructions around 1945.[14]

Ambersons – like all of Welles's subsequent Hollywood films except for the two versions of *Macbeth* (1948 and 1950) – is impossible to consider a finished work by Orson Welles. But thanks to the investigative work of Peter Bogdanovich, Robert L. Carringer, Jonathan Rosenbaum, and others, extensive documentation about the longest version has been recovered and published. This research has drawn on the shooting script, the cutting continuity, still photographs, and frame enlargements from the cut sequences. Bernard Herrmann's complete score manuscript also survived and has been re-recorded commercially.

Many of the cuts and alterations by RKO weakened the status of *Ambersons* as a city film. Mostly faithful to the Tarkington novel, the provisional 131-minute version maintained emphasis on the transformation of the material structures of Indianapolis amid the rise of the automobile. The RKO release version diminishes that emphasis. Fortunately Wise retained the dinner scene where the characters discuss the impact of automobile-based suburbanisation on real estate values in the old town centre, undoubtedly because it is a key moment in the dramatic conflict between George and Eugene. The film's other reflective moments about the changing urban landscape were deemed least essential to the basic story of a wealthy family evaporating amid death and financial ruin.[15]

These deletions include discussions between Isabel, Lucy, George, Jack, and Fanny as they ride in Eugene's automobile through the snow on the outskirts of town at Christmas, 1904. Their distance allows a perspective on its changes:

> ISABEL: When we get this far out you can see there's quite a little smoke hanging over town.
> JACK: Yes, that's because the town's growing.
> EUGENE: Yes, and as it grows bigger it seems to get ashamed of itself, so it makes that big cloud and hides in it.
> ISABEL: Oh, Eugene.
> EUGENE: You know, Isabel, I think it used to be nicer…

As they drive on George notices that "those fences are smeared!"

LUCY: That must be from soot.

FANNY: Yes ... there're so many houses around here now.

GEORGE: Grandfather owns a good many of them, I guess ... for renting.

FANNY: He sold most of the lots, George.

GEORGE: He ought to keep things up better. It's getting all too much built up. Riffraff! He lets ... these people take too many liberties. They do anything they want to...

The subplot concerning the gradual subdivision of Major Amberson's estate was almost entirely cut. Following the surviving scene in the Amberson kitchen, after George and Jack tease Aunt Fanny about Eugene's intentions, George was to have been startled by a vision through the window. He runs into the rain to examine "excavations under the raging storm, partly erected buildings in the background". Uncle Jack follows in pursuit.

GEORGE: What is this? Looks like excavations... Looks like the foundations for a lot of houses! Just what does grandfather mean by this? (*He rushes toward the building sites, Jack following.*)

JACK: My private opinion is he wants to increase his income by building these houses to rent. For gosh sakes, come in ... out of the rain...

GEORGE: Can't he increase his income any other way but this?

JACK: It would appear he couldn't. I wanted him to put up... (*Jack tries to put up an umbrella over both of them.*) ... an apartment building instead of these houses.

GEORGE (*shouting*): An apartment building! Here!

JACK (*shouting*): Yes, that was my idea.

GEORGE (*shouting*): An apartment house! (*George looks to right, shocked, water streaming down his face.*) Oh, my gosh!

JACK (*off*): Don't worry ... your grandfather wouldn't listen to me, but he'll wish he had, some day.

GEORGE: But why didn't he sell something or other, rather than do a thing like this?

JACK: I believe he *had* sold something or other, from time to time.

George is ignorant of the family's declining wealth. Major Amberson's speech on the town "rolling right over" his heart survived in RKO's version, but a few lines of subsequent conversation with Jack were cut. The Major complains about "those devilish workmen yelling around my house and digging up my lawn". Jack advises: "When things are a nuisance, it's a good idea not to keep remembering 'em." That elected obliviousness proves to be the Amberson style, and it will be their downfall. Also cut: in 1910, during George and Isabel's absence, Major Amberson and Aunt Fanny sit on the porch of the mansion and observe those houses recently built on Amberson property:

> MAJOR: Funny thing – these new houses were built only a year ago. They look old already … cost enough money, though… I guess I should have built those apartments, after all.
> FANNY: Housekeeping in a house is harder than in an apartment.
> MAJOR: Yes. Where the smoke and dirt are as thick as they are in the Amberson Addition, I guess the women can't stand it. Well, I've got one painful satisfaction – I got my tax lowered.

His satisfaction is painful because the tax reduction merely reflects the decline in the overall value of his properties. Prices are high in the periphery of the growing city where Eugene and Lucy live, and also apparently in the town centre, but not in the declining Amberson Addition.

Dialogue was changed in the sequence where Jack visits Eugene and Lucy in their "Georgian instead of nondescript Romanesque" version of the Amberson Mansion in the upland Indianapolis suburbs. Jack was to have originally commented on the inner-city pollution the Morgans had escaped. George's last walk home to the mansion through the "strange streets of a strange city" was shortened, and the final sequence was completely rescripted and reshot to eliminate Eugene and Fanny's talk in the boarding house, and the grim shots of Eugene driving away into the anonymity of the twentieth-century city.

* * *

> That small city, the Indianapolis where I was born, exists no more than Carthage existed after the Romans had driven ploughs over the ground where it had stood. Progress swept all the old life away.
>
> – Booth Tarkington[16]

Tarkington's *Magnificent Ambersons* is the middle novel between *The Turmoil* (1915) and *The Midlander* (1923) in a trilogy he later republished in a single volume called *Growth*. Tarkington was born in Indianapolis in 1869. The city began to rapidly transform around the time he reached maturity. His comparison with the razing of Carthage was hyperbole, of course, but of a piece with Tarkington's conservative myth of Indianapolis's decline.

The Turmoil begins with a racist and apocalyptic rant against the spirit of 'Bigness' that had flooded a midland city with new people: "The negroes came from the South by the thousands and thousands, multiplying by other thousands and thousands faster than they could die." Immigrants came from across the world; Tarkington itemises twenty-three nationalities or races and adds "every hybrid that these could propagate. And if there were no Eskimos nor Patagonians, what other human strain that earth might furnish failed to swim and bubble in this crucible?" The modernising streets were soon filled with "a cockney type [...] a cynical young mongrel barbaric of feature, muscular and cunning".[17]

African-Americans, long-time residents of Indianapolis, play no crucial part in the novel of *The Magnificent Ambersons*. Stereotypical "darkey" servants are mere cheerful period detail, recalled in a narrative voice that consequently excludes a black readership. *Ambersons* won the Pulitzer Prize and was a bestseller, making its appeal to the nostalgia of a white, middle-class readership for an idealised pre-urban way of life. For most of that initial readership, the 1880s and 1890s were still within living memory. That topicality probably explains the book's relative obscurity by 1942.[18]

While Welles remained a great admirer of Tarkington's fiction, he was aware of the author's limitations. He admitted in 1970 that Tarkington's children were "hopelessly dated now" in comparison to the characters of Mark Twain, "who wasn't writing about children in a middle-class atmosphere [...] on Main Street under the shadow of the elms".[19] But Welles claimed on several occasions that his father had been Tarkington's friend and that it had "long been a family assumption that the author had my father in mind when he created [the character Eugene Morgan]".[20] No evidence has emerged beyond Welles's anecdotes to support a record of this friendship or inspiration, but Welles clearly found a deeply personal resonance in Tarkington's novel. On several occasions Welles recalled childhood visits to the town of Grand Detour, Illinois, where his father ran the Sheffield Hotel. It was the "one place" he desired to return:

> Where I do see some kind of 'Rosebud', perhaps, is in that world of Grand Detour. A childhood there was like a childhood back in the 1870s. No electric

The Sheffield Hotel in Grand Detour, Illinois
owned by Richard Head Welles and destroyed by fire in 1928

light, horse-drawn buggies – a completely anachronistic, old-fashioned, early-Tarkington, rural kind of life [...] Grand Detour was one of those lost worlds, one of those Edens that you get thrown out of. It really was kind of invented by my father. He's the one who kept out the cars and the electric lights. It was one of the 'Merrie Englands.' [...] I feel as though I've had a childhood in the last century from those short summers.[21]

Welles probably confounded his followers on the left with this nostalgic, tender, and vastly forgiving reverie on declining nouveau aristocracy from a firmly bourgeois and, even by 1942, antiquated point of view. It is true that Welles's narration, judiciously edited from Tarkington's own third-person text, is given enhanced irony in the early scenes when juxtaposed with comic images of the town's customs. But except for its conclusion and avoidance of the book's overt racism, the 131-minute version of *Ambersons* is a faithful adaptation of Tarkington's novel. Welles's film acquiesces to Tarkington's conservative myth of the midland town's "spreading and darkening" into a city. It's an indication of Welles's priorities in adaptation.

The power of Welles's drama overcomes a nagging question: why is the passing of the Ambersons' "magnificence" worth lamenting? The family contribute little to the city apart from symbol, spectacle, and ritual. Uncle Jack Amberson is only a US congressman because "the family always like to have somebody in congress", according to George. Eugene's uncritical, decades-long glorification of Isabel Amberson is a mystery. Superficial in her early rejection of him for his drunken serenade, she verges on idiotic in her vague passivity.

Aunt Fanny Minafer is emotionally warped by bitterness, vindictiveness, and self-pity. And George is no more than an uncritical vehicle for his class's prejudices – certainly no tragic hero.

The decline and fall of this short-lived nouveau aristocratic family – three generations and bust – is the surface melodrama pasted onto the story of the transforming midland town. The cause of the Ambersons' fall is their obliviousness to the coming of modernity. Major Amberson makes some effort to stave off the family's financial decline when with reluctance he subdivides his estate in the Amberson Addition. Everybody else, except for the sardonic realist Jack, is oblivious to the changes until they hit hard. George's "comeupance" is merely the vanishing of his wealth and privilege and his alienation from the modern city.

Welles's lost conclusion wildly departs from Tarkington's silly fantasy of Eugene contacting the dead Isabel through a medium. The final scene of the film was probably the reason Joseph Cotten negatively assessed the mood of the film as "more Chekhov than Tarkington".[22] Eugene visits Fanny in her run-down boarding house and, as Welles later described it,

> There's just nothing left between them at all. Everything is over – her feelings and her world and his world; everything is buried under the parking lots and the cars. That's what it was all about – the deterioration of personality, the way people diminish with age, and particularly with impecunious old age. The end of the communication between people, as well as the end of an era.[23]

This conclusion seems to have left a powerfully bleak impression at the previews – the obliteration of people by the growth of a modern city – and RKO refused to accept it.

* * *

Ambersons is not a western – it might be considered the finest example of a *Mid*western – but it adapts a key trope from the genre. The coming of the transcontinental railroad to the frontier had been "the dominant symbol of progress" in westerns such as *The Iron Horse* (John Ford, 1924), *The Union Pacific* (Cecil B. DeMille, 1939), and *Dodge City* (Michael Curtiz, 1939).[24] In *Kane* the railway connects the Colorado frontier back east to Chicago and New York, to the moneyed soullessness represented by Thatcher. The coming of the automobile to Indianapolis in *Ambersons* has the same symbolic function as the herald of modernity.

Welles created Indianapolis's 'National Avenue' at the RKO Ranch in the San Fernando Valley.[25] Like the few exterior street sets in *Kane*, the avenue has the slightly artificial appearance of a Hollywood backlot. Welles enlivens the *mise-en-scène* by emphasising various period-signifying components of the streetscape. The scenes of the turn of the century employ generic motifs of the western: a wagon wheel, the period costumes of the townsfolk, the town's bank and hardware store, and one of several horse-drawn carts George drives in the movie.

1

2

3

4

The town in 1894 (figs 1–2) and 1902 (figs. 3–4)

For the later scenes in 1905 and 1912, National Avenue is modernised with automobile traffic and picture theatres.[26] The soundscape was designed to increasingly register the noises of automobiles.[27]

Tarkington never directly identifies the novel's setting as Indianapolis, but the fictional midland town is universally regarded as a personal reimagining of his birthplace.[28] In his film adaptation, Welles directly identifies the

Indianapolis, 1905

city only once by a brief insert shot of an *Indianapolis Inquirer* headline. That insert also features a cameo by *Kane*'s Jedediah Leland, by-lined and pictured above his dramatic column. It is the sole intertextual hinge between Welles's two American history films.

The city by the White River was chosen in 1820 as the state capital in the mistaken belief that the river was navigable for transport. The plan for the capital was conceived around institutions of government, with the governor's house at its centre. Indianapolis's emergence as a commercial nexus followed in the middle of the nineteenth century. This has been attributed to the construction of interurban railroads which linked Indianapolis to the Ohio River; it eventually became the 'hub of the wheel' and so assumed a dominant commercial role in the state.[29]

In the middle of the century the population swelled. As of 1860, at least twenty per cent of the population was foreign-born, immigrants mainly from Germany and Ireland.[30] The interwar half-century between 1865 and 1917 saw a vast transformation in Indianapolis's industrial economy, demographics, and physical infrastructure. Booth Tarkington explicitly cites the year 1873 as the beginning of the Amberson family's "magnificence", a particularly short social dominance of less than forty years. The novel's first line describes how in that year "Major Amberson had 'made a fortune' when other people were losing fortunes." Tarkington was referring to the Panic, an international recession that plunged Indianapolis into economic stagnancy for fifteen years and probably contributed to the preservation of its mid-nineteenth-century social hierarchy.[31]

Economic growth restarted with the discovery of natural gas in north central Indiana in the late 1880s; Indianapolis lurched towards becoming a centre of manufacturing. The city pushed through a recession in the mid-1890s to expand until the end of the century. As the gas supply declined, so did the Indianapolis economy, but the decline was partly stalled by two factors: the city's centrality to the interurban railway network and the growth of a local automobile industry.[32] Indianapolis became a representative Midwestern site of a dynamic historical antagonism: different modes of interurban and intraurban transport would compete for the next century to drag the cityscape towards conflicting material forms.[33]

In other words, Indianapolis experienced waves of growth and decline, and the periodic realignment of its industrial resources in a changing America. The physical infrastructure of the city changed in response to industry, technologies, and a growing population.

The period just before World War I was the peak of Indianapolis's railways – an average of four hundred electric interurban trains arriving and departing every day in 1910. But these services dropped away as the Midwest banked its future on the automobile.[34] Major automobile firms including Ford, Stutz, and Duesenberg produced cars in Indianapolis.[35] The city was for a time the production centre of shock absorbers.[36] The world-famous Indy 500 race was established in 1911. Indianapolis's material cityscape continued to change as the automobile grew in dominance. Electric streetcars replaced horse-drawn cars in the 1890s. A 1913 strike by streetcar workers led to riots, a police mutiny, and the imposition of martial law. The streetcars endured until 1953.[37] The increase in private traffic in the early twentieth century had demanded the replacement of gravelled streets with expensive hard surfaces. To protect this municipal investment in roads, the city had to take control of underground utilities.[38]

City transit had been a background issue in *Kane*, just one of Kane's social crusades, but in *Ambersons* it defines the shape of the city and the economic fortunes of its citizens. *Ambersons* argues for technology's transformative power and laments its casualties.

***

In Welles's *Ambersons* Indianapolis is reduced to National Avenue, the Amberson Mansion and its surroundings in the Amberson Addition, the city's train station, Eugene Morgan's house and factory, the rural outskirts of town, and finally Fanny's boarding house.

Welles's narrator, like Tarkington's, takes on the retrospective point of view of Indiana's middle class. The opening shots, however, paradoxically assume the point of view of the Amberson Mansion itself, looking across the street to the less magnificent house of Mrs Johnson, who will years later be censured by George for spreading gossip about his mother (Mrs Johnson appears to be the woman who hollers for the horse-drawn streetcar).

The opening sequence of the 131-minute version maintained this point of view and framing across four successive shots, creating a time lapse of the Johnson house in the dress of different seasons and times of day. This is a variation of the opening of *Kane*, where Xanadu looms in a succession of progressively closer shots, always with Kane's lighted window occupying the same pivotal position in the upper right of the frame – a spatial lapse rather than a temporal one. In *Ambersons*, Eugene's disastrous serenade intrudes into the summer shot. He rushes into the foreground and the fixed shot pans slightly downwards to take in his spectacular fall backwards through the bass fiddle; the counter-shot representing his point of view up towards Isabel Amberson's window establishes his location in the Amberson's front garden. The time lapse depicting the Johnson house was interrupted by RKO's reordering of the early sequences: the survey of the period's fashions was interpolated between the Johnson house's autumn and winter.

The Johnson house

In the novel the Amberson Mansion is the residence of Major Amberson. Isabel and Wilbur live in a nearby house. Welles relocates the whole family inside the same impressive residence, a dramatically efficient change. The exteriors of the mansion on Amberson Boulevard were shot at the RKO Ranch with a false front and a matte painting. The mansion also appears in several back projections.[39]

As in *Kane*, much of the action of *Ambersons* centres on a house that is a symbolic expression of personality. The interior designs of the mansion were

The Amberson mansion embellished by a matte painting; and with back projection

based on photographs in a publication called *Artistic Houses; Being a Series of Interior Views of a Number of the Most Beautiful and Celebrated Homes in the United States* (1883–1884).[40] The set was constructed at the RKO-Pathé Studio in Culver City. Welles would never again have such large financial resources to build sets. That limitation led to creative solutions and helped determine his later aesthetics.

Welles's long sequence at George's Christmastide ball, comprising several elaborate tracking shots, would have taken the audience from the mansion's front door and upstairs through all three storeys. The many interwoven conversations and asides establish the leading characters and set in action both Eugene and Isabel's renewed fascination and George's courtship of Lucy. RKO's cuts to this sequence diminish the mansion's spatial coherence.

Welles assigned Stanley Cortez to film another long and difficult tracking shot that would have represented George's subjective point of view as he entered the mansion after his 'last walk home' from the train station. On this occasion Welles seems to have rejected the shot from the outset, because it does not appear in the continuity of the 131-minute version.

* * *

Around 1800 [sic] Major Amberson had bought two hundred acres of land at the end of National Avenue; through this tract he had built broad streets and cross-streets, paved them with cedar block, and curbed them with stone. He set up fountains, here and there and at symmetrical intervals placed cast-iron statues, painted white. And all this Art showed a profit from the start. The lots had sold well and there was a rush to build in the new Addition. Its main thoroughfare was called Amberson Boulevard, and here, now stood the new Amberson Mansion which was the pride of the town.

– Orson Welles's narration for his *Campbell Playhouse* production

Welles's 1939 radio production quickly establishes the neighbourhood surrounding the Amberson Mansion as the Amberson Addition. That name, taken from the novel, is first mentioned in the 131-minute version of the film by Major Amberson when he speaks to Aunt Fanny on the mansion porch in 1910. The RKO version only mentions the Amberson Addition during George's 'last walk home'.

As of 1890, the dominant form of dwelling across all social classes in Indianapolis was the single family house.[41] The wealthiest of Indianapolis lived in Woodruff Place, an early suburb established a mile and a half from the city centre, a proto-gated community and the widely acknowledged inspiration for Tarkington's Amberson Addition. The Amberson Mansion itself was said to be inspired by the Knights of Columbus Headquarters on Delaware Street.[42]

A postcard representing Woodruff Place in the early twentieth century

The planning and construction of Woodruff Place was a typical Midwestern development in America's Gilded Age, the parcelling of urban space into pockets of socio-economic distinction. In that significant year of 1873, James O. Woodruff bought eighty acres east of the city centre to create a park neighbourhood for the well-to-do. Woodruff's prosperity was short-lived and the development of his suburban enclave was slowed by his bankruptcy. He died outside Indianapolis in 1879, aged only thirty-nine.[43] The plan of Woodruff Place ostentatiously insisted on its residents' wealth and status by the installation of fountains and statuary (which were quickly vandalised). Its boulevards were thirty feet wider than the streets of some of Indianapolis's contemporary middle-class suburbs. Woodruff Place's founding covenant established its exclusivity and aloofness from the rest of the city: fenced-off, its private streets and alleys, to be maintained by the owners of the houses, would not permit use by non-residents. It was said to have forbidden cows and chickens.[44]

Woodruff Place kept its political independence from Indianapolis while contracting its municipal services. It was not incorporated into the city itself until 1962.[45] Its population grew from twenty inhabitants in 1880 to almost five hundred at the turn of the century. There were no streetcars to or from the Indianapolis city centre, but the wealthy inhabitants of Woodruff Place could probably afford private carriages.[46] Tarkington's novel does not locate a streetcar line outside the Amberson Mansion; by including one in the cinematic Amberson Addition, Welles was able to compress the diverse activities of the city to a manageable zone.

Woodruff's exclusive zone of pretentious splendour was short-lived. In the twentieth century many of the stately homes were transformed into apartment houses.[47] Tarkington's Amberson Addition accurately anticipated this decline.

In the film, following Jack Amberson's departure by rail to Washington in search of a consulship, George walks home to spend his final night at the Amberson Mansion. On the way he confronts the much-changed Indianapolis of 1911 as if for the first time. For the first time in his career, Welles was able to realise the subjective camera technique he had planned for the entirety of *Heart of Darkness*. The shooting script has the camera following George as he walks up a street "until it is so close that his body creates a dark screen for a DISSOLVE" to a new shot in which the camera "is now George". The 131-minute version as assembled did not include that dissolve but instead transitioned from the railway station immediately to George's point of view in the street.

Welles's narration in this sequence is very carefully adapted from two different sections of Tarkington's novel. It explains George's alienation from modern Indianapolis:

> George Amberson Minafer walked homeward slowly through what seemed to be the strange streets of a strange city; for the town was growing and changing as it had never grown and changed before. It was heaving up in the

middle incredibly; it was spreading incredibly; and as it heaved and spread, it befouled itself and darkened its sky.⁴⁸

The narration was to have itemised a few of George's childhood memories of the neighbourhood, closely adapted from the novel (this part of the narration was cut by Wise). The scripted images are also taken directly from the novel: shots of a 'Stag hotel', boarding houses, a dry cleaner, a funeral home, and a benevolent society (the novel reveals this to be the former house of George's father's family). This sequence was ultimately filmed from George's point of view as a series of upwards-looking shots tracking along empty streets: the camera takes in telegraph wires, streetcar cables, grain elevators, an electrical generator, a factory, steel scaffolding, and grimy apartment houses.⁴⁹ In the RKO version, the shots slowly dissolve into each other. Welles claimed he shot this sequence himself with a handheld camera in downtown Los Angeles, using found spaces rather than the drastically transformed locations he would use in later films.⁵⁰

In Tarkington's novel, George's moment of urban alienation comes as a negative reaction to the racial diversity of the city. Welles's adaptation is

Los Angeles doubling as Indianapolis

THE DARKENING MIDLAND

delicate. He took the sentence on the "befouled" city from chapter 28, which is not actually from George's point of view at all, but occurs during George and Isabel's long absence abroad. Tarkington immediately follows the passage with the observation:

> But the great change was in the citizenry itself. What was left of the patriotic old-stock generation that had fought the Civil War, and subsequently controlled politics, had become venerable and was little heeded. The descendants of the pioneers and early settlers were merging into the new crowd, becoming part of it, little to be distinguished from it. What happened to Boston and to Broadway happened in degree to the Midland city; the old stock became less and less typical, and of the grown people who called the place home, less than a third had been born in it. There was a German quarter; there was a Jewish quarter; there was a negro quarter – square miles of it – called 'Bucktown'; there were many Irish neighbourhoods; and there were large settlements of Italians, and of Hungarians, and of Rumanians, and of Servians and other Balkan peoples. But not the emigrants, themselves, were the almost dominant type on the streets downtown. That type was the emigrant's prosperous offspring: descendant of the emigrations of the Seventies and Eighties and Nineties, those great folk-journeyings in search not so directly of freedom and democracy as of more money for the same labour. A new Midlander – in fact, a new American – was beginning dimly to emerge.[51]

And in chapter 31, the actual scene of the 'last walk home', from which Welles took the line about the "strange streets of a strange city", the strangeness is actually related to the faces George encounters among the "begrimed crowds of hurrying strangers":

> Great numbers of the faces were even of a kind he did not remember ever to have seen; they were partly like the old type that his boyhood knew, and partly like types he knew abroad. German eyes with American wrinkles at their corners; he saw Irish eyes and Neapolitan eyes, Roman eyes, Tuscan eyes, eyes of Lombardy, of Savoy, Hungarian eyes, Balkan eyes, Scandinavian eyes – all with a queer American look in them. He saw Jews who had been German Jews, Jews who had been Russian Jews, Jews who had been Polish Jews but were no longer German or Russian or Polish Jews. All the people were soiled by the smoke-mist through which they hurried, under the heavy

sky that hung close upon the new skyscrapers; and nearly all seemed harried by something impending…[52]

Next, from Welles's narration, again closely adapted from the novel: "this was the last walk home [George] was ever to take up National Avenue to Amberson Addition and the big old house at the foot of Amberson Boulevard". In the script – but not the 131-minute version – the boulevard has already been renamed 10th Street. In the novel the stone pillars that marked the entrance to the Amberson Addition have vanished, although a fountain of Neptune remains. Welles's narrator:

> The city had rolled over his heart and buried it under as it rolled over the Major's and the Ambersons' and buried them under to the last vestige. Tonight would be the last night that he and Fanny were to spend in the house which the Major had forgotten to deed to Isabel. Tomorrow they were to 'move out'.

Welles's plan was to continue with another subjective tracking shot that moved through the interior of the Amberson Mansion. It was shot but not included in the 131-minute version, which cuts from the walk home to George kneeling before Isabel's bed. The following narration, cut from RKO's version and closely adapted from Tarkington, accompanied that shot in his mother's bedroom:

> The very space in which tonight was still Isabel's room would be cut into new shapes by new walls and floors and ceilings. And if space itself can be haunted as memory is haunted, then it may be that some impressionable, overworked woman in a 'kitchenette', after turning out the light, will seem to see a young man kneeling in the darkness, with arms outstretched through the wall, clutching at the covers of a shadowy bed. It may seem to her that she hears the faint cry, over and over, of George crying, "Mother, forgive me! *God*, forgive me!"

This is a powerful projection into the city's future working-class space. Welles's narrator now announces that George had received his "come-upance", "three times filled and running over. But those who had so longed for it were not there to see it, and they never knew it. Those who were still living had forgotten all about it and all about him."[53]

The reshaping of the spaces of the modern city provided new opportunities for interaction between the classes, and this found expression in literature. Charles Baudelaire's prose poem 'Eyes of the Poor' (from *Paris Spleen*, published posthumously in 1868) focuses on a wealthy couple in a luxurious new café who differ profoundly in their reactions to a poor family looking through the window. Marshall Berman wrote of how Baudelaire announced that Baron Haussmann's Paris boulevards had "opened up the whole of the city, for the first time in its history, to all its inhabitants"; the city had become "a unified physical and human space".[54]

George's alienating encounter with the Indianapolis of 1911, as it was presented in Tarkington's novel, is one such confrontation with the open modern city; George, with the probable sympathy of the author, reacts like Baudelaire's snob, who wishes the poor to disappear from her sight. Welles's adaptation of the 'last walk home' in the 131-minute version delivers the same alienating effect on George – for the better, it turns out, because it shocks him into admitting the irrevocable mistake of his treatment of his mother and Eugene. He attempts to redeem himself by working to support Aunt Fanny. But in Welles's version George's alienation is a reaction to the grim material condition of the empty cityscape rather than to the crowd. The narrator's projection of some future "impressionable, overworked woman in a 'kitchenette'" where there was once Isabel's bedroom is another abstraction of the poor. In Welles's script George had a brief encounter outside the mansion with some apparently well-to-do "riff-raff" in an automobile; by the time of the 131-minute version, George's experience of urban alienation is stripped entirely of human interaction. The streets are eerily empty. The subjective point of view of the camera only makes the Indianapolis inner city appear more of an abandoned wasteland.

It's a big change from Tarkington's description of George moving through "thunderous streets" and "begrimed crowds of hurrying strangers", but a necessary one for Welles to avoid carrying over the sympathetically presented racism of the original scene. But that moment in Tarkington's novel was typical of the widespread bigotry of contemporary Indianapolis. Once a nexus of immigration, the proportion of foreign-born residents had declined to only nine per cent by 1910.[55] City life was persistently segregated, particularly in the 1920s. Soon after the publication of *The Magnificent Ambersons*, Indiana would claim the largest Ku Klux Klan organisation in the country – an estimated 300,000 members at its peak in the early 1920s. The Klan dominated the city's municipal election of 1925, and one of its members, Edward L. Jackson, ruled as a corrupt state governor from 1925 to 1929.[56]

Orson Welles's solution as an adaptor was to be modest rather than critical: he simply eliminated the racism that was a key part of Tarkington's provincial myth of decline. But Welles's political radicalism was only beginning to stir and seek expression in film. Just days after recording his tender *Ambersons* narration, his lament for an idealised middle-class Eden, Welles was in Rio de Janeiro improvising a Technicolor documentary film about the city's Carnaval. In Portuguese Welles found the word that best defined his sweet ache for the imagined past – *saudade*. 'Carnaval' quickly developed into a radical celebratory project that attempted to directly interrogate the racial politics of urban space and present a utopian vision of joyous racial mixing in the streets of a modern city.

NOTES

1 'The Magnificent Ambersons', *The Campbell Playhouse* (Orson Welles, 1939). Original broadcast: 29 October (CBS Radio Network)
2 Carringer, *The Making of Citizen Kane*, 125.
3 Carringer, *The Making of Citizen Kane*, 130.
4 Welles and Bogdanovich, *This Is Orson Welles*, 165; Berthome and Thomas, *Orson Welles at Work*, 97.
5 Benamou, *It's All True*, 36.
6 Benamou, *It's All True*, 41–2.
7 These details are drawn from Jonathan Rosenbaum, 'Welles' Career: A Chronology', in Welles and Bogdanovich, *This Is Orson Welles*, 365–70; and Berthome and Thomas, *Orson Welles at Work*.
8 Carringer, *The Making of Citizen Kane*, 126.
9 Jonathan Rosenbaum, 'The Original *Ambersons*', in Welles and Bogdanovich, *This Is Orson Welles*, 456.
10 This synopsis of the 131-minute version has drawn on the readable summary by Jonathan Rosenbaum, 'The Original *Ambersons*', in Welles and Bogdanovich, *This Is Orson Welles*, 454–90; and the full textual reconstruction in Carringer, *The Magnificent Ambersons: A Reconstruction*.
11 Clinton Heylin, *Despite the System: Orson Welles Versus the Hollywood Studios* (Edinburgh: Canongate, 2005), 116–7; Callow, *Orson Welles: Hello Americans*, 86.

12 Carringer, *The Making of Citizen Kane*, 127.
13 Berthome and Thomas, *Orson Welles at Work*, 92.
14 David Kamp, 'Magnificent Obsession', *Vanity Fair*, April 2000, at http://www.vanityfair.com/hollywood/2010/04/magnificent-obsession-200201 (accessed 17 June 2015).
15 The following dialogue and description of sequences here are taken from Rosenbaum, 'The Original *Ambersons*', 465–7 (I have edited out most of Rosenbaum's shot-by-shot notations).
16 Booth Tarkington (n.d.) quoted in Frederick D. Kershner Jr, 'From Country Town to Industrial City: The Urban Pattern in Indianapolis', *Indiana Magazine of History*, Vol. 45, No. 4, December 1949, 330.
17 Booth Tarkington, *The Turmoil* (New York: Grosset & Dunlap, 1915), 3–4.
18 Carringer remarks on Tarkington's obscurity by 1942 in *The Making of Citizen Kane*, 124.
19 Welles quoted in Welles and Bogdanovich, *This Is Orson Welles*, 96.
20 Welles, 'My Father Wore Black Spats'.
21 Welles quoted in Welles and Bogdanovich, *This Is Orson Welles*, 93.
22 Joseph Cotten, letter to Orson Welles, 28 March 1942, in Callow, *Orson Welles: Hello Americans*, 90.
23 Welles quoted in Welles and Bogdanovich, *This Is Orson Welles*, 130.
24 See Richard Slotkin, *Gunfighter Nation: The Myth of the Frontier in Twentieth-Century America* (New York: Harper Perennial, 1993), 287.
25 Berthome and Thomas, *Orson Welles at Work*, 83.
26 George and Lucy's final walk together occurs in 1905, although the film posters decorating the Bijoux Theatre date mysteriously from 1912. The date of 1905 is both consistent with the film's chronology and noted in the shooting script, making the 1912 posters an apparent historical inaccuracy. The care with which the theatre sets were dressed is indicated by the fictional film poster starring Tim Holt's father, Jack. See Bordwell, '*The Magnificent Ambersons*: A Usable Past'.
27 Berthome and Thomas, *Orson Welles at Work*, 90.
28 David J. Bodenhamer and Robert G. Barrows (eds), *The Encyclopedia of Indianapolis* (Bloomington: Indiana University Press, 1994), 956.
29 Jon C. Teaford, *Cities of the Heartland: The Rise and Fall of the Industrial Midwest* (Bloomington: Indiana University Press, 1993), 27–8, 38–9.
30 Kershner, 'From Country Town to Industrial City', 329.
31 Kershner, 'From Country Town to Industrial City', 328.
32 Kershner, 'From Country Town to Industrial City', 328.
33 Teaford, *Cities of the Heartland*, 27–8.
34 Teaford, *Cities of the Heartland*, 110–11.
35 Dennis E. Horvath and Terri Horvath, *Indiana Cars: A History of the Automobile in Indiana* (Indianapolis: Hoosier Auto Show and Swap Meet, 2013), 3.
36 Teaford, *Cities of the Heartland*, 109.
37 Bodenhamer and Barrows, *The Encyclopedia of Indianapolis*, 1,488.

38 Kershner, 'From Country Town to Industrial City', 334.
39 Carringer, *The Making of Citizen Kane*, 131.
40 Carringer, *The Making of Citizen Kane*, 130.
41 Teaford, *Cities of the Heartland*, 79.
42 See Susanah Mayberry, *My Amiable Uncle: Recollections About Booth Tarkington* (West Lafayette: Purdue University Press, 1983), 13; also Bodenhamer and Barrows, *The Encyclopedia of Indianapolis*, 1,453.
43 Timothy J. Sehr, 'Three Gilded Age Suburbs of Indianapolis: Irvington, Brightwood, and Woodruff Place', *Indiana Magazine of History*, Vol. 77, No. 4, December 1981, 306–7, 314.
44 Sehr, 'Three Gilded Age Suburbs of Indianapolis', 323.
45 Bodenhamer and Barrows, *The Encyclopedia of Indianapolis*, 1,453.
46 Sehr, 'Three Gilded Age Suburbs of Indianapolis', 326–7.
47 Bodenhamer and Barrows, *The Encyclopedia of Indianapolis*, 1,453.
48 Orson Welles, *The Magnificent Ambersons* 'Final Script' (7 October 1941), A-155. Orson Welles Manuscripts, Lilly Library.
49 Carringer, *The Magnificent Ambersons: A Reconstruction*, 243–5.
50 Welles and Bogdanovich, *This Is Orson Welles*, 128.
51 Booth Tarkington, *The Magnificent Ambersons* (New York: Modern Library, 1998), 203.
52 Tarkington, *The Magnificent Ambersons*, 228.
53 In the novel, George's "come-upance" is announced later, after the Ambersons' mansions have been razed, when he discovers that Amberson Boulevard has become Tenth Street and the Ambersons have been excluded from a vanity publication containing "Biographies of the 500 Most Prominent Citizens and Families in the History of the City".
54 Marshall Berman, *All That Is Solid Melts into Air: The Experience of Modernity* (New York: Penguin, 1988), 151.
55 Kershner, 'From Country Town to Industrial City', 329.
56 Richard B. Pierce, *Polite Protest: The Political Economy of Race in Indianapolis, 1920–1970* (Bloomington: Indiana University Press, 2005), 3; Leonard J. Moore, *Citizen Klansmen: The Ku Klux Klan in Indiana, 1921–1928* (Chapel Hill: University of North Carolina Press, 1991), 11, 91, 144.

PAN-AMERICA

CHAPTER 4

DARKNESS AND FEAR
The Early Anti-fascist Thrillers

Aside from *Citizen Kane* and *The Magnificent Ambersons*, most of Welles's creative energies in Hollywood were devoted to contemporary political films about the American hemisphere. He attempted to interrogate the threat of fascism in a string of projects dating from 1939. Most never reached production.

Recurrent and politically significant settings of the Pan-American film projects include urban political frontiers (port cities and the border town) and the impoverished urban periphery (the shantytown). These are spaces of authoritarian control and social exclusion where fascist manoeuvers frequently burst to the surface. Welles would consistently develop experimental techniques to illustrate such manoeuvers.

Later in the 1940s, a number of Hollywood directors would pursue synoptic overviews of urban space, often in films shot on location on the theme of police investigation and surveillance, such as *The Naked City* (Jules Dassin, 1948) and *Side Street* (Anthony Mann, 1950).[1] Earlier in the decade, and through his perspective of anti-fascism, Welles had frequently pursued comprehensive visions of the total city. In this pursuit he attempted to synthesise the ambitions of the international 'city symphony' cycle of the silent era with Hollywood narrative filmmaking of the 1940s. He experimented with long and mobile shots that would track ambulatory characters, vehicles, and ritual human and animal processions through diverse passages of urban space. He conceived ambient sound schemes, planned intercutting between contrasting social spaces, and the integration of synoptic maps and architectural models into the *mise-en-scène*. In his early years at RKO (1939–1942) he had access to expensive studio sets, miniatures, matte paintings, and optical printing. As he shifted from studio-based to location-based filmmaking, Welles sketched and was sometimes able to implement innovative methods of transforming found urban spaces into cinematic spaces that expressed his ideological and personal vision. This programme reached its zenith in *Touch of Evil*, when he converted Venice Beach in Los Angeles into his fictional Texan-Mexican border town, 'Los Robles'.

* * *

Welles's first feature project under contract to RKO was an experimental and Americanised anti-fascist adaptation of Joseph Conrad's *Heart of Darkness*. It was never produced, despite extensive scripting and pre-production planning. Following *Kane* and *Ambersons*, he shot but was unable to finish *It's All True*, a celebratory semi-documentary anthology intended as an emissary for President Roosevelt's Good Neighbor Policy. Although Welles rather dubiously disavowed any particular fondness for the thriller genre – "I can pretend no special interest or aptitude"[2] – the rest of his anti-fascist Pan-American film projects fall into that genre.

The Mercury production of Eric Ambler's 1940 novel *Journey into Fear* was the first of these spy thrillers to reach cinemas, under Welles's (partial) supervision. Of the other many Pan-American thrillers Welles developed at least until the end of the 1970s, only *The Stranger* (1946), *The Lady from Shanghai* (1947), and *Touch of Evil* were actually finished and released, and all three were travesties of the director's editorial wishes. These three were later categorised as film noirs. Welles's Pan-American and anti-fascist emphases in these three films were frequently blunted by studio interference. As the earlier, more Wellesian versions of these three films no longer exist (or were never finished), scholars have long found it fruitful to examine evidence of the director's original conceptions in production documents. In fact, the long-term Pan-American strain of Welles's oeuvre can only be comprehensively appraised with recourse to such scripts, treatments, correspondence, and pre-production art for both his produced and his unmade films. These documents contain sketches for innovative approaches to creating cinematic cities that did not find fruition in any of the commercially released films. Welles accrued masses of written texts during the sometimes permanent pre-production stage of a project. The surviving documents are, however, often fragmentary and occasionally of ambiguous authorship. In the early to mid-

1940s, Welles commissioned writers such as Norman Foster, Paul Trivers, John Fante, Paul Elliot, Brainerd Duffield, Fletcher Markle, Les White and Bud Pearson to draft treatments and screenplays which would be the rough material for Welles's rewrites and final revisions (as he had used Herman J. Mankiewicz's preliminary drafts in the writing process of *Citizen Kane*).[3] He had managed to stamp his personality on a vast turnover of weekly radio dramas by the same method. But these collaborations complicate Welles's *auteur* status and demand a careful appraisal of the many surviving documents, which range from Welles's own meticulously detailed and industry-standard 'Revised Estimating Script' for *Heart of Darkness* ("I did a very elaborate preparation for that, such as I've never done again – never could"[4]) to an uncredited, incomplete, hand-annotated draft adaptation of Michael Fessier's novel *Fully Dressed and In His Right Mind* (1934). There are also drafts annotated with studio censorship guidelines, storyboards, and other types of production artwork.

The best approach is to contextualise these pre-production documents, by Welles's own definition totally provisional, as best as possible within the known details of his creative process. From early on Welles showed no particular loyalty to conventional industry-standard screenplay formats and much interest in expanding the definition of screenwriting as a practice. During the making of the 'Carnaval' segment of *It's All True* in 1942, he explained to RKO that he considered the 'minutes' of his detailed nightly discussions with research collaborators "the nearest thing we have to a script". These minutes recorded the fruitful debates within the collaborative creative process, provided a clarifying recap of the segment's thematic and structural evolution, and determined the logistical approach to realising new ideas on film, even if they were not comprehensible to everyone; the minutes "can mean little to anybody except ourselves", stated Welles.[5]

* * *

Welles had already performed *Heart of Darkness* in a radio script by Howard Koch in 1938. For his own screenplay, he altered Conrad's late nineteenth-century Congo setting to a contemporary unnamed 'dark country'.[6] Welles declared, "The film is frankly an attack on the Nazi system."[7] He intended to play both the American narrator, Marlow, and the object of his search in the jungle, the insane ivory agent Kurtz. In preparation Welles commissioned a comprehensive study of tribal anthropology,[8] similar to the exhaustive research into Brazilian culture he would gather while making *It's All True*.

Welles's 'Revised Estimating Script' of *Heart of Darkness* is dated 30 November 1939, less than three months after Great Britain declared war on Nazi Germany. Following an introduction to the film's unprecedented technique – a first-person method that will present the action almost entirely through the eyes, ears, and inner monologue of Marlow – the action proper begins in New York Harbor, a port setting that will turn up again in drafts of *The Smiler with the Knife*, *Don't Catch Me*, *The Lady from Shanghai*, and *The Cradle Will Rock*. The city appears in long shot, "seen from the East River just at dusk", followed by a "SERIES OF DISSOLVES showing the movement of traffic on the river".[9] We see Manhattan from afar against the sunset sky. Marlow narrates, "Further west – on the upper reaches – the place of the monstrous town marked ominously on the sky, a brooding gloom in the sunshine, a lurid glare under the stars."[10] Then we see a series of 'lap dissolves' to various places in the city at the very moment its lights illuminate: bridges over the Hudson and East Rivers, parkways, boulevards, and skyscrapers.

In his first Hollywood script, Welles brings his extensive radio experience to the task of attempting to revolutionise cinema sound. He makes notes for a now commonplace ambient use of fragmentary diegetic sound sources to help convey the city's spatial distinctions:

> As we move down the length of the Island, snatches of sound and music, the beginnings of life of the city at night, are heard on the sound track. In Central Park, snatches of jazz music is heard from the radios in the moving taxicabs. The sweet dinner music in the restaurants of the big hotels further West. The throb of tom-toms foreshadow the jungle music of the story to come. The lament of brasses, the gala noodling of big orchestras tuning up in concert halls and opera houses, and finally as the camera finds its way downtown below Broadway, the music freezes into an expression of the empty shopping district of the deserted Battery – the mournful muted clangor of the bell buoys out at sea, and the hoot of shipping.[11]

Welles would sketch versions of this sound scheme for different projects throughout the years – most notably to accompany *Touch of Evil*'s long opening tracking shot through Los Robles – but he was consistently thwarted.[12] Despite his innovations on *Kane* and *Ambersons* in collaboration with RKO sound editor James G. Stewart, Welles was frequently constrained in experimenting with sound in Hollywood.

This plan for the beginning of the film suggests a miniature city symphony that emphasises New York as a port city. Its "sleepless river" leads to "the mystery of an unknown earth. The dreams of men, the seeds of commonwealths, the germ of Empires."[13] Marlow leans against the single mast of a ship in the harbour and narrates how New York, the towering modern city, was once "one of the dark places on the earth … they must have been dying here like flies four hundred years ago." His narration then closely follows Conrad: "It's not a pretty thing when you look into it too much, the conquest of the earth which mostly means the taking it away [sic] from those who have a different complexion or slightly different shaped noses than ourselves."[14]

There is a flashback to another harbour in "some Central European seaport town".[15] These are the first two instances of a dramatically pregnant and cosmopolitan setting that frequently occurs in Welles's films: the international seaport where characters of diverse and ambiguous backgrounds intermingle and scheme. Welles would use seaport settings in *Journey into Fear* (Istanbul and Batumi), *The Stranger* (a Buenos Aires-like port in South America), *The Lady from Shanghai* (New York, San Francisco, and Acapulco), *Mr. Arkadin* (Naples, Cannes, Juan-les-Pins, Tangier, and Acapulco), *The Immortal Story* (Macau), and the unproduced late 1960s script *Santo Spirito* (a fictional island in the Caribbean).[16]

Marlow the sailor is "used to clearing out for any port in the world with less thought than most men give to crossing a street".[17] Parts of this Central European seaport were intended to be created with miniatures by RKO's special effects department. Welles inserts a note to special effects artist Vern Walker: "when making long shots of harbor and settlement from the miniature, suggest the following to give movement in the shots: a dredge working near the railroad track, dynamite explosions with accompanying dust and smoke, etc."[18] At the beginning of the seaport town sequence Marlow looks at a map of the "dark country" through a shop window. "I've always had a passion for maps," he narrates. "When I was a child there were many blank spaces on the earth, and when I saw one that looked inviting – I'd put my finger on it and say, 'When I grow up I'll go there.'"[19] Maps were frequently interpolated into Welles's *mise-en-scène* in this period as one way of providing an economical geographical synopsis. They would be used in *Citizen Kane*, the pre-release cuts of *Journey into Fear*, and the script for *The Smiler with the Knife*. At a later stage in *Heart of Darkness* Kurtz's fiancée, Elsa, draws a map of the dark country's river.

When Marlow accepts the job to find Kurtz, the script enters the jungle and ceases to concern city culture. Welles's projected budget of more than a million dollars, twice the target amount for Welles's first film, made the experimental film unworkable for RKO.[20]

* * *

Early on Welles was attracted to the contemporary anti-fascist incarnation of the spy novel epitomised by the work of English writers Graham Greene and Eric Ambler. Cultural historian Michael Denning calls this new type of spy novel the 'serious thriller', although that does not necessarily imply grimness of execution in the age of Hitler and Mussolini. In fact, the novels are wildly entertaining. Aside from the considerable literary qualities of Ambler's and Greene's work, the 'serious thriller' surely appealed to Welles because it abandoned the genre's traditionally conservative political orientation to embrace the cause of the Popular Front.[21]

Welles would eventually come to adapt Ambler and, much later, Greene. To Denning, the archetypal narrative of the Ambler–Greene 'serious thriller' novel is as follows:

> An educated, middle-class man (a journalist, teacher, engineer) travelling for business or pleasure on the Continent … accidentally gets caught up in a low and sinister game (no longer the Great Game) of spies, informers, and thugs. He is innocent both in the sense of not being guilty, and in the sense of being naive. He is an amateur spy, but not the sort of enthusiastic and willing amateur that [John Buchan's Richard Hannay] is; rather he is an incompetent and inexperienced amateur in a world of professionals.[22]

In novels of the 1930s Ambler and Greene present a European milieu of spies, criminals, lowlifes, and refugees whose ethnic and national identities have been obscured by the political disruptions of World War I. The stories are frequently set in cosmopolitan crossroads in upheaval following the end of the Ottoman and Austro-Hungarian Empires or in transit between such cities by railway (Greene's *Stamboul Train*, 1932), by ship (Ambler's *Journey into Fear*), or by foot (Ambler's *Cause for Alarm*, 1938).[23]

Welles was ideologically opposed to political borders and the nationalism (he was loyal to more antiquated, romantic, and inclus identifications). His strong antipathy to police, government bu borders, and passports would be expressed in his British television documen taries several times in the mid-1950s. He found a kindred thinker in Ambler, whose novels frequently focus on hapless but sympathetic characters rendered stateless by the vicissitudes of war and occupation, or on the difficulties, anxieties, and sometimes arbitrary violence of bureaucratic control over human passage across political frontiers.[24]

In a 1975 conversation, Ambler recalled:

[C]ertainly to anyone who came to maturity during the Fascist years the importance of papers became overwhelming. People are denied passports – that means now the right to travel freely – for often, it seems to me, illogical reasons. [...] it's a question of control to deny him freedom of movement. [...] diplomatic documents, papers and such have become a 20th century means of control, and I make use of them in my work.[25]

In the cinema the new category of European spy novel found an analogue in Carol Reed's *Night Train to Munich* (1940) and Alfred Hitchcock's *Foreign Correspondent* (1940). Although Welles was critical of Hitchcock's later work, at least in posthumously published private conversations, his early thrillers are firmly in the tradition of Hitchcock's early work.

Welles prepared two anti-fascist novels by Popular Front novelists as prospective projects at RKO: *The Smiler with a Knife*, by Cecil Day-Lewis (writing as Nicholas Blake, 1939), and *The Way to Santiago*, by Arthur Calder-Marshall (1940). Along with the later adaptation of Richard Powell's *Don't Catch Me* (1943), they make for a progressively sophisticated and entertaining trilogy of Hitchcockian thrillers. Welles did not restrain himself to realism but exploited the genre for its theatrical, carnivalesque, and comic potential. No script in this Hitchcockian trilogy was produced.

* * *

An unsigned memo, probably written by Welles (or possibly by John Houseman), makes a self-critical summary of an early draft of *The Smiler with the Knife* and gives insight into the creative process of adaptation. The memo confesses that one scene, written in haste, contains "just whatever I could get down on paper".[26] Such a provisional quality – rough assemblies of scenes, gestures towards structure – must be assumed of many other Welles scripts. What seems to be the latest draft, the 178 page "Revised Estimating Script", is dated 9 January 1940, and bears no writer credit. Welles seems to have created about half the script's plot and taken the rest from the source novel.[27] Despite its anti-fascist orientation, this draft's politics are not nuanced. The fascists are cartoon villains and the script is plagued by implausibilities. The dialogue is in the vein of the sometimes inscrutable banter that would characterise Welles's later original scripts *The Other Side of the Wind* and *The Big Brass Ring*. There is a note that a "*March of Time* sequence", a fictional newsreel, will be interpolated into the script as an expositional device. The idea would be revived for *Kane*.

The action of *Smiler* commences at a wedding ceremony at the remote country house of a parson. The far-fetched MacGuffin is a locket in the beak of a crow. Two strange men separately chase the crow to the parson's house, but newlyweds Johnny and Gloria evade surrendering the locket, which is engraved 'S.S.' and contains a vintage photograph of an old woman.

The couple take the mysterious find to Johnny's father, John Strangeways Sr, the head of the US Department of Justice in Washington, DC. He connects it to a secret fascist organisation about which nothing is known but its name: 'S.S.' stands for 'Stars and Stripes'. Strangeways makes a speech for democracy. The politically indifferent Johnny wants to know what his father is yammering on about. The answer? "Shirts. I like to pick my own color. I like to go on a ballot with more than one name. Get it?"[28] Strangeways lectures the newlyweds on similar international fascist conspiracies, such as the recent action by the Cagoulards against the French Third Republic. He worries about the USA because "one seventh of the munitions manufactured in this country can't be accounted for. We don't know how big this is, but we can guess. And the worst of it is we haven't an idea in the world who's behind it." When Johnny protests, "The American people will never stand for a dictator," his father rejoins: "You mean they'll never give a politician that much power. How about a hero? We like heroes over here and this one won't talk like a dictator. He'll look like a movie star and everybody'll love him."[29]

Shortly after, an aviator hero in the mould of Nazi sympathiser Charles Lindbergh lands his 'stratosphere' machine in Washington, DC, in an atmosphere of public ecstasy. The hero's name is Anthony Chilton and he would surely have been played by Welles. He is feted on the radio by "militant Broadway columnist" and democracy defender Wally Winters (a barely disguised Walter Winchell).

The newlyweds meet Chilton at a party where the guests play games. Chilton dresses in drag and, in one of the script's heavier demands on the audience, will be recognised as a dead ringer for the woman in the locket photograph – his female ancestor. Chilton tries to romance Gloria, who quarrels with her husband; the newlyweds separate for the rest of the film. The structural conceit of separated newlyweds would be repeatedly revisited in Welles's thriller scripts, although it made the screen only once, in *Touch of Evil*.[30]

Gloria accompanies Chilton to Rosa's restaurant, "a rather sinister establishment outside the city limits of Washington" (the script suggests as a model Ernie Byfield's Pump Room at the Ambassador East in Chicago).[31] This is the beginning of an extra-marital romance, although the political intrigue builds. The urban settings are briefly swapped for rural Kentucky, where Chilton owns a country house. There Gloria discovers Chilton to be the head of Stars and Stripes. He mobilises his organisation to capture her in a dash across the United States. In one car chase sequence through the country the visual action occurs off screen: a contrast between static shots and "wild screeching of police sirens in a constantly building pattern of sound. Big chase music."[32] The script comes most alive during a chase sequence in a crowded urban shopping street in Zenith, Pennsylvania. Gloria escapes capture by the very Hitchcockian solution of dressing as Santa Claus.

Welles incorporates maps in a moment of Hitchcockian hokum. Gloria realises the miniature golf course on Chilton's country property in Kentucky really represents a secret map of the United States indicating the fascist organisation's "twenty-six secret arsenals and munitions dumps". She annotates a map of the United States in an atlas with the locations – and "the resemblance of the map to the miniature golf course is striking enough to make the idea clear".[33] Chilton has also hidden secret papers inside a terrestrial globe. She sends it all to Strangeways in Washington.

Although the action skips from the nation's capital to the rural south, to Cincinnati and Columbus, Ohio, to Zenith and even to the Welles's alma mater, the Todd School for Boys (which was in Woodstock, Illinois), the urban settings would have been filmed in the studio using sets and process shots. The street scenes of Zenith would have been created on the RKO Ranch.[34] It's a challenge to imagine how Welles would have overcome the generic quality of the urban settings based on this draft of the script. In other ways *The Smiler with the Knife* would have needed substantial reworking to rise above this draft's weaknesses and implausibilities. Welles would continue to marry serious and urgent political themes to screwball comedy and the carnivalesque, but this early exploration of a fascist conspiracy is not at all sophisticated. Welles abandoned the project and made *Citizen Kane*.

* * *

A superior stab at the fascist-infiltration suspense plot is Welles's adaptation of Calder-Marshall's *The Way to Santiago*. The title of the film adaptation never graduated beyond the working titles *Mexican Melodrama* or *Orson Welles #4*. What seems to be the latest draft, a 'Third Revised Continuity' script, is dated 25 March 1941, just over a month before the premiere of *Kane*. The practical purposes of this version of the script should not be overlooked: marked 'For Budgeting Purposes Only', it was also the version submitted to Mexican authorities for official approval to film on location in the country (which was granted). That said, this draft seems to represent an advanced state of development. James Naremore persuasively argues for *Mexican Melodrama* as a reworking of *Heart of Darkness* within a more commercial, less experimental form.[35]

Welles doesn't seem to have planned to direct the project, although he would have starred in the lead role. With this project Welles moved away from the USA as a setting. The script is prefaced by the declaration that Mexico "shares with us the American dream of freedom".[36] Under President Lázaro Cárdenas, Mexico had nationalised its oil in 1938, expropriating the assets of international firms. President Roosevelt maintained a pacific stance against retaliatory intervention in line with the Good Neighbor Policy.

The Way to Santiago explored the fascist threat to Mexico in the period. One innovation in Welles's script is its usual first-person subjectivity, which is distinct from the near-total observance of Marlow's point of view in *Heart of Darkness*. The lead character – named 'Me' – wakes up naked in an anonymous empty room surrounded by representatives of "every race in the world, every color". Me has no documents and does not remember who he is. The amnesia motif would be used in several future Welles films, including *Mr. Arkadin*, although in this story the condition is genuine.

Me is helped by a newspaper man named alternately Gonzalez or Johnson; the draft is evidently an indecisive composite of versions. They are in Mexico

City, and Gonzalez/Johnson mysteriously offers to take Me to a party at the presidential palace to "get friendly with the most beautiful girl in the world". Me's presence makes a shocking impression on the guests, including the beauty, Elena. She identifies him as Lindsay Keller, a fascist connected with a Mexican revolutionary group, led by one General Torres. Gonzalez/Johnson's stunt at the palace is designed to pry further information from the General about his fascist plot to take over Mexico. Torre's organisation has stockpiled ammunitions and set up a radio station on the island of Santiago. We later discover Keller is the charismatic fascist radio personality 'Mr England', who has been brought to the Americas to propagandise to the "hundred and thirty million people [who] speak English in this hemisphere". Mr England was based on the English Nazi broadcaster William Joyce (aka Lord Haw Haw).[37]

Me and Gonzalez/Johnson leave the presidential palace and walk into the city's *zócalo*, its enormous central square. The mob scene as sketched promises grand spectacle and threatening overtones: thousands of patriots enjoying the Mexican Independence Day ritual of the presidential *grito*, a cry of "Viva Mexico! Viva la República! Viva la Revolución!" There is "a hurricane of voices – a typhoon of confetti – and finally, fireworks".[38] In a particularly Hitchcockian moment, Gonzalez/Johnson is shot as the fireworks explode; the bullet was surely intended for Me. The police allow Me to leave, but the "unanimously sinister" crowd suspects Me's guilt.[39] The ecstasy of the patriotic mob turns threatening. Me briefly hides among a busload of gauche American tourists.

Me meets Elena at the city's El Chango, a nightclub featuring flamenco entertainers in exile from Spain. Me learns that Elena is not part of Torres's conspiracy, but instead a Mexican spy. The amnesia has left Me with total naivety about fascism itself, so Elena provides him (and the audience) a definition: "It means tyranny. It means everything that isn't human or beautiful. It means the ant hill, darkness, and death."[40] Me accepts her definition and confesses, "I can't remember what I liked about it. I guess fascism is something that happens to you – like disease. I guess everybody is born innocent. Well, I was born this afternoon."[41]

And so Me and Elena conspire to destroy the fascists' munitions dump in Santiago. Me makes a long and dangerous journey out of the teeming capital city to Santiago, with a side adventure in a remote jungle village saloon, where since the oil nationalisation, "business is so bad nobody's drinking".[42] Further along Me meets the real Keller (his physical double) and is captured.

Later the cadre of conspirators sit on the sundeck of General Torres's yacht and rather didactically share their theories of fascist rule. A Spanish aristocrat states: "the lesson we learned from Spain was that a military minority with the help of foreign sympathizers and the principal of non-intervention can overthrow a government which had strong support at home and institute a military dictatorship in its place."[43]

The real Keller adds:

> The terrorist provocation must break out simultaneously all through the country so that the public will be stunned and bewildered. They'll realize that only a strong man with dictatorial powers can save them. … Mexico at last a country where the rich can live in security.[44]

But Me's voice interrupts from a loudspeaker. He has escaped and infiltrated the radio station in Santiago to broadcast a passionate anti-fascist message, "another Grito", which we see reach listeners across the Americas. Me participates in capturing General Torres, but Mr England drowns trying to reach a submerging German submarine.

Unlike *The Smiler with the Knife*, the *Way to Santiago* project was to have been shot extensively on location. Despite some initial resistance from the Mexican government,[45] pre-production was underway in Mexico in the second half of 1941. RKO editor Jose Noriega, representing Mercury Productions in Mexico City, successfully negotiated with the Secretary of State for the authorisation to make two films in the country: 'My Friend Bonito' and the *Way to Santiago* project. Although Welles had yet to sign up to officially represent the Good Neighbor Policy in Latin America, Noriega was already arguing that *Santiago* would "enhance the better ethical and social values of Mexico by the light of the policy of Continental and democratic solidarity that Mexico is pursuing".[46] Authorisation was granted and both scripts were approved with the proviso of the presence of an on-set representative from Mexico's Department of Cinematographic Supervision – in other words, a censor.[47]

Around the same time a tentative shooting schedule and detailed budget were drawn up for *Santiago*, presumably by Noriega. A month of location work would begin in April 1942, followed by inexpensive Mexico City studio filming. Noriega essays the possibilities of location filming in the capital itself. El Patio bar, supposedly the inspiration for El Chango, would either be used as found or reconstructed on a stage; a custom-made neon sign would have to be fitted to the exterior. Perry Ferguson, the art director for *Kane*, seems to have been already lined up. No director was yet locked in, but it is noted that "a man like [Norman] Foster" should be paid about $15,000. Mexico's eminent Gabriel Figueroa was pitched as cinematographer.[48]

In September Welles visited the Yucatán to scout locations for the *Santiago* project; 16mm footage, possibly shot by Welles himself, has survived from this expedition.[49] That same month Norman Foster began shooting 'My Friend Bonito' on location with 'co-director' status. Foster was also probably set to direct the *Santiago* project the following year, but Welles's plans had to be changed after the attack on Pearl Harbor. On 10 December, between takes of *The Magnificent Ambersons*, Welles wrote to Foster in Tlaxcala about 'Bonito': "On the phone tonight I'm going to try to tell you how really and truly beautiful and important is the picture you're making [but also that] war has broken out and I have broken down."[50]

Foster was withdrawn from Mexico to direct the Welles-Cotten script of *Journey into Fear*, allowing Welles to wind up his Hollywood commitments faster. In early February Welles went to South America to make the Brazilian portions of *It's All True*, now officially under the umbrella of the Good Neighbor Policy.

Around the same time this draft of the *Way to Santiago* project was completed, in early 1941, Welles showed interest in another Mexican-set anti-fascist screenplay, by Paul Trivers, with the working title *Unnamed Mexican Story*. The story involves striking labourers on a Mexican ranch who battle a military force employed by the cruel ranch owner. It is difficult to ascertain the extent of Welles's involvement in this strongly Marxist screenplay's development.[51]

＊ ＊ ＊

Welles's departure from RKO following *It's All True* did not put an end to his work in the thriller genre. In fact, the most enjoyable of his early unmade anti-fascist screenplays, and the third of his Hitchcockian trilogy, is *Don't Catch Me*, "a farce melodrama" based on a 1943 novel by Richard Powell that had been serialised in *American Magazine*. A press release was drafted by Mercury Productions in April 1944 to announce imminent production and that Welles would write the final shooting script.[52] The most realised version of the script is an undated 103-page draft that credits Welles alongside co-writers Bud Pearson and Les White.[53] This time the story varies the device of a separated newlywed couple by allowing their joint adventure to prevent the consummation of their marriage.[54]

The script begins with an evocative night scene as a German submarine dispatches Nazis in rubber rafts to New York City. By the next morning the Nazi agents are dispersing into the United States via Penn Station, where their conspiracy intersects with the reunion of the soon-to-be-married Arab and Andy. Like Susan Alexander in *Kane*, Arab suffers a "coothache".[55] James Stewart would have been well cast as Andy, a hapless army lieutenant and antiques dealer. But except for the regularly employed New York Harbor and the scenes at Penn Station, *Don't Catch Me* is mostly set around rural Long Island. The settings actually closely resemble those of Welles's less cosmopolitan early drafts of *The Lady from Shanghai*.

Don't Catch Me was promised but not delivered. In 1945 Welles announced a radio version starring his wife, Rita Hayworth, on the CBS show *This Is My Best*, but the show's official director was unhappy with Welles's choice – and possibly his conflict of interest as rights holder – and cancelled the promised broadcast.[56]

The scripts for Welles's Hitchcockian trilogy, thematically unified around the threat of a fascist conspiracy, were prepared for very different approaches to creating urban space on screen: Hollywood studio re-creations in the case of *The Smiler with the Knife*, authentic Mexico City locations and studio work for the *Way to Santiago* project. It's difficult to determine what approach Welles would have taken with *Don't Catch Me* had he been able to progress with production.

* * *

The Mercury production of Eric Ambler's *Journey into Fear* was exceptional among Welles's early 1940s run of anti-fascist thrillers because its settings were not transferred to the Americas. It was also the only one of Welles's thriller projects to be actually filmed and released to theatres during Welles's stint at RKO, albeit in a much mutilated and censored form.

The embryonic scripts of *Journey into Fear* are more politically sophisticated than the shortened, watered-down version finally released to cinemas in 1943. They illustrate the challenges Welles faced as a political filmmaker during wartime, even within such a commercially orientated genre. The 'Budget Script', the next-to-last draft, is dated 1 August 1941 and was written by Welles and actor Joseph Cotten. Numerous blue replacement pages were inserted up until January, when a new final shooting script was typed for production. Norman Foster's copy of this 'Budget Script' contains annotations in pink pencil from somebody at RKO to guide revisions that would satisfy both the moral censorship of the Production Code and the political sensitivities of the State Department now that the United States had entered World War II. Anti-fascism had obviously become the official stance all around, but many of Welles's and Cotten's nuances were stripped out at the outset.

The pre-censorship version of the 'Budget Script' (incorporating the blue pages) begins in a grimy Istanbul hotel. Banat, a silent assassin armed with a revolver, listens to a "very sentimental French song" on a skipping gramophone record – his aural signature. He wanders into the street and observes the arrival of an American couple at the Hotel Adler-Palace. The Americans are Howard Graham, a timid American ballistics expert on assignment to survey the armaments of the Turkish navy, and his wife, Stephanie. Kopeikin, the obsequious local representative of Graham's firm, goes to great effort to pull Graham away from the comforts of a hot bath and dinner. Graham is uninterested in Kopeikin's promise of "girlies" but is eventually dragged away from his wife.

At Le Jockey Cabaret, a cosmopolitan nightclub, Graham meets the beautiful Serbian singer Josette. During a magic act, the magician is shot by Banat. Kopeikin and Graham visit Colonel Haki, chief of the Turkish secret police, who reveals an assassination plot by a Nazi agent, Moeller, to delay the rearmament of the Turkish navy. Banat's bullet was intended for Graham. Haki decides Graham will escape Turkey via a cargo ship (the *Persephone*) bound for Batumi in Soviet Georgia, and assures him that Mrs Graham will meet him at his destination. With Graham now out of the way, Haki will pursue the seduction of Mrs Graham, allowing her to believe her husband is involved with another woman.

Meanwhile, Graham is onboard the *Persephone* with Josette and her Basque manager, Gogo, as well as mysterious characters of various nationalities and political attitudes. Josette seems to propose an affair, although it is later revealed as more of a financial proposal administered by Gogo. Banat appears in the ship's dining room and intimidates Graham. One of Haki's secret agents, Kuvetli, is killed shortly after revealing his true identity to Graham. Haller, a polite German archaeologist, in turn reveals himself to be the Nazi Moeller. Graham is bundled off the boat in Batumi by Moeller and his henchmen, but he escapes and seeks his wife at the Grand Hotel. Alas, Moeller is already with Stephanie (and there are hints that Haki has made progress in his seduction of the woman). Graham winds up in a rooftop duel with Banat. Moeller is shot, Colonel Haki turns up for the shootout and is killed, and finally Banat slips to his death. Graham survives. The script ends incomplete, with a "TAG TO FOLLOW".

The film was nominally directed by Norman Foster under the heavy pre-production guidance of Welles, who was a key supporting player as well as the film's uncredited producer and co-writer with Joseph Cotten. Early scripting work was also contributed by Richard Collins and Ellis St. Joseph, but Cotten was assigned sole screenplay credit.[57] Virtually every scene was carefully storyboarded in pre-production. The storyboards, which have survived, were very closely followed in execution by Foster, which is hardly surprising considering the short time he had to prepare for filming.[58] For these reasons *Journey into Fear* is best considered an ensemble work of the Mercury company. Everett Sloan, who played Kopeikin, remembered that Welles directed his own scenes, and said, "I think it retains much of Orson's original conception of the picture."[59]

Joseph Breen, in between stints as Hollywood's chief film censor, was in 1941–42 the general manager at RKO and effusive with praise for what he had seen of *The Magnificent Ambersons*.[60] The annotations to Foster's copy of the 'Budget Script' of *Journey into Fear* make clear that Breen had read the script and passed along his comments. The moral objections mainly concerned Josette and Graham's proposed transactional adulterous affair. The censorship annotator also cautions against negative comments about Turks, who had signed a non-aggression pact with Germany in mid-1941. Colonel Haki's casual mockery of "the American point of view" is pencilled out because it "presents Turks (and a ranking officer at that) without morals".[61] The character of Josette describes Turks as "heathen animals" who in the last war "killed babies with their bayonets" ("Mr. Breen cautions that not only censorship but our own State Department will strenuously object to this"[62]). The wide diversity of political opinions presented in dialogue onboard the cargo ship was to be stripped of controversy. The Basque Gogo is in favour of appeasing Germany as long as business can continue; this was objectionable because the film would be watched by "thousands in places (Latin America) where agreement with speeches could bring applause and even riot".[63] Gogo recalls he had taken no sides in the Spanish Civil War, either, but another passenger,

Madame Mathews, shudders to imagine "if the Reds had won… They violated Nuns and murdered Priests." RKO's legal advice: "Church Legion of Decency positively will fight to the end on this … same thing State Dep't … very delicate. *Reds are our allies*."[64] The political situation would be drastically reversed in Hollywood five years later.

A 102-minute version was previewed in Pasadena on 17 April 1942, in a double feature with the Charles Laughton comedy *Tuttles of Tahiti*. The comment cards ranged from high praise to total dismissal. A dialogue continuity has been preserved but the long version is lost.[65]

RKO amended this long cut to an unconventionally brief 71-minute version, which was previewed in August 1942 and has survived. Welles later remembered it as "the opposite of an action picture" but that RKO "just took out everything that made it interesting except the action".[66] Although estranged in other ways from RKO, Welles was allowed a short time to revise this cut in October 1942 for a 68-minute version that was commercially released the following year.[67] Welles reframed the narrative to play via the point of view of Howard Graham (Cotten); Cotten voiced an amusing narration that comically emphasised Graham's husbandly devotion. The changes demoted Stephanie (Ruth Warwick) to genial one-dimensionality; the restriction to Graham's point of view meant eliminating the scene where Colonel Haki prepares to seduce Mrs Graham, and downplayed Welles's separated couple motif. Welles filmed a new single-shot ending with Cotten that resurrected the dead Haki, who had only suffered a mere flesh wound. Welles also removed his producer and co-writer credits.

Journey into Fear remains an enjoyable orientalist spy fantasy that never takes its anti-fascist agenda too seriously. To be fair, this was true even before RKO's censoring of the script. The opening page of Welles and Cotten's 'Budget Script' insists: "The names 'Athens' and 'Alexandria' are used in this draft only for convenience. Pay no attention to geographic correctness."[68] That's the general spirit; Ambler's novel was written without the experience of visiting the Central Asian settings.[69] The film was created almost entirely inside RKO Studios in the manner of Hollywood orientalist concoctions such as *Algiers* (John Cromwell, 1938), *Casablanca* (Michael Curtiz, 1943), and the adaptations of Ambler's novels *Background to Danger* (Raoul Walsh, 1943) and *A Coffin for Dimitrios* (as *The Mask of Dimitrios*, Jean Negulesco, 1944). In *Journey into Fear*, Istanbul is briefly glimpsed in exteriors by night as Banat (Jack Moss) stalks the Grahams outside their hotel; sandbags mounted alongside the street suggest wartime. At the city's shadowy Bosphorus port Ambleresque anxieties play out when Colonel Haki takes Stephanie's passport from Graham and establishes arbitrary control over the fate of the couple. At the end of the journey at the port of Batumi, a convincing neighbourhood in the Soviet city is created on the Hollywood backlot by signs in Cyrillic (although not in Georgian script) and large portraits of Joseph Stalin.

Joseph McBride has described *Journey into Fear* as "at best a very rough draft for some of Welles's later films".[70] When Welles returned to the anti-

The port at Istanbul

The port at Batumi

fascist thriller in the mid-1940s, with the valuable experience of location work in South America, he would pursue new techniques of putting urban spaces on screen.

NOTES

1. See Bond Love, '"Architectural jungle" or the "sum of its people"? Policing Post-War Urban Space in Anthony Mann's *Side Street* (1950)', in Jens Martin Gurr and Wilfried Raussert (eds), *Cityscapes in the Americas and Beyond: Representations of Urban Complexity in Literature and Film* (Tempe, AZ: Bilingual Press/Editorial Bilingüe, 2011), 243–56.
2. Welles quoted in Heylin, *Despite the System*, 200.
3. Bret Wood, *Orson Welles: A Bio-Bibliography* (Westport, CT: Greenwood Press, 1990), 194.
4. Welles quoted in Welles and Bogdanovich, *This Is Orson Welles*, 31.
5. Orson Welles, 'Carnaval' (memo to RKO and Treatment), n.d. (probably late May 1942), 10–12. *It's All True* file, box 17, folder 7, Lilly Library.
6. A three-page plot treatment by Welles's assistant Herbert Drake describes a jungle river of "no particular continent or island. It is just a place of mystery." Quoted in Marguerite H. Rippy, *Orson Welles and the Unfinished RKO Projects: A Postmodern Perspective* (Carbondale: Southern Illinois University Press, 2009), 91.
7. Welles quoted in Denning, 'The Politics of Magic: Orson Welles's Allegories of Anti-Fascism', 186.
8. According to Marguerite H. Rippy, Welles's commissioned research into the primitive was in order to create a "composite native" for the project, "a familiar Other based on sights and sounds of 'primitive' cultures that fit the fantasies of the white American public." He also scouted for existing jungle footage. See Rippy, *Orson Welles and the Unfinished RKO Projects*, 91.
9. Orson Welles, *Heart of Darkness* 'Revised Estimating Script' (30 November 1939), 1. Box 14, folder 16, Lilly Library.
10. Welles, *Heart of Darkness*, 2.
11. Welles, *Heart of Darkness*, 2.
12. See Jonathan Rosenbaum, 'The Voice and the Eye: A Commentary on the *Heart of Darkness* Script', in *Discovering Orson Welles*, 33; and Heylin, *Despite the System*, 127. The 1998 version of *Touch of Evil* featured a soundtrack remixed by Walter Murch that attempted to honour Welles's intentions as set out in his now-famous 58-page memo to the studio.
13. Welles, *Heart of Darkness*, 3.
14. Welles, *Heart of Darkness*, 3–4.
15. Welles, *Heart of Darkness*, 5.

16. Santo Spirito, the initial setting of the rip-roaring early nineteenth-century pirate adventure of heroes Dinty and Beauregard, is a Caribbean island. The historical note remarks that the island has been colonised successively by the Spanish, the English, the French, the Dutch, the Spanish (again), and the English (again). "Only the Africans are permanent. If there's a point to this history, it's the rich cultural mixture which makes for so cosmopolitan flavor in the location of our next adventure." *Santo Spirito* – Scripts – [Final?] Draft (photocopy of typescript, n.d.) (2 folders), 1. Box 3, Orson Welles–Oja Kodar Papers, Special Collections Library, University of Michigan.
17. Welles, *Heart of Darkness*, 12.
18. Welles, *Heart of Darkness*, 14.
19. Welles, *Heart of Darkness*, 5.
20. Carringer, *The Making of Citizen Kane*, 12.
21. See Michael Denning, *Cover Stories: Narrative and Ideology in the British Spy Thriller* (London: Routledge and K. Paul, 1987), 65.
22. Denning, *Cover Stories*, 67.
23. Denning, *Cover Stories*, 78.
24. Denning, *Cover Stories*, 71.
25. Joel Hopkin, 'An Interview with Eric Ambler', *Journal of Popular Culture*, Fall 1975, 290.
26. Uncredited 'Summary' of *Smiler with the Knife*. Box 14, folder 24, Lilly Library. Bret Wood speculates the author is Welles or Houseman. See Wood, *Orson Welles: A Bio-Bibliography*, 159.
27. Wood, *Orson Welles: A Bio-Bibliography*, 160.
28. Uncredited [Orson Welles], *The Smiler with the Knife* 'Revised Estimating Script' (9 January 1940), 20. Box 14, folder 20, Lilly Library.
29. Uncredited [Welles], *The Smiler with the Knife*, 23.
30. Bret Wood identifies this trend in the thriller scripts. See Wood, *Orson Welles: A Bio-Bibliography*, 157.
31. Uncredited [Welles], *The Smiler with the Knife*, 50.
32. Uncredited [Welles], *The Smiler with the Knife*, 123.
33. Uncredited [Welles], *The Smiler with the Knife*, 110, 134.
34. Uncredited [Welles], *The Smiler with the Knife*, 131.
35. Naremore, *The Magic World of Orson Welles*, 20.
36. Uncredited [Orson Welles], *Orson Welles #4* [*The Way to Santiago*] 'Third Revised Continuity' (25 March 1941). Box 15, folder 18, Lilly Library.
37. McBride, *Whatever Happened to Orson Welles?*, 33.
38. Uncredited [Welles], *Orson Welles #4*, 18.
39. Uncredited [Welles], *Orson Welles #4*, 23.
40. Uncredited [Welles], *Orson Welles #4*, 42.
41. Uncredited [Welles], *Orson Welles #4*, 46.
42. Uncredited [Welles], *Orson Welles #4*, 71.
43. Uncredited [Welles], *Orson Welles #4*, 119.

44 Uncredited [Welles], *Orson Welles #4*, 122.
45 Carringer cites a *Variety* article of 16 April 1941 that reports the Mexican rejection of the project. See Carringer, *The Making of Citizen Kane*, 123.
46 Jose Noriega, letter to Secretario de Gobernacion, 29 August 1941 (translated copy). Box 15, folder 18, Lilly Library.
47 F. Gregorio Castillo, letter to Jose Noriega, 5 September 1941 (translated copy). Box 15, folder 18, Lilly Library.
48 Uncredited, shooting schedule and production notes for *Way to Santiago* project. Box 15, folder 22, Lilly Library.
49 Benamou, *It's All True*, 27, 324.
50 Welles to Norman Foster, 10 December 1941. Correspondence, 1941, December 1–15, boxes 1–4, Lilly Library.
51 Wood, *Orson Welles: A Bio-Bibliography*, 172–4.
52 I found no evidence that this press release was ever issued. Uncredited, Mercury Production draft press release for *Don't Catch Me*. Box 21, folder 8, Lilly Library.
53 Bud Pearson, Les White, and Orson Welles, *Don't Catch Me: A Farce Melodrama* (n.d.). Box 20, folder 34, Lilly Library.
54 See Wood, *Orson Welles: A Bio-Bibliography*, 195.
55 Pearson, White, and Welles, *Don't Catch Me*, 79.
56 Callow, *Orson Welles: Hello Americans*, 243–4.
57 Berthome and Thomas, *Orson Welles at Work*, 97.
58 Uncredited, *Journey into Fear* storyboards, n.d. Box 20, folder 14, Lilly Library; Berthome and Thomas note some divergences between the storyboards and the ultimate framing in the final rooftop chase in *Orson Welles at Work*, 98–9.
59 Sloan quoted in Joseph McBride, *Orson Welles* (New York: Da Capo, 1996), 89–90.
60 Joseph Breen, inter-department communication to Orson Welles, 2 December 1941. Correspondence, 1930–1959, boxes 1–4, Lilly Library.
61 Uncredited [Orson Welles and Joseph Cotten], *Journey into Fear* 'Second Revised Budgeting' ('Norman Foster Censorship') (1 August 1941), 40. Box 20, folder 12, Lilly Library.
62 Uncredited [Welles and Cotten], *Journey into Fear*, 48.
63 Uncredited [Welles and Cotten], *Journey into Fear*, 56.
64 Uncredited [Welles and Cotten], *Journey into Fear*, 57.
65 Berthome and Thomas, *Orson Welles at Work*, 100; *Journey into Fear* comment cards from 17 April 1942 preview at U.A. Theatre, Pasadena, document dated 18 April 1942. Box 20, folder 19, Lilly Library.
66 Welles quoted in Welles and Bogdanovich, *This Is Orson Welles*, 166.
67 Benamou, *It's All True*, 131; Berthome and Thomas, *Orson Welles at Work*, 100.
68 Uncredited [Welles and Cotten], *Journey into Fear*, unpaginated.
69 Mark Mozower, 'Introduction', in Eric Ambler, *The Mask of Dimitrios* (London: Penguin Modern Classics, 2009), vi.
70 McBride, *Orson Welles*, 90.

CHAPTER 5

THE RAUCOUS RAGGLE-TAGGLE JAMBOREE OF THE STREETS
It's All True (unfinished, 1942)

Orson Welles's lifelong enthusiasm for the exotic was founded on a thoughtful and humanistic embrace of the foreign: languages, social rituals, food, music, and literature. Few other prominent Americans of the time gave such energy to the promotion of a cosmopolitan sensibility. To be cosmopolitan was to be inclusive, open-minded, committed to social justice, and orientated to an internationalist future. Nevertheless, many of Welles's cosmopolitan enthusiasms were steeped in the same romantic nostalgia for pre-industrial society he had invested in the vanished America of *Citizen Kane* and *The Magnificent Ambersons*. Welles continued to combine the political and the romantic within the same vision.

In the 1930s and 1940s his cosmopolitanism was instilled with moral seriousness and urgency. Fascism not only was destroying Europe but threatened the rest of the world. The OCIAA, implementing Roosevelt's Good Neighbor Policy, sought to improve relations across the Americas to ward off the influence of fascist Europe and to increase Pan-American economic and cultural ties.[1] Welles's inclusive, cosmopolitan persona and charismatic mastery of the mass media made him a likely Good Will Ambassador, even though he was only twenty-six years old at the time.

Welles's interpretation of the mission of the Good Neighbor Policy was idealistic and radically progressive. He employed a staff of researchers to educate him in Latin American history and culture.[2] His approach was to seek an unusual depth of cultural knowledge which he would then filter through his personal artistic sensibility. For the Rio Carnaval segment of *It's All True*, he expanded his attention from street parades and elegant nightclubs to the city's favelas – its hillside slums – in order to seriously explore the Afro-Brazilian roots of samba music. He quickly became an enthusiast. The surviving Technicolor footage of the 1942 Carnaval, both documentary and re-staged, suggests a celebratory vision of racially integrated urban life rarely, if ever, seen in Hollywood films of the era.[3]

Welles's radically *simpatico* reading of the Good Neighbor Policy did not prove entirely palatable to all the participating authorities. Officials in the Brazilian government's Departamento do Imprensa e Propaganda, who had originally proposed filming the Carnaval to attract tourists to Brazil, objected to aspects of Welles's approach as it developed, as did commentators in the local press.[4] Elements within RKO were completely at odds with Welles. Production Manager Lynn Shores's reports to the home office damned Welles's footage as "just carnival nigger singing and dancing".[5] On 11 April, Shores secretly informed the Brazilian Department of Propaganda that Welles had filmed in the city's favelas, and a few days later complained to RKO, "[Welles] ordered day and night shots in some very dirty and disreputable nigger neighborhoods throughout the city." The local press complained that Welles was filming "no good half-breeds ... and the filthy huts of the favelas which infest the lovely edge of the Lake, where there is so much beauty and many marvelous angles for filming".[6] It is a sad fact that even during the brief window when US political pragmatism allowed Welles's cosmopolitanism an official platform, a fifth column of racist provincialism helped crush the project.

Of course, there were many other reasons for the film's incompletion, most to do with executive politics at RKO, of which Welles's long version of *The Magnificent Ambersons* was another casualty.

Despite his occasional pastoral evocations – the Colorado frontier, sleigh rides outside Indianapolis, the fishing community in Fortaleza – Welles projected an essentially urban sensibility. He defined civilisation as 'city culture'. Aside from the implicitly critical contrast between the racially segregated spaces of Rio de Janeiro, the surviving traces of the Carnaval film gesture towards a utopian vision of cosmopolitan city living: the population united by an inclusive Pan-American identity, its public spaces open to the people, and socially progressive urban planning.

The unusual challenges of filming *It's All True* in Brazil also seem to have been pivotal for Welles's development as an urban filmmaker. Barely two weeks after he'd finished filming *The Magnificent Ambersons* at RKO in Hollywood, he was in South America trying to film a wild, uncontrollable, and uncontainable real-life event: "shooting a storm", he called it. The unorthodox process forced him to grapple with new challenges of representing a city on screen.

The trajectory of Welles's Brazilian filmmaking in 1942, from Rio de Janeiro to Fortaleza, was a little like that of Welles's film career in miniature: it began with a 27-person Hollywood crew and a plane's worth of movie equipment, as well as anti-aircraft searchlights seconded from the Brazilian military;[7] it ended with non-professional actors and a skeleton crew shooting with a single silent film camera.

***

It's All True was intended to be a multi-part anthology of stories based on actual events. In its pre-Good Neighbor Policy phase, the focus was North America: stories about Canada, the United States, and Mexico. After Pearl Harbor it expanded to include South American narratives. But Welles never finalised a definitive structure, and at least seven segments were developed. Three were fully or partially shot but never edited: 'My Friend Bonito', 'Carnaval', and 'Jangadeiros'.

During the early development of *It's All True*, Welles assigned preliminary scripting duties to writers including John Fante, Norman Foster, and Elliot Paul. Welles's own revisions would come at a later date, his method for radio dramas. But some of these scripts were never pursued further, and the extent of Welles's involvement in their development is unclear. Some of the segments used urban settings, and there was a recurring interest in architects, but it can only be speculated how Welles might have pursued these aspects on film.[8]

'The Story of Jazz' was to have dramatised the life of Louis Armstrong, playing himself – "except in knee pants", Welles noted.[9] Duke Ellington was contracted to write the music and participate in the development of the story. An early treatment from July 1941, written by Elliot Paul, was titled 'Jazz Sequence'. Welles appended a page of comments which clarified his conception of the segment as "a dramatised concert of hot jazz with narrative interludes by real people".[10] The treatment follows Armstrong's career from New Orleans to Chicago to New York. It is remarkably observant of the growth of jazz within specific urban spaces. It uses a New Orleans railway track as a recurring motif; Louis, first as a five-year-old boy, collects "usable pieces of coal which have fallen from the train".[11] Louis meets his mentor King Oliver in a New Orleans funeral band. There are marching band battles, 'cutting contests', and legendary New Orleans locations such as Mahogany Hall and the Frenchman's.

One passage in this early treatment, which surely shows the guidance of Welles, outlines another incarnation of his *Heart of Darkness* sound scheme: diegetic music to spatially orientate the viewer outside Mahogany Hall in Storyville. Paul's treatment notes:

> As we go from one fanlight to another we hear band music to match: that is to say, Oliver's music fades out under somebody else's; then somebody else's is taken over by still somebody else's. Sometimes the music is fast – sometimes slow – sometimes its just piano music. Always it representative New Orleans jazz.[12]

Later in Paul's treatment there is crosscutting between two Chicago nightclubs: the banal performance of the white Original Dixieland Jazz Band – "with all the stunts and gags" – and the exciting black Armstrong and Oliver band.[13] This kind of juxtaposition occurs in Welles's later sketches for the Rio Carnaval material, an emphatic contrast between the black originators of authentically American music and the white musicians who create a commercially acceptable version for white listeners in segregated spaces.[14]

Further continuity draft screenplays were written by Paul in August and September 1941.[15] Duke Ellington formally signed his contract with Mercury as composer in May 1942 while Welles was in Brazil, but the segment was never shot.[16]

Nevertheless, Welles's concept had an afterlife. *New Orleans* (1947), a later RKO jazz film made entirely without Welles's participation, seems to have evolved from Elliot Paul's material (he was co-credited for 'original story'). The film featured Louis Armstrong in a small role and its plot mirrored the "geographic trajectory" of 'The Story of Jazz'. Following the film's release, Welles's associate producer Richard Wilson sought legal advice on its similarities with Welles's project.[17] Later, Ellington and Billy Strayhorn's CBS television special and album *A Drum Is a Woman* (1957) used a jungle-to-nightclub narrative to tell the history of jazz. At the time of the broadcast Ellington recalled Welles's invitation to participate in *It's All True*: "Then there never was a movie,"

Ellington told *Newsweek*, "but I never forgot the theme." One Ellington critic notes that *A Drum Is a Woman* "implicitly portrayed music as a historical and cultural link between African, African American, and Latin American peoples, and implicitly argued for a Pan-African unity".[18]

Another untitled and uncredited script about jazz partially survives in typescript in Welles's archives. It is undated but was probably written around 1945.[19] This fictional story also follows the origins of the music from the jungles of Africa, across the Atlantic by slave ship, to New Orleans, and then to Chicago and New York. The story properly begins at the turn of the century and involves Kit, a white foundling in New Orleans, and Reggie, the son of her adoptive father's black housekeeper. Despite the lack of a credit, there is enough Welles-style humour to suggest he had a strong role in its writing. A courtroom sequence, in which the grown-up Kit, a jazz pianist, defends jazz as an art form against the 'Pure in Heart League', has a humorous quality which anticipates the farcical courtroom in *The Lady from Shanghai*. One racist commentator, who believes jazz is "the ignorant clamor of savage black men", is called as an "expert" witness for the prosecution. The "expert" works backwards through his professional experience – six years as a critic with the *Evening Telegram*, eight years with the New York Opera House, twelve with the Paris Symphony, fourteen with the Milan Opera Company, eighteen years with the Budapest choir, and so on. When he finishes, Kit's attorney cross-examines the witness: "Just one question, Mr. Travers. For how many years now have you been dead?"[20] It's difficult not to imagine a flustered Erskine Sanford smashing down his gavel to silence the uproarious laughter of the court.

Even more so than 'The Story of Jazz', the script seems to gesture towards connecting the development of jazz to the development of cities; Kit's father, Latimer, is a New Orleans architect conveniently involved in designing "cheap bungalows" and "modern housing".[21] But little evidence about this project survives in the Welles archive.

'Love Story' was to have focused on a romance between Italian immigrants in the United States. It was supposedly based on the parents of its writer, John Fante, author of the novel *Ask the Dust* (1939). In Fante's '1st Draft Continuity' script, finished in the summer of 1941, Rocco is a hod carrier who wants to be an architect, and pretends to have achieved material success to impress an Italian girl and her family. The setting is the San Francisco Bay Area in 1909. The script takes in the city's cable cars, a vaudeville theatre, a skating rink, a beach, a ballroom, a ferry, and a suburb at the end of the street car line in

Sausalito, a "block of scattered, cheap homes, treeless and lonely" where Rocco has a "box-like, two-story, weather beaten frame house".[22] The variety of historical urban settings suggests that the film could have become another part of Welles's *U.S.A.* alongside *Kane* and *Ambersons*. Catherine Benamou, the dean of *It's All True* research, notes that the world depicted in 'Love Story' is modernising, and its characters interact with a built cityscape and mixed population representative of these changes.[23] But the settings show more promise than Fante's weak melodramatic romance and its ethnic stereotypes. It does not seem that Welles revised Fante's work.[24]

Beyond the San Francisco setting, there are other hints at what would later become *The Lady from Shanghai*. The early scenes move between a penny arcade, a scenic railway, a 'Foolish House', a midway, and a crystal maze inside an amusement park.[25] The hall-of-mirrors concept would also feature in the unproduced *Don't Catch Me*.[26]

Another part of *It's All True*, 'My Friend Bonito', was based on a story by the filmmaker Robert Flaherty about the friendship between a Mexican boy and a bull raised to die in the *corrida de toros*. The bull would escape death after exhibiting exceptional bravery. Its screenplay was written by Fante and director Norman Foster, who began production in Mexico in September 1941. After he recalled Foster to Hollywood to direct *Journey into Fear*, Welles intended to himself film the missing scenes in Mexico on his way back from South America. This proved impossible after RKO's cancellation of *It's All True*.[27] 'Bonito' was never finished, but some of the black-and-white negative survived and several minutes were presented in the posthumous documentary *It's All True: Based on a Film by Orson Welles* (1993). In this assembly the boy and Bonito are seen playing together in material shot at the La Punta hacienda in Jalisco. There is another sequence showing the blessing of animals by a village priest. This part was shot at the Zacatepec ranch in Tlaxcala.[28]

***

> They're closing down Praça Onze
> There will be no more samba schools
> The tamborim cries, the shanty towns cry…
> put away your instruments,
> the samba schools won't be parading today.
> – 'Adeus, Praça Onze' by Herivelto Martins and Grande Otello[29]

Amid the maelstrom of his daily activities in Rio, Welles commissioned detailed research reports to help him understand Brazilian culture. The research helped him find a meaningful structure for the documentary film material he had shot during the four tumultuous days of Carnaval and guided the re-staging of the festivities. Welles's assistant Richard Wilson said: "As we learned more down there, the structure of the Carnaval subject altered. As Orson filmed more, it altered. There were several structures conceived for this subject, and several structures for the whole film."[30]

Many of these reports survive in the Mercury archives. Welles read about Brazil's 'macumba' ceremonies ("a kind of fetish lethargy"), the history of the rubber business, "Primitive Inhabitants of Rio Grade do Sol", the "History of Rio Grande do Norte and Legends, Customs and Traditions of the Northeast", "The Origin of the Word *Gaucho*", "Brazilian Independence and Jefferson", and "Holy Week in Ouro Preto". There is a long report on how Rio had developed from its beginnings to the imminent razing of the city's Praça Onze (Square Eleven) to make way for Avenida Getúlio Vargas, "an 80 meter wide avenue constituting an important longitudinal axis of the city". The "colossal" Avenida, already in progress, would require the destruction of entire blocks, four churches, and many other tall buildings.[31]

The city's samba schools, which researcher Robert Meltzer reported had replaced the banned *cordãos* (local gangs), traditionally fought in Praça Onze.[32]

A research paper by future Brazilian director Alex Viany explains:

At first, Praça Onze was – as it was … with all new public places in Rio and other world capitals – almost a privilege of the rich or the whitemen. When the city grew and life in the center began to get more and more expensive, the negroes and the poor went to the suburbs and the hills. They get back to town in Carnaval. Praca Onze is like the African embassy in Rio during Carnaval … [its] feasts are like Harlem jam-and-swing sessions elevated to the highest degree. […] The white workers also go to Praça Onze during Carnaval. There, among their negro brothers they are happier and more free than in the middle-class Carnaval hangout, Avenida Rio Branco, or than in beautiful but snobbish Copacabana. Praca Onze can be taken as a democratic symbol, as a center of irradiation… there you'll find the most genuine freedom in thinking and speaking. […]

The reaction of the negroes to the demolition of Praca Onze was one of resignation. They know that someday their hills shall be demolished too. But they also know that they must have better houses in better conditions by then. They believe in progress and want to cooperate. But they want to see progress working – not in promises. That's why they are building an obelisk to President Getúlio Vargas near Praca Onze. They (the workers of Brazil) believe in his promise but want to see them working. The obelisk is something of a reminder.[33]

Viany adds that the obelisk was actually the initiative of government-controlled workers' syndicates, not a spontaneous move by the workers themselves.

These commissioned papers, many by Brazilian scholars, indicate Welles's serious intent to film more than a colourful background for a propagandistic travelogue. He would reimagine Rio de Janeiro on screen with a grounding in its history, culture, economy, flows of communication, racial politics, and power relations, all in aid of Pan-American unity against fascism.

* * *

Through to the end of May, Welles and his crew filmed re-stagings of the festivities at Cinédia Studio, at the Teatro Municipal, and in the Quintino neighbourhood. He also entered the city's favelas to film with both a handheld camera and his Technicolor crew.[34] He later said the crew was attacked in one place by mysterious thugs who threw rocks and empty bottles.[35]

Welles had by now conceived an additional Brazilian segment for *It's All True*, a re-enactment of the recent ocean journey of four peasant fisherman by *jangada* raft some 1,650 miles from Fortaleza on the north-eastern Brazilian coast to Rio de Janeiro to appeal to dictator Getúlio Vargas for basic social benefits.[36] In March Welles temporarily left Rio to scout locations in Fortaleza. He intended to return in the winter to film the rituals of the fishing community and the commencement of the *jangadeiros'* journey. But before that Welles brought the four original *jangadeiros* to Rio to film the conclusion, a re-staging of their arrival in the city – which, contrary to history, would now coincide with the Carnaval festivities. However, during preparations for filming on 19 May, the *jangadeiro* leader, Jacaré, drowned in an accident off the coast of Rio.

Shortly after Jacaré's death, Welles wrote a long defensive memo to RKO.[37] His filming methods had been reported with persistent negativity by RKO finks such as Lynn Shores, and he had been pressed to explain and justify his

Surviving frames from Welles's Technicolor footage from the favelas of Rio de Janeiro, 1942 (Source: *It's All True: Based on a Film by Orson Welles*, 1993)

unorthodoxy to the brass back in Hollywood. *The Magnificent Ambersons* had already been removed from his editorial authority, and RKO had begun to reduce Welles's financial and logistical resources for *It's All True*. They refused to supply Technicolor stock for the upcoming *jangadeiro* segment in Fortaleza, which would now have to be shot in black and white at the cost of aesthetic continuity with the Carnaval material.[38]

In the memo Welles defined *It's All True* as "neither a play, nor a novel in movie form" but instead a "magazine", with the Carnaval sequence "a feature story" within that format. He added with enthusiasm that "the sheer immensity of Rio's Carnival is hopelessly beyond the scope of any Hollywood spectacle". There was only one possible approach considering the little preparation he'd been afforded:

> We often had no choice but to set up our camera and grind away until we got something usable. We shot without a script. We were forced to… I as director, was always the one to be informed rather than the people working under me.

Welles wrote that he immediately recognised that Carnival was too complex to be comprehensively documented on the fly and that re-stagings were inevitable. What's more, the cemented structure normally provided by a screenplay in advance of production had to be postponed until the film and sound recordings could be assembled and synchronised back in Hollywood; the crew were obliged to "take out all the paying dirt and ship it halfway around the world from the place where it was mined. We won't get the gold until we get back to where operations are possible."

Welles's memo is a key provisional document about the 'Carnaval' segment while he was still working on it in Rio. It is his attempt to define the themes and structure of the work-in-progress under duress. Although Welles appended, at RKO's request, a more traditional treatment – "a design for the main architectural lines of the Carnival film" – he did so under gentle protest. Both *Kane* and *Ambersons* had been meticulously scripted and planned shot by shot; it's clear Welles was exhilarated to be improvising on location without a traditional script as he had done three and a half years earlier making the film segments of *Too Much Johnson*.

The memo emphatically makes the case for the exceptionalism and cultural importance of 'Carnival'. With great clarity Welles argues that logistical challenges had made it necessary to invent a new process of filmmaking. He clearly thrived on the challenge, but felt it unfair to be criticised for circumstances outside his control.

> It was understood by all concerned before I left that Carnaval would be shot on the cuff. [...] The task of learning about Carnaval, and translating what we learned into film, has been very far from easy.

It was, after all, a semi-documentary. Welles claimed he and his collaborators had been "writing the Carnaval picture every night" in the form of extensive discussions with local experts. This was "the sort of daily work which has necessarily taken the place of actual writing". As an example, Welles appends excerpts of "minutes of these meetings" that document a democratic, well-informed debate on incorporating a romantic *choro* song and the practicalities of how the *choro* scene should be filmed. Welles makes a bold pitch for these notes as "the nearest thing we have to a script". By this method, the 'script' serves as a detailed record of the collaborative creative process rather than a meticulous pre-plan to be executed with a minimum of needless expense. It leaves open wide space for improvisation during both the filming and post-production.

In the future Welles would write screenplays that met strict industry standards only when he was working within an institutional context or when he was attempting to independently raise finances. Discussing his bullfighting project *The Sacred Beasts* in 1966, he said he planned to discard the many scripts he had written and shoot without one.[39] Writing was a crucial part of Welles's creative process – the mountains of messy drafts in the archives prove that – but as he said in 1964, "I prepare a film but I have no intention of making *this* film. The preparation serves to liberate me."[40]

Nevertheless, also appended to the memo is that 'Treatment for the Film Itself' demanded by RKO. It is possibly Welles's earliest surviving attempt to lay out a formal plan for the Carnaval footage he was still shooting. He intends to use as the structuring conceit samba, which, in the words of Catherine Benamou, will provide "the lens through which to gauge the effects of modernization on human relations and social identity" in Rio de Janeiro.[41] Welles writes:

> Samba comes from the hills that rise above Rio, from the people who live in those hills – but there are those authorities who maintain that Samba is principally a product of Rio's Tin Pan Alley. The best opinion and, most importantly, dramatic interest, sustain the hill theory… The point needs to be proved and illustrated…[42]

This 'hill theory' had not been unanimously supported by Welles's 'brain trust' of experts. Local researcher Rui Costa reported:

> To say that the samba was born in the hills is as much a matter of opinion as to say that Venus was born in the waves of the sea… the truth is that all elements of the city, from all the sections, cooperate to produce the samba.

Costa notes the one-time usefulness of the favelas as a rehearsal space because it had been easier there to evade the police, who tried to prohibit late-night noise. However, the composers deserted the favelas following the invention of radio and recording studios down in the city. He describes the subsequent state of the favelas' samba schools as "mediocre affairs, without any of the choral discipline of the old times". Costa concludes:

> At any rate, perhaps it's just as well to allow the people and the literal-minded to keep the sweet conviction that the samba was born in the hills. It's a sweet and poetic tale which after all doesn't harm the real trend of things...[43]

The American Robert Meltzer's long and entertaining memo to Welles on the musical genealogy of samba lamented the lack of existing written studies, which meant that the music's origins were still mythical and debated. He sought advice in Rio from such experts as composer Heitor Villa-Lobos and encountered conflicting opinions. Meltzer settled for the imprecise conclusion that

> it's neither the Colonist of the North nor the composer of Rio, neither the barefoot bacteria from the hills nor the Fireman's Band, neither the European and American influence nor the troubadours, neither the denizens of Villa Isabel nor the sons of the slaves – none of these can claim responsibility for Samba's birth and appearance. All of them together, each in its own way, had a great deal to do with that appearance, too, a very great deal. [...]
> It takes all sorts of things to make a world, but it seems to take even more to make a Samba.[44]

Perhaps unsurprisingly, Welles went for the sweet and poetic 'hill theory' as the structural device of this version of 'Carnaval'. This served to highlight the central contribution of Afro-Brazilians to Rio de Janeiro's culture and to recognise the city's peripheral, impoverished underclass. It also provided the opportunity to canvas the city's many diverse spaces.

Welles mentions Rio's "kinship" with New Orleans and how "between American Jazz and American Samba there is much in common" (one of several instances where Welles's Good Neighborliness extends to calling the entire hemisphere 'America' in the South American fashion). Meltzer, himself a jazz pianist, had come to the conclusion that samba is quite different from jazz because it privileges composition over performance.

But no matter. Welles lays out his plan:

> Here we are, up in the hills. Here is the jungle, trying to push its way back down into the city; and below us, profuse and glittering, is the city itself, the bays and the beaches, the skyscrapers – beyond, the breathtaking monuments of other hills. We're up the Favellas [sic] now, rude dwellings (now being

replaced by the Government of Brazil with better homes for the people). Here, in a special place of its own, distinguished by its special structure, its flowers, its curtains, its large fenced-in yard, is a typical School of the Samba.[45]

Welles introduces the Afro-Brazilian composer, musician, and dancer Grand Otello as a central figure. In the weeks before Carnaval, Otello introduces a new samba to the musicians at a samba school. The film will cut to the same song being recorded in one of the city's radio stations by a sophisticated female singer. Now "the city has taken up the new Samba".

Welles introduces the percussion instruments of samba, as well as other props of Carnaval: "perfume-throwers … masks, serpentina, confetti, noise-makers". He then cuts to four representative and "widely contrasting locations"[46] of the *bailes* or dance venues: the Teatro Municipal, the Independencia, the Teatro da Republica, and the Rio Tennis Club. Each represents a different class of *carioca* and each is alive with festivities and music ('marchas' rather than 'sambas'). A woman in the Tennis Club sings a romantic *choro* during an interlude before the festivities resume.

> The people come down from the hills early, dressed up in the costumes they've been preparing for weeks: clowns, Hawaiians, Cossacks, Bahianas, tramps, animals, Indians, monsters – everything and anything. Down they come from the hills, down the paths and rough roads to the paved streets and the little plazas in the suburbs […] The crowds jamming the city's outskirts choke the narrow streets and the wide streets: a rising river of humanity that moves together in the channels defined by the shops and houses. There is nothing placid about this movement. It is all whirlpools and eddies. And always there are the rhythms of Carnaval's music, the gay noise of thousands of voices singing without inhibition in the open air.[47]

The revellers appropriate the city's public transport in their movement towards the city centre. An open street car is so overcrowded it becomes

> a great clinging globule of humanity with a trolley sitting on top. By this and by other means, the people move and gather in the center of Rio. The tens have become hundreds, the hundreds thousands, and the thousands a million. Their voices combined in song now produce a mighty roar that sifts into the farthest alley and rises up to the top of the tallest skyscraper.[48]

Surviving frames from Welles's Technicolor footage of the Carnaval of Rio de Janeiro, February 1942 (Source: *It's All True: Based on a Film by Orson Welles*, 1993)

* * *

Next, Welles includes a fictional scene, playing himself as a newcomer to Rio:

> A roof garden on top of a skyscraper in the middle of the city. All around are more skyscrapers, some finished, some in work. Beyond are Rio's sumptuously beautiful hills. From the street there rises the huge roar of Carnaval, throbbing like a powerhouse. Close to us people are singing the samba 'Farewell, Praça Onze'. This is distinct from the multiplicity of other sounds, other rhythms – increasingly so during the following scene.
>
> An architect's stand on trestles displays a plaster model of part of the city. Standing beside this is a young lady whom we will call Donna Maria. She looks efficient and attractive. There is no mistaking her officialdom or her sex appeal.

Welles and Donna Maria discuss the samba song and the important public square whose imminent disappearance it laments. Welles remarks that "now it has to go to make room for a big new street".

DONNA MARIA

The people love it very much – so they made up this song about it to bid it goodbye. Senhor Orson, you've never been to Rio before, so you can't know how our city's been changing. Over there we used to have a mountain. A little while ago we moved it away. Now the city is several degrees cooler and the traffic problem is simplified.

WELLES

I think Rio can spare a few mountains and still be the loveliest city in America.

DONNA MARIA

We thought so, too. Now here's a model of our new Avenue – Avenida Getulio Vargas.

INSERT – MODEL OF AVENIDA GETULIO VARGAS

WELLES

Right there (my hand points) – Isn't that where Praça Onze is now? (back to scene)

DONNA MARIA

It won't be by the time this picture's shown onscreen. The city's going to be tremendously improved, but, of course, lots of people will still have *saudades* for Praça Onze.

WELLES

Saudades – Ladies and gentleman, I'm no interpreter, but I now offer you a Portugese expression the English language ought to adopt because we haven't got its equivalent – saudades.
DISSOLVE during the next few words to title:

S A U D A D E S

Over this I continue.

WELLES (Cont'd)

It means heartache – something like that – Sentimental memory, lonesomeness – a longing remembrance of something past, or of someone gone away…

Welles believes 'Farewell, Praça Onze' will become a standard like 'Basin Street Blues' or 'Swanee River'.

WELLES

No, Donna Maria, I don't think you Cariocas are going to forget Praça Onze – that song won't let you. Next year, of course, there'll be a new samba about the new street, and I'm all for that – for new sambas and new streets. (to camera) You know, Rio's one of the only beautiful old towns where new things are even more beautiful than the old ones. Of course, it's just as hard here as it is anywhere else to say goodbye to the past – but you can always keep your mind off the past if you're busy enough with the future, and Rio's plenty busy. Right, Donna Maria? You've got even more plans here than you've got memories – more hopes than regrets, more dreams than saudades.

DONNA MARIA

The hills up there, for instance, where the poor people live, where the Schools of Samba come from – you were up there photographing one of them, Senhor Orson – do you know we've got new housing projects for all those places – model homes? They're going up right now.

WELLES

That's fine.

DONNA MARIA

Just wait and see…

The 'Praça Onze' tune sounds louder, more insistently. She smiles, acknowledging its effect.

DONNA MARIA (Cont'd)

Of course, we can't deny we're sentimental.[49]

Welles's dialogue with this fictional Brazilian official is characteristic of his interpretation of his mission on behalf of the Good Neighbor Policy. It would have been another exercise in charismatic but calculated diplomacy. Rather than attack the cynicism of the Vargas regime in what was surely an authoritarian usurpation of public space, Welles calls the dictatorship's bluff, accepts its urban development plans at face value, and pushes the most utopian and progressive reading of those plans. The destruction of the culturally important square is permissible because it is linked, Welles indicates, to socially progressive aspects of the city's modernisation, including the housing projects that will replace the slums of the favelas. It would have been a passive-aggressive attempt on Welles's part to publicly defy the Brazilian dictatorship not to come up with the goods – in other words, the internal radicalisation of a policy by excessive endorsement. As pitched, Welles's 'Carnaval' segment would have served like that ambiguous workers' obelisk to President Vargas near Praça Onze – both a commissioned tribute and a reminder.

In this interpretation 'Farewell, Praça Onze' is not exactly a protest song against authoritarian control of the spaces of the city. Instead, the song gives popular expression to a very Wellesian sense of loss. Welles's discovery of the Portuguese word *saudade* couldn't have been more timely. His work in film to date is seeped in it.

Carnival had been increasingly institutionalised under Vargas; the samba schools had been forced to register with the authorities.[50] Simon Callow is right to describe Welles's endorsement of the Vargas regime as an "extraordinary piece of ideological flexibility".[51] At the same time Welles does not compromise on his radical commitment to celebrate the city's marginalised black and indigenous people. And to be fair, this scene was sketched in a memorandum directed to RKO in the midst of trouble, as he was losing control of *Ambersons*.[52] Welles had been forced to justify the *It's All True* project and his methods, defend himself against damaging accusations, and present the segment as both commercially viable and in line with the OCIAA propaganda mission. But Welles was in risky territory. Welles had alienated officials in the Vargas regime by focusing on Afro-Brazilian and *caboclo* culture in both his documentary footage and his recreations.[53]

* * *

The treatment continues. Welles plans a "montage concert" of what he calls the 'Praça Onze Suite' which will show varied arrangements of the song as it is played in many venues of the city, beginning in Praça Onze itself. A similar montage occurs for the other samba hit of the year, 'Amelia', and introduces the character of a lost young boy named Pery who seeks his mother in the crowd. The two songs merge in the square and the competing singers busy themselves with a *capoeira*, the Brazilian fight dance.[54]

Welles intends to show the singer Linda Baptista performing in the racially segregated Casino de Urca, where Carmen Miranda was discovered;[55] this is to be intercut with the same samba, 'Batuque no Morro', as sung in the streets in a parody of Carmen Miranda by Grand Otello, who has appropriated various pieces of women's clothing. Welles explains:

> The contrast is not only of voices, but of directions: the Carnaval of tradition is a celebration of the streets alone. But recent years have send a trend indoors to the Baile and the Casino. The contrast, as it's illustrated by this song, isn't extreme – but the raucous raggle-taggle jamboree of the streets and the more professional, if equally enthusiastic atmosphere of the nightclub, is interesting in juxtaposition…
>
> We've seen people inside the clubs and dance halls at night; we've seen them outside during the day. Now we see them outside at night. We see them from the level of the streets themselves, and from the roofs of buildings. The total effect is breathtaking.

Welles also dubiously lauds the "unpoliced good behavior of Carnaval's mob. Drunkenness has no part of the world's biggest good time, since only champagne and beer are obtainable on Carnaval days, and besides, Brazilian good humour is so unaggressive that brawls are hard to find."

The segment continues with footage of the parade down the city's main avenue. There is an orgy of Pan-American propaganda. One float depicts five tall columns, the fifth symbolically toppled – "as the people believe it should be". Then there are several spectacular musical numbers played by the Ray Ventura Orchestra in the Urca Casino, which ends as

> Rio's Carnaval becomes Pan-America's Carnaval. Here, you realize, is one way of saying something that all of us in the Western Hemisphere are coming to recognise. The Americas, all the Americas together, are joined in fact as well as in idea, today rather than in the future.[56]

There is a brief return to the nearly deserted Praça Onze. 'Farewell, Praça Onze' plays in a minor key. A policeman carries the boy Pery home. Grand Otello wakes up and discards his broken tamborim.

A short coda shows the *jangadeiros* returning by plane to Fortaleza after their heroic quest. Welles as narrator dedicates the picture to the late Jacaré and "to his dream of the future!"[57]

* * *

Benamou considers Welles's 'Carnaval' treatment in the tradition of the international cycle of city symphonies, and singles out comparison with *Man with a Movie Camera*, which goes beyond presenting mere social contrasts to show the city as "a collective consciousness" in flux.[58]

Welles's treatment aims for an expansive reimagining of the city on screen. He approaches the challenge by proposing several innovative techniques. By mapping the passage of the music-making Carnaval revellers from the favelas – "this huge conservatory of the samba"[59] – to Praça Onze, Welles illustrates the centripetal flow of Rio's geographically marginal dwellers through the built passages of the city. This also radically asserts the cultural centrality of impoverished non-whites. Surviving Technicolor footage of the massed crowds moving through the streets, some shown at the conclusion of the 1993 documentary, depicts the happy and uninhibited mingling of races.[60]

Then there are the stark, ideologically loaded juxtapositions between different spatial and social zones of the city: Grand Otello's authentic creation of a song in the favela samba school matched with a tamer performance of the same song in a radio studio; and the four venues for *bailes* with clear distinctions of race and class.

The dialogue with Donna Maria provides the film with a synoptic overview of the city as well as an ideological guide to interpreting that vision. The expansive point of view of the camera from the skyscraper roof in the centre of the city shows the Carnaval procession in its totality. The plaster model of the new Rio, including Avenida Getúlio Vargas, allows for an immediate visual comparison between the city of the present and the city of the future. The genial dialogue between Welles-the-outsider and Donna Maria as government official determines authoritatively the progressive significance of the urban changes.

The memo is a typically persuasive sketch by a cinematic visionary, but

Welles was overly optimistic to believe he could get away with it. RKO continued to withdraw financial and logistical support for *It's All True*. Undoubtedly moved to pay tribute to the drowned Jacaré, Welles prefaced his memo on 'Carnaval' with the assertion that he was now by necessity at work writing a "wholly new attack on the Jangadeiro story... No effort will be spared to hasten its completion."[61] And although RKO stopped further shooting of the Carnaval segment in Rio, they allowed Welles to continue making the *jangadeiros* story in Fortaleza on a paltry budget of $10,000 with a tiny crew rather than risk bad press after the death of Jacaré.[62]

* * *

Years later Welles would recall the new regime at RKO blaming him for having tried to make a film in South America without a script. He said, "I entirely sympathized with them, but it wasn't my idea or project."[63]

Even after *It's All True*'s cancelation, Welles tried to persuade RKO to allow him to finish the film. He did some editing of the Carnaval and Rio-based *jangadeiro* material in Hollywood in September 1942,[64] but plans for Twentieth Century Fox and Warner Bros. to take over the release of the film fell through. In another treatment pitched to RKO in September 1943, Welles persisted in including images from the favelas, "the real jungle, which still makes long hopeless war on the capital of Brazil".[65] This pitch was not accepted by RKO's executives.

Welles kept trying. He bought the rights to the footage from RKO for $200,000 in 1944, and attempted to devise new fictional films that would draw upon the extant material.

One thriller script, also titled *Carnaval*, involved an American fighter pilot with amnesia named Michael Gard who slowly pieces together his memories of the 1942 Carnaval. It turns out his Czechoslovakian lover had almost been killed by Nazi soldiers, and her survival and escape to Mexico had inspired him to sign up to fight in the war. Grand Otello appears as himself.[66]

A treatment and production outline also survive for a mooted romance to be called *Samba* that was planned around 1945.[67] *Samba* uses a framing narrative similar to that Welles planned for a contemporaneous film of Oscar Wilde's *Salome*: a story told at a café table. The setting is a Copacabana all-night restaurant called the Samba School, which may have been inspired by the Café Nice on the Avenida Rio Branco, where, as Robert Meltzer had reported to Welles, many sambas were composed.⁶⁸ By now, from afar, Welles perceived Rio as a romantic locale of foreign exiles, artists, and bohemians: "As we'll learn, Rio de Janeiro is to the American hemisphere what Budapest is to Europe. This should partly help to explain 'The Samba School' and it's customers."⁶⁹

He makes the case that he will be able to create a believable cinematic version of Rio by integrating the location-based Carnaval footage with new Hollywood material shot on cheap sets:

> The street fronts the beach. Enough stage space should be allowed for cut-offs of buildings (in forced perspective) and a feeling of real distance for the mountains painted on the sky backing. The cafe is never seen except by night and early sunrise, so there is no need for this to look at all phoney.⁷⁰

Welles notes what of the existing footage can be used for "processes and plates"⁷¹ (he also asserts his viability as a romantic lead: "If you don't think I can play it, wait till I take off another 40 pounds!"⁷²). In this treatment Welles revived key aspects of his earlier sketches. The 'hill theory' on the origins of samba is now voiced by that "dark cupid", Grand Otello, who shines shoes at the café.⁷³ 'Ave Maria' is sung as a samba, as it had been in the May 1942 treatment, and there is the juxtaposition of a new favela samba with its "slick and polite"⁷⁴ interpretation on commercial radio. While the melodramatic love story is not particularly interesting, the treatment does provide insight into Welles's practicality when working with very limited resources.

Welles would never be able to finish any incarnation of the Carnaval material. The rights reverted to RKO in 1946 when Welles was in financial difficulties.⁷⁵

* * *

First the city, then a contrasting pastoral. Welles spent weeks from mid-June 1942 in Fortaleza and other cities on the Brazilian coast filming a re-creation of the preparations and voyage of the four *jangadeiros*.⁷⁶ In Fortaleza's traditional fishing community, Welles found another pre-modern paradise to celebrate and romanticise, this time in the context of a dignified political struggle for basic social benefits. The footage of the fishing community scrupulously avoids depicting any aspect of Fortaleza's urban modernity.⁷⁷ The exclusive emphasis is on the *jangadeiro* rituals of the sea and the coast. The wild human processions from favela to city centre in 'Carnaval' would have been counterpointed by an austere *jangadeiro* funeral procession across the coastal landscape of north-eastern Brazil.

Although Welles was never able to edit the *jangadeiro* footage, and never apparently even viewed the rushes, much of the original negative was rediscovered in 1981.[78] Richard Wilson was behind the effort to edit the segment after Welles's death, although he did not live to see it. An essentially complete silent film of almost fifty minutes named 'Four Men on a Raft', with sound effects and a score by Jorge Arriagada, provided the conclusion to the 1993 documentary. Despite somewhat lethargic pacing, this posthumous film is one of the most impressively realised items to emerge from the shadows of Welles's oeuvre. It's also a reminder that the canon of commercially released films does not give a full account of Welles's artistic development. The segment was an adventure in the extremely low-budget, under-resourced, and improvisatory filmmaking Welles would not resume until he made *Othello* in Europe at the end of the decade.

NOTES

1. Benamou, *It's All True*, 10.
2. Benamou, *It's All True*, 46–7.
3. Surviving images are included in the documentary *It's All True: Based on a Film by Orson Welles* (Bill Krohn, Myron Meisel, and Richard Wilson, 1993).
4. Benamou, *It's All True*, 100–1, 235.
5. Shores quoted in Benamou, *It's All True*, 139.
6. Quoted in Heylin, *Despite the System*, 134–5.
7. Benamou, *It's All True*, 47.
8. Of such unrevised scripts by other writers, Welles scholar Bret Wood says that at best we can appreciate "the broad themes which attracted [Welles] to the project". Wood, *Orson Welles: A Bio-Bibliography*, 181.
9. Orson Welles 'Note', included in Uncredited [Elliot Paul], *It's All True: Jazz Sequence* (July 1941), 18. Box 16, folder 17, Lilly Library.
10. Uncredited [Paul], *It's All True: Jazz Sequence*, 18.
11. Uncredited [Paul], *It's All True: Jazz Sequence*, 1.

12 Uncredited [Paul], *It's All True: Jazz Sequence*, 6.
13 Uncredited [Paul], *It's All True: Jazz Sequence*, 9.
14 See Benamou, *It's All True*, 121–2.
15 Benamou, *It's All True*, 325n27.
16 Duke Ellington to Mercury Productions, 1 May 1942. Correspondence, 1942, May 1–6, boxes 1–4, Lilly Library.
17 Benamou, *It's All True*, 282, 361n21.
18 Harvey G. Cohen, *Duke Ellington's America* (Chicago: University of Chicago Press, 2010), 330.
19 Wood, *Orson Welles: A Bio-Bibliography*, 176–7.
20 Uncredited, untitled (jazz script), 72. Box 22, folder 24 (Films – Untitled), Lilly Library.
21 Uncredited, untitled (jazz script), 10, 16.
22 Uncredited [John Fante], *It's All True: Love Story* '1st Draft Continuity' (8 August 1941), 36. Box 16, folder 1, Lilly Library.
23 Benamou, *It's All True*, 31.
24 Wood, *Orson Welles: A Bio-Bibliography*, 180.
25 Benamou, *It's All True*, 31, 325n32. Benamou also cites James Naremore, 'Between Works and Texts: Notes from the Welles Archive', *Persistence of Vision*, No. 7, summer 1989, 21–2.
26 Wood, *Orson Welles: A Bio-Bibliography*, 195.
27 Benamou, *It's All True*, 57.
28 Benamou, *It's All True*, 311.
29 Translation is taken from the subtitles of the documentary *The RKO Story: Tales from Hollywood* (episode 4: 'It's All True') (Charles Chabot and Rosemary Wilton [producers], 1987).
30 Wilson quoted in Wood, *Orson Welles: A Bio-Bibliography*, 183.
31 Uncredited, 'Transformation of the City from Its Founding to the Present Time', *It's All True* Research Materials, 19. Box 20, folder 1, Lilly Library.
32 Robert Meltzer, memorandum to Orson Welles, 'Subject: The Genealogy of Samba and Other Aspects of an Unquiet Life', n.d., *It's All True* Research Materials, 14. Box 20, folder 7, Lilly Library; Benamou, *It's All True*, 114.
33 Alex Viany, 'Samba Goes to Town', n.d., 3–4. *It's All True* Research Materials, 14. Box 20, folder 7, Lilly Library.
34 Benamou, *It's All True*, 47–51.
35 Welles quoted in Heylin, *Despite the System*, 135.
36 Benamou, *It's All True*, 37.
37 Welles, 'Carnaval', 1–11.
38 Benamou, *It's All True*, 51–2.
39 *Orson Welles in Spain* (Albert and David Maysles, filmed 1966 [unreleased]). Available at https://www.youtube.com/watch?v=Z3gcp9-_bfI (accessed 28 June 2015).
40 Welles quoted in Juan Cobos, Miguel Rubio, and J. A. Pruneda, 'A Trip to Quixoteland:

Conversations with Orson Welles', in Estrin (ed.), *Orson Welles: Interviews*, 100.
41 Benamou, *It's All True*, 113.
42 Welles, 'Carnaval', 13–14.
43 Rui Costa, 'The Truth About The Samba', n.d., *It's All True* Research Materials, 1–2. Box 20, folder 7, Lilly Library.
44 Meltzer, memorandum to Orson Welles, 16, 21.
45 Welles, 'Carnaval', 14–15.
46 Welles, 'Carnaval', 17.
47 Welles, 'Carnaval', 21.
48 Welles, 'Carnaval', 22.
49 Welles, 'Carnaval', 23–7
50 Benamou, *It's All True*, 240.
51 Callow, *Orson Welles: Hello Americans*, 74.
52 Benamou also warns about reading the treatment as an "isomorphic reflection of the authorial text". Benamou, *It's All True*, 114. The scene with Donna Maria would endure in the 2 September 1943 treatment Welles submitted to RKO for 'Carnival'; it is this incarnation to which Callow refers.
53 Benamou, *It's All True*, 240.
54 This shot can be seen in the 1993 documentary.
55 Benamou, *It's All True*, 45.
56 Welles, 'Carnaval', 34–8.
57 Welles, 'Carnaval', 42.
58 Benamou, *It's All True*, 113.
59 Welles, 'Carnaval', 14.
60 Benamou, *It's All True*, 109; RKO vice president Phil Reismann claimed to have given Welles the idea of using the hills-to-city samba trajectory as a narrative device (Callow, *Orson Welles: Hello Americans*, 71).
61 Welles, 'Carnaval', unpaginated.
62 Benamou, *It's All True*, 52–3.
63 Welles quoted in Welles and Bogdanovich, *This Is Orson Welles*, 161.
64 Benamou, *It's All True*, 131.
65 Welles quoted in Heylin, *Despite the System*, 137.
66 Wood, *Orson Welles: A Bio-Bibliography*, 188–90.
67 Wood, *Orson Welles: A Bio-Bibliography*, 176.
68 Meltzer, memorandum to Orson Welles, 19.
69 Uncredited [Orson Welles], *Samba* 'Screen Treatment and Production Outline', 9. Box 16, folder 24 (Films – *It's All True*), Lilly Library.
70 Uncredited [Welles], *Samba*, insert page between 8 and 9.
71 Uncredited [Welles], *Samba*, insert page between 36 and 37.
72 Uncredited [Welles], *Samba*, 6.
73 Uncredited [Welles], *Samba*, 7.

74 Uncredited [Welles], *Samba*, 37–8.
75 Benamou, *It's All True*, 133.
76 Benamou, *It's All True*, 54.
77 Rosenbaum, *Discovering Orson Welles*, 219.
78 Benamou, *It's All True*, 278.

CHAPTER 6

RATLINE TO MAIN STREET
The Stranger (1946)

Back in the United States, Welles resumed a typically heavy schedule but was temporarily estranged from directing films. Aside from his ongoing work in radio drama, his performance as Rochester in Robert Stevenson's *Jane Eyre* (1943), and magic performances for the military in the Mercury Wonder Show, his activities were political. He gave anti-fascist lectures, campaigned for President Roosevelt's 1944 re-election, broadcast political commentaries, and wrote a daily column for the *New York Post* that was syndicated across the country through much of 1945.

He continued to support the Good Neighbor Policy. In March 1944 he wrote:

> [I]n spite of all the dictators supporting it, in spite of its stumbling caution, its blind snobbishness, in spite of itself, the Good Neighbor Policy is an anti-fascist alliance, a community of nations bound together in the name of democracy. As such it is a preliminary sketch for world organisation.[1]

Later that year, Welles defined fascism as "always … some form of nationalism gone crazy".[2] Welles's post-national vision of world government after World War II in some ways overlapped with Soviet-style internationalism, although he pushed a progressive rather than revolutionary agenda.[3] At a 1943 convention sponsored by the United Nations Committee to Win the Peace, Welles had said:

> The scaly dinosaurs of reaction (if indeed they notice what I'm writing here) will say in their newspapers that I am a Communist. Communists know

otherwise. I'm an overpaid movie producer with pleasant reasons to rejoice – and I do – in the wholesome practicability of the profit system. I'm all for making money if it means earning it. Lest you should imagine that I'm being publicly modest, I'll only admit that everybody deserves at least as many good things as my money buys for me. Surely my right to having more than enough is canceled if I don't use that more to help those who have less. This sense of humanity's interdependence antedates Karl Marx.[4]

After the war, Welles aggressively denied he had ever been a communist and sued the vice president of the American Federation of Labor for claiming he had communist tendencies. When grilled by gossip columnist Hedda Hopper in July 1947, he insisted he was "opposed to political dictatorship" and that "organized ignorance I dislike more than anything in the world".[5] By now everybody should have realised that Orson Welles wasn't to be easily tamed by any organisation. However, throughout the 1930s and 1940s Welles had many Communist Party associates and participated in the campaigns of various front organisations.

In fact, Welles's key political mentor, close friend, and future producer of his ill-fated *Mr. Arkadin* was Louis Dolivet, a secret Soviet agent. Born Ludovicu Brecher in Polish Galicia, Dolivet spent his childhood in Romania.[6] He was in the service of the French Comintern from 1929[7] and was also an operative of the KGB. For a time in the 1930s and 1940s Dolivet was married to the sister of Michael Straight, an aristocratic communist spy within the US State Department who was also connected to the Soviet spy cell at Cambridge University.[8] Dolivet seems to have first encountered Welles in Hollywood around 1942.[9] He invited the young director to join his International Free World Association. Welles became an editor and penned articles for the association's journal. It is not certain whether Welles knew about Dolivet's covert Soviet activities, or that the International Free World Association was a Comintern front. Nevertheless, whatever its hidden objectives, the public message to which Welles lent support was progressive anti-fascism with the aim of international political cooperation.[10]

For a time Welles was mooted as a statesman and politician. Surviving letters between Dolivet and Welles testify to the mentor's enduring belief in the young man's extraordinary potential to be a key figure of the age.[11] Dolivet supposedly believed that Welles would make an ideal Secretary-General of the nascent United Nations; Welles later claimed he'd been unenthusiastic about the idea.¹² Welles later recalled, "Oh, he had great plans! He was organise it so that in fifteen years I was going to get the Nobel Prize."¹³ wasn't alone in his optimism. If Welles is to be believed, President R personally encouraged him to run for political office. Welles also considered running for the senate in his home state of Wisconsin in 1946 against newcomer Joseph McCarthy, the eventually disgraced politician who would come to define the reactionary mood of the coming years.¹⁴

In 1945 Welles edited a daily newspaper and made broadcasts from the United Nations Conference on International Organization in San Francisco. Around this time his utopian hopes for postwar world government dimmed. Welles later reflected to his former school master Roger Hill:

> I remember driving to the airport after witnessing and reporting on the founding charter of the United Nations that established "equal rights for large and small nations," thinking that the starry-eyed days were over. Even then you could see that the lines were drawn between the east and west. You could see from the Russians that there was no hope of a dialogue. I went to San Francisco starry-eyed as you say, but I left pretty much the realist I've remained ever since.¹⁵

Welles's postwar anti-fascism increasingly focused on race issues. Unlike many of his peers, Welles directly equated racism with fascism, and was more fearlessly outspoken on civil rights than probably any other white American of his celebrity. His campaign for justice over the blinding of black veteran Isaac Woodard, Jr, by the Georgia policeman Linwood Shull was a particular passion in mid-1946.

In the midst of this consuming political life, Welles produced an ambitious stage adaptation of Jules Verne's *Around the World in Eighty Days*, with original songs by Cole Porter. He also continued to try to make films. He had fruitlessly pursued new dramatic ideas to make use of the Rio Carnaval footage and worked on editing 'My Friend Bonito' with Jose Noriega. He bought the rights to *Don't Catch Me* and Antoine de Saint-Exupéry's *The Little Prince* and developed their screenplay adaptations. He developed projects for independent producer Alexander Korda, including *War and Peace*, *Cyrano de Bergerac*, and Oscar Wilde's *Salome*.¹⁶ None of these films were made, but Welles was able to return to cinema with two thrillers that responded to the postwar political order.

***

Leftist filmmakers such as Edward Dmytryk, Abraham Polonsky, Jules Dassin, and Robert Rossen enjoyed a short-lived prominence in Hollywood after the war. These particular directors were active in the production of those crime melodramas retrospectively categorised as film noir. Noir came to be defined by mythical character types, dark and fatalistic narratives, and bleak urban settings, and drew on a visual language indebted to German Expressionism but which could nevertheless extend to semi-documentary realism. The cinematography of *Citizen Kane* (and its complicated flashback structure) had also been a seminal influence. Noir proved to be a language to express the moral and political darkness beneath the supposed tranquillity of the postwar years, and was briefly a venue for a politically radical perspective on big business, political corruption, and crime.[17]

This brief opportunity for left-wing filmmakers coincided with labour unrest and mass strikes across the nation – and also at Hollywood's film studios. American workers had long postponed demands for improved working conditions and pay during the war (Welles began directing his independently produced noir *The Stranger* at the Universal Studios lot in October 1945, just after the national strikes began). But the reactionary backlash was swift. The Taft-Hartley Act of 1947 effectively outlawed strikes and the House Un-American Activities Committee began to purge leftists and labour organisers from various industries under the banner of anti-communism.[18] In the film business, left-wing filmmakers were intimidated into allegory or silence. Some were imprisoned, others blacklisted, exiled, or pushed into betraying others. Welles all but vanished into a long European exile.

Dennis Broe's political historiography of film noir traces a consequent shift away from the immediate postwar period's "outside-the-law fugitive protagonist" – the sympathetic working-class character, often a war veteran, forced into crime, usually by someone in a dominant class position. Key examples include the protagonists of *The Strange Love of Martha Ivers* (Lewis Milestone, 1946) and *Raw Deal* (Anthony Mann, 1948). By contrast, the heroes of noirs from 1950 to 1955 tended to be authoritative law enforcement protagonists.[19]

Welles more or less fits into this political historiography of noir. The trajectory of his Pan-American thrillers from the late 1930s to the late 1950s reflects his growing sophistication as a political thinker alongside his expanding cinematic virtuosity. During the Roosevelt era Welles scripted variations on the fascist infiltration plot, presenting fascism as an alien ideology that would be crushed by strong democratic institutions and international support for the war effort. Welles's role as an ambassador for the Good Neighbor Policy and a campaigner for Roosevelt was compatible with this view. In his wartime screenplays and in his activism he endorsed the progressive anti-fascism of official intentions from a position within the political establishment, even if this demanded some overly generous – or even disingenuous – interpretations of Allied policy.

But *The Stranger* and *The Lady from Shanghai*, his back-to-back postwar noirs, straddle a pivotal shift in Welles's political identification from the centre of power to the periphery after the death of Roosevelt. *The Stranger* revives the infiltration plot and presents an American Nazi-hunter protagonist as the heroic embodiment of postwar internationalist justice.[20] But soon after making that film Welles abruptly abandoned his optimistic depiction of American officialdom. Moreover, fascism ceased to be an alien force infiltrating democratic society; it was now a danger arising from within the institutions of power.

Perhaps inevitably, the heroic anti-fascist crusader was pushed into the margins. Welles described Michael 'Black Irish' O'Hara, the near-penniless drifter hero of *The Lady from Shanghai*, as "a poet and a victim" who "represents an aristocratic point of view" as had Jedediah Leland in *Kane*. In Welles's terms, 'aristocratic' was a superior moral quality rather than a class position, "something connected to the old ideas of chivalry, with very ancient European roots". The aristocratic figure lives outside "sentimental bourgeois morality".[21] Mike's naive medieval chivalry leads him to be compared to Don Quixote, but he is the only character with a shred of real conscience in the cynical world of the rich. He is unimpressed by their wealth and believes it "very sanitary to be broke". He has impeccable anti-fascist credentials as a veteran of the Spanish Civil War. A legendary rabble-rouser to his fellow sailors, the radio labels him a "notorious waterfront agitator". He is an anti-authoritarian with good reason to distrust the police. The wealthy frame him in a labyrinthine plot and use the institutions of American law to railroad him to the gas chamber. The studio's heavy post-production control of *Shanghai* only somewhat dulled the film's anti-authoritarianism.

Why this sudden change in political identification? Welles wrote the *Lady from Shanghai* script through the summer and early autumn of 1946, exactly the time he was engaged in a public crusade against racist police brutality in the Isaac Woodard case. The following year he left the United States as reactionary forces abused the power of American political institutions to crush left-wing activism in the name of anti-communism. Welles's subsequent anti-fascist projects abandoned the infiltration plot in favour of vastly more nuanced illustrations of institutionalised corruption. In fact, his politics became more deeply radical.

* * *

Film noir is overwhelmingly an urban mode of cinema, situating its melodrama in the alienation, violence, sex, and corruption of the mid-century city. Noir's cinematic cities draw on many sources, including the traditions of hardboiled crime fiction, German Expressionism and the related *Kammerspiel* and street film of the 1920s, Hollywood gangster films, documentary street photography, and existentialism.[22] Within the cycle are cinematic reimaginings of actual cities, most commonly the distinct locales of New York and Los Angeles. There are also fictional cities that exist more in the realm of myth, such as the comprehensively corrupt and isolated small industrial city, an archetype descended from Dashiell Hammett's Poisonville in his novel *Red Harvest* (1928).

The noir worldview – bleak, violent, fatalistic – bridges these diverse urban settings and stylistic modes. What Richard Slotkin writes about the imaginary landscape of the western is equally applicable to the cities of noir:

> The history of a movie genre is the story of the conception, elaboration, and acceptance of a special kind of space: an imaged [sic] landscape which evokes authentic places and times, but which becomes, in the end, completely identified with the fictions created about it. [...] The genre setting contains not only a set of objects signifying a certain time, place, and milieu; it invokes a set of fundamental assumptions and expectations about the kinds of events that can occur in the setting, the kinds of motive that will operate, the sort of outcome one can predict.[23]

The settings of *The Stranger* and *The Lady from Shanghai* are in fact rather atypical for the noir cycle, but they served Welles's themes in a rapidly disintegrating political climate. After an early sequence in a dangerous South American port city, *The Stranger* is set in a mythical American small town with pastoral fringes. Port cities – New York, Acapulco, San Francisco – dominate the settings of *The Lady from Shanghai*. The port city, already a key setting in the *Heart of Darkness* screenplay and in *Journey into Fear*, provided an aptly cosmopolitan milieu for Welles's political melodrama as anti-fascism was squeezed from its place in the wartime political establishment out to the periphery and soon into exile. These are crossroad cities whose spaces occasion the meeting of characters of different nationalities and classes in the postwar upheaval. In these cities everybody is under surveillance, but Ambleresque anxiety over identity documents is offset by the prospect of wiping clean the slate of identity and thereby dodging responsibility for the horrors of history.

***

The Stranger is probably Welles's least admired film. Independently produced by Sam Spiegel and International Pictures, *The Stranger* evolved from a story treatment called 'Date with Destiny' by Victor Travis and Decla Dunning (an earlier version of the story by Travis dated back more than ten years).[24] John Huston and Anthony Veiller, who had recently worked on the adaptation of Ernest Hemingway's story 'The Killers' for the eponymous 1946 film directed by Robert Siodmak – a noir masterpiece indebted to *Citizen Kane* – developed the adaptation of *The Stranger* before Welles was invited to star and direct. The story concerns the exposure of a German Nazi posing as a respectable American citizen in a small town shortly after the end of World War II. Welles's performance as the Nazi is relatively weak.

Welles worked on a 'Temporary Draft' of the script dated 9 August 1945, co-credited with Huston; it reflects Welles's provisional ideas for the film before officially signing his contract. But that temporary script was subject to pre-production cuts on the order of editor Edward Nims, who favoured retaining only what he deemed to be essential to the plot. A particular casualty was the long sequence in South America. About twenty-five pages of material from the 'Temporary Draft' was lost.[25]

Welles's working copy of his subsequent 24 September shooting script, as it survives in the Mercury files, was embellished with coloured replacement pages until after the start of shooting on 1 October. This copy also contains Welles's pencilled rewrites and crossed-out sequences. Researchers have had trouble establishing exactly what was dropped from the shooting schedule and never filmed, and what was filmed but eliminated in the editing room by Nims without Welles's participation.[26] Some of the pencilled-out sequences in the shooting script actually survive in the final cut of the film, which suggests Welles may have been using his script to prepare an edit he was never able to realise himself. In any case, the shooting script sketches a more psychologically complex and visually interesting version of what ultimately made the producer's final cut.

It begins one night in the fictional town of Harper, Connecticut. Mary Longstreet is drawn from her bed in a dreamlike state to cross town to the church clock tower. The church is soon surrounded by a mob of armed townsfolk; a scream announces a fight at the top of the tower, and two unidentifiable figures fall. Then we flashback to Wilson, a pipe-smoking American with the Allied War Crimes Commission, who decides that war criminal Conrad Meinike should be allowed to escape from prison in a risky gambit to lay a trail to a Nazi mastermind.[27] Wilson tracks Meinike by ship to a South American city, where Meinike reconnects with the Nazi underground, is provided with a new identity and passport, and learns the present whereabouts of Franz Kindler. One of Wilson's South American agents, Señora Marvales, is murdered by dogs during the surveillance of Meinike.

The story shifts to Harper, where Kindler is posing as a history teacher with a passion for antique clocks named Charles Rankin. Rankin meets and romances Mary, the naive daughter of a Supreme Court judge.

Meinike arrives in Harper by bus and lures Wilson, who has followed him without much discretion, to a brutal ambush in the local high school gymnasium. Meinike tracks down Kindler-Rankin and preaches spiritual redemption. Rankin leads him into the woods and strangles him. He then proceeds to church to marry Mary as scheduled.

Meanwhile, Wilson has recovered from the attack and remains in town under cover as an antiques dealer. On that pretence he meets the Longstreets and, soon after, Rankin himself. Wilson comes to believe that Rankin is really Kindler after he expresses the bizarre opinion that Karl Marx was not German because he was Jewish. Wilson confronts Mary's brother and father with the truth and begins to close in on Rankin. After Meinike's body is found, Wilson shows Mary footage of the liberation of a Nazi death camp. Meinike is shown in the film under arrest. Mary, however, continues to believe her husband's explanation that Meinike was merely a blackmailer he'd been forced to kill and that Wilson is laying a trap.

Rankin plots to kill Mary by beckoning her to the top of the church clock tower; the ladder has been booby-trapped. However, she is prevented from arriving by her housekeeper, and in her place Noah and Wilson are almost killed. Rankin goes into hiding and Mary unravels psychologically (there is an "impressionistic montage" or dream sequence). We return to the opening sequence: Mary crosses town at night, seeking to kill Rankin in his hideout in the clock tower. Wilson intervenes. During a gun battle, Rankin is impaled on a sword brandished by an angel statue in the gothic clock mechanism. He and the statue fall to the ground as a mob of the townsfolk gather at the foot of the church.[28]

***

A handwritten correction in Welles's copy of the shooting script names the South American port city 'Puerto Indio', although the name is not mentioned in the final cut of the film. There are a few indications to suggest this fictional city is based on Buenos Aires, including a reference in the script to tango. Welles had visited that city in 1942 on his Good Will tour.[29] In January 1945, Welles called for direct Allied involvement in Argentina's affairs, due to the Nazi wealth invested in the country.[30] Nazi influence in Argentina was topical: Edward Dmytryk's *Cornered* (1945) cast Dick Powell as a Canadian war veteran hunting a Nazi in Argentina to avenge his wife's death. That film created its Buenos Aires in Hollywood. Welles's Puerto Indio is similarly a studio creation, and what survives is stunning. Later Welles described the South American section as "the only chance to be interesting visually in the story".[31]

Following the incompletion of *It's All True*, Welles indeed re-emerged with a Latin American story, but instead of an uplifting celebration of Pan-American unity, Welles created a dark and murderous South American port city devoid of the appealingly exotic. Puerto Indio is the end of a ratline for escaping Nazis. Here war criminals change their names and nationalities, and go underground.

The shooting script, while cut down from the more expansive Welles–Huston temporary draft, nevertheless covers more spaces of this imagined city than the final cut.[32]

After the *S.S. Bolivar* docks in Puerto Indio, an immigration official and ship's purser check through a Romanian man, a Dutch woman, and Konrad

Meinike (under the Polish passport of one 'Stefan Podowski'). The mentally disturbed Meinike rehearses his explanation: "I am travelling for my health". He is waved through the border check. The camera cranes up to Wilson observing from an overhead ramp. He confers with local agents Señor and Señora Marvales, who will trail Meinike through the city. During filming, Welles apparently extended the crane shot to take in Señora Marvales's pursuit of Meinike beyond the border post, but the shot was pointlessly abridged in the release version by a clumsy slow dissolve. It is the only crane shot of this South American section to make the release version of the film, although several others are noted in the shooting script.

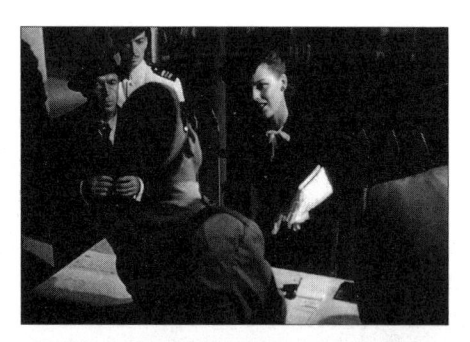

Three surviving frames of the abridged crane shot:
Meinike at immigration, observed from above by Señora Marvales, and followed

As Meinike crosses a "rustic bridge" he is compared to a "small, scuttling spider". Once again, Welles sketches a scheme to use diegetic music to help enhance the illusion of a city's space. When Meinike passes the door of a "cheap nightclub" we hear a "slow, sad tango". Further on, "through a group of archways", Meinike passes another bar, where we hear "hot exciting rhythm played by a small, corny band" (only a murmur of Latin American dance music underlines this scene as it survives in the film, in shortened form).

All the while Meinike is under almost omniscient surveillance: the Marvales have access to private telephones in bizarrely convenient buildings around the city. The silhouette of Señor Marvales observes Meinike from a window as he telephones a report to Wilson at the Hotel Nacionale.

At this point the shooting script presents a number of powerfully evocative Puerto Indio scenes that did not make the final cut. The first setting is terrifying, even on the page: the Farbright Kennels, a warren of dog cages adjoining a multi-storey building. Fierce German police dogs are kept in order by a whip-brandishing trainer in a wire face mask. A vertiginous crane shot was to have moved from the dog cages to track up the side of the building, where Meinike observes from a ramp. He then ascends to the top of a circular staircase to meet Farbright, another Nazi fugitive. Meinike seeks the current whereabouts of Franz Kindler. Inside "a shabby room" at the top of the building, Farbright and a seedy doctor drug Meinike and interrogate him to confirm his loyalty. Farbright is sufficiently convinced to direct Meinike to a contact who will provide a new passport. Señora Marvales observes the meeting from ground level beside the cages. As the dogs growl, she can see light escape from the fringes of the burlap sack that covers the shabby room's window.

At dawn Meinike continues along a "high rampart above the city" en route to collect his passport from a Nazi who works in a morgue. Señora Marvales reports Meinike's whereabouts to Wilson from a telephone in a basement. Meinike reaches the morgue on a deserted street. A woman appears leading a goat and selling milk. In the earlier temporary draft, however, Meinike was to have seen instead the shadow of a crucifix fall on the street. He falls to his knees and interprets it as a message from God. His subsequent comment to his passport photographer – that he comes in the name of the "all highest" – was meant to play on the photographer's confusion between God and the Führer, an irony lost by the time of the shooting script (in fact, many of the script's religious references were cut by the time of the release version).[33]

Señor Marvales, again observing Meinike from yet another convenient window, makes a telephone report to Wilson; by now, however, Señora Marvales has gone missing. Inside the morgue, the Nazi hands Meinike his new passport (still lacking an identity photograph) in the name of 'Phillipe Campo'. Before Meinike departs, "two bruisers", including the sinister dog trainer from the Farbright Kennels, wheel in the corpse of Señora Marvales under a "rough cloth". The audience will identify her by a distinctive golden hoop earring. She has been savaged by wild dogs.

Now Meinike proceeds to a photographer's studio to complete the passport. The release version of the film resumes here, skipping the kennels and morgue scenes entirely. Considering the excision of the intervening scenes, it is entirely possible the dissolve from Señor Marvales's initial report to the

The dissolve from Señor Marvales to the passport photographer

photographer's studio scene was not designed by Welles. Nevertheless, the matching framing of the silhouette of Marvales and the shadowy photographer perfectly suits this city of fluid identities.

In the surviving three and a half minutes, Puerto Indio appears as a shadowy city of cavelike passages. The camera pans from low angles to follow Meinike and Señora Marvales in pursuit. Welles and cinematographer Russell Metty film silhouettes and Meinike's monstrous shadow as it plays over rough walls. The pair would repeat this brilliantly expressionist use of shadows when they reunited for *Touch of Evil*.

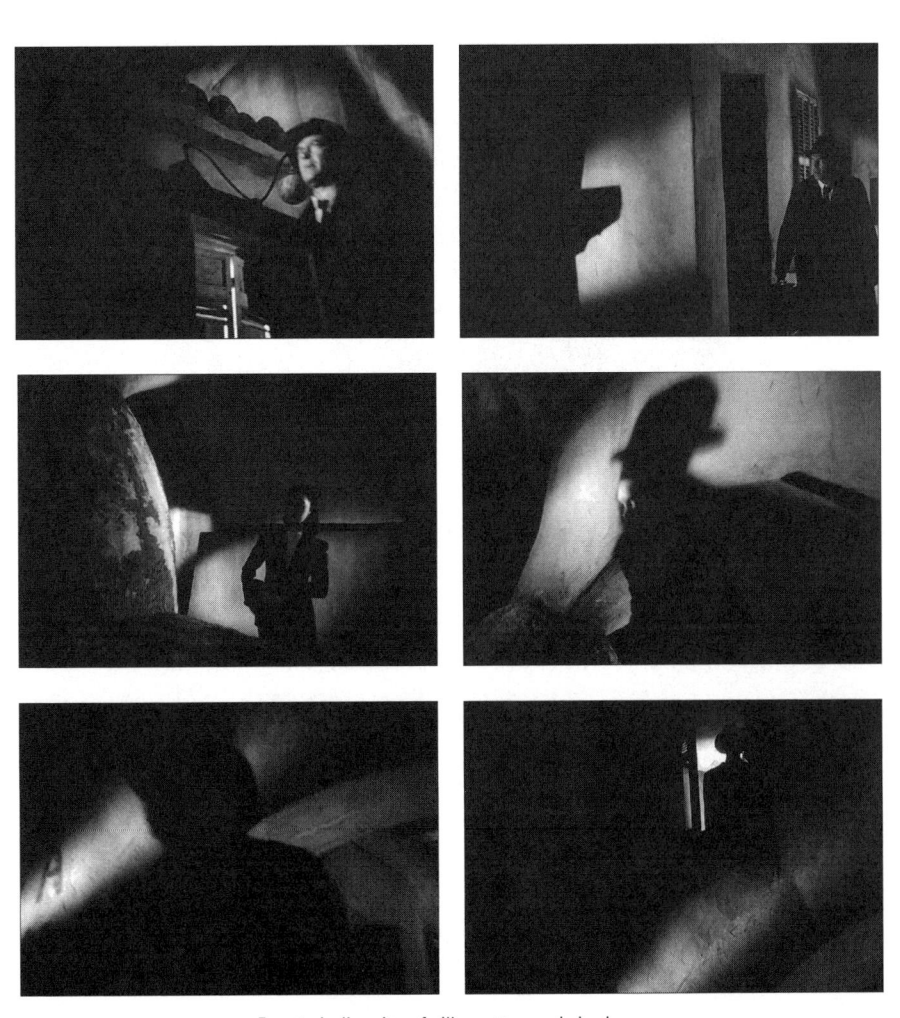

* * *

Puerto Indio: city of silhouettes and shadows

The remainder of *The Stranger* takes place in the very different setting of Harper. Its pastoral qualities are established in the shooting script by the courtship of Rankin and Mary.[34] "Let's go through the fields," he tells her at their first meeting. "It's my favorite walk… It's beautiful that way … through the cemetery, over the little brook and then the woods." Rankin encourages her to cross the stream over a plank; in this way Mary temporarily overcomes her fear of heights (this scene was cut or possibly never filmed). Rankin will quickly pollute the town's pastoral tranquillity by his murder and burial of Meinike in the woods.

Harper as postcard

The mythical smalltown setting with pastoral fringes had also featured in Huston and Veiller's *Killers* script as Brentwood, New Jersey. But otherwise it was the rare setting of noirs such as *Shadow of a Doubt* (Alfred Hitchcock, 1943) and *Out of the Past* (Jacques Tourneur, 1947). They all share narratives of murderous urban forces invading the peace of an idyllic small town. *The Stranger*, which uses the conceit in the context of a political rather than straightforward crime thriller, is surely inferior to each of these other films, but Welles is alone in introducing an ambiguous undertone to the small town setting.

He was not quite so eager to evoke the virtues of smalltown life as he had been four years earlier for *Ambersons*. Harper is a quirky but provincial town that has been too long closed to the sobering political urgencies of the world. In the shooting script (but cut from the film), the discovery of Meinike's corpse prompts one of the baffled locals to wonder, "What would a

South American ... just off the boat ... be doing in our incosmopolitan little town?"[35]

The broken clock crowning the church tower, found by the production at a Los Angeles museum,[36] serves as both a plot point – repairing clocks is Rankin's tell-tale hobby – and a flexible metaphor. In the shooting script, Rankin describes the "ideal social system in terms of a clock".[37] But it also represents the town's stasis. When Rankin manages to repair the mechanism, one citizen complains, "Charles Rankin, I wish you'd left that clock alone. It was a nice quiet place until it began banging." Mary's naivety regarding the extremes of human depravity verges on a dangerous moral complacency. Even when Wilson confronts her with (real) documentary footage of a Nazi camp, Mary refuses to accept her husband's true identity and moral responsibility for mass murder. She has a psychological breakdown.

* * *

Welles initially intended to construct the Harper town set from the plan overleaf at Twentieth Century Fox (the art director was *Kane*'s Perry Ferguson). That plan would have better established a concentrated sphere of action and a coherent spatial relationship between the film's key settings – Potter's drug store, the Harper Inn (where Wilson lodges), the church and cemetery bordering the woods, and the Rankin home.[38] The centre of the town was intended to be the church and clock tower, which the shooting script describes as "fronting a green around which the township itself is clustered, cradled by the gentle slopes of the Berkshire foothills".[39]

Welles had to compromise for budgetary reasons and shoot the film on the permanent Universal Studios smalltown set.[40] Numerous other films had been shot there, and to moviegoers the familiarity of the town layout, based around a central square, would have only increased the mythical unreality of Harper. The town appears antiseptically clean with its polished gymnasium floors and its raked late autumn lawns. Once again Welles employs paper detritus to dress his setting: the high school boys' paper chase through the woods, which almost leads to the accidental discovery of Meinike's murder scene, temporarily litters the *mise-en-scène*. The shooting script has Rankin desperately tear pages from Meinike's Bible to create an alternative trail leading away from the corpse. This audacious act of Bible destruction was abandoned when the film was shot.

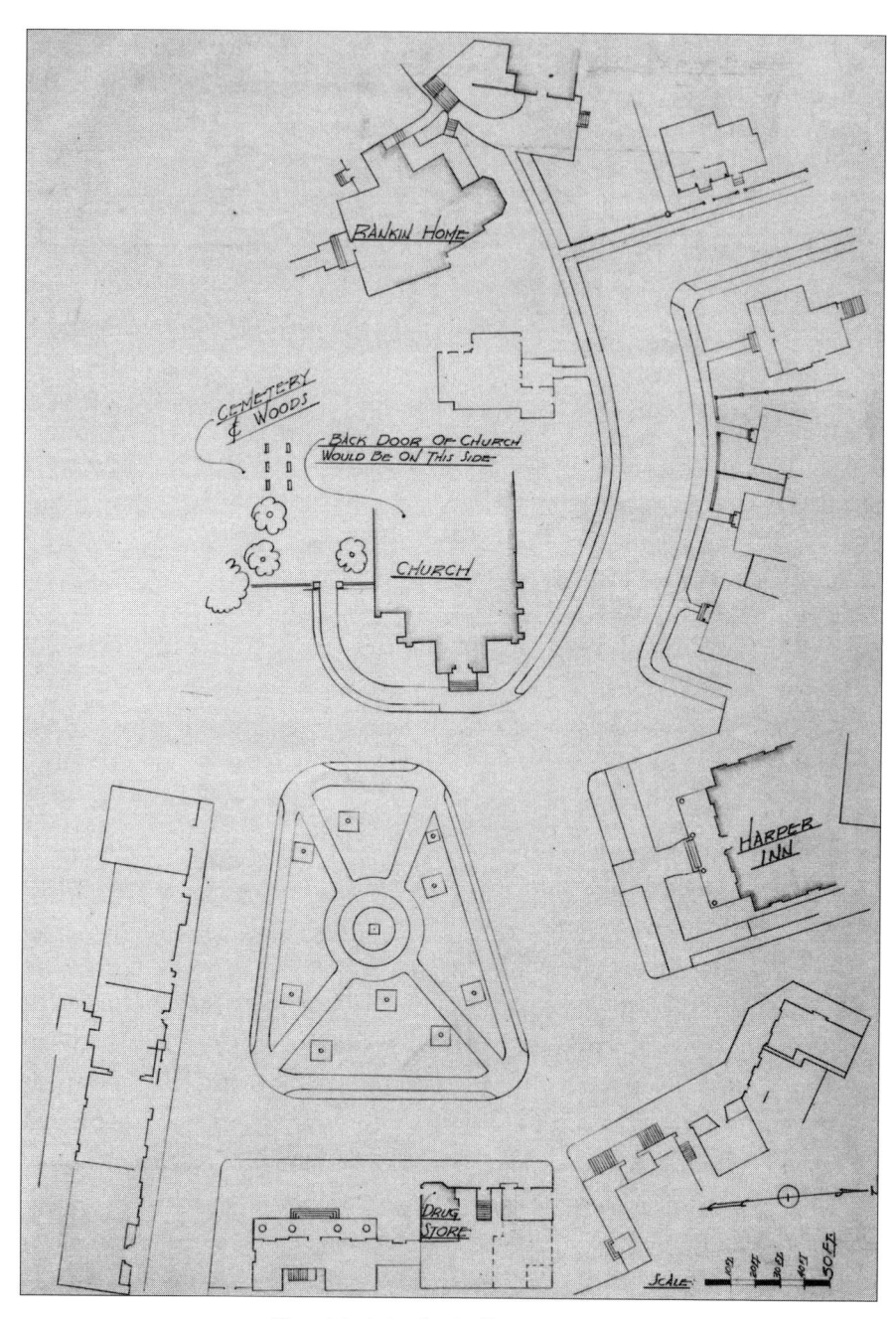

The original plan for the Harper town set
Courtesy, The Lilly Library, Indiana University, Bloomington, Indiana

Welles's camera was becoming increasingly mobile, at least while he still had access to Hollywood's ace technicians. There are many tracking shots of characters navigating Harper by foot, which emphasises its smalltown compactness, although the coherence of the spatial relationships between the settings beyond the central square was lost owing to the abandonment of the original town plan.⁴¹

Walking through Harper

* * *

Like Puerto Indio, Harper is dominated by surveillance. The shooting script repeatedly describes the act of looking. In a comment anticipating a more famous line in *The Third Man*, Rankin looks down from the clock tower on the mob and says he feels "like God looking at little ants".⁴² Often the gaze is cast through obscuring windows. In a shot described in the script that didn't make the final cut, Meinike hides from Wilson in the doorway of a store, behind the "plate glass windows" that "angle gently out from the deeply recessed entrance… He is able to look out through the glass cases and thus can observe the street without being seen."⁴³ The looking-through-windows motif was realised mostly in shots set in the vicinity of Potter's Drugstore.

The act of looking in Harper

Potter's Drugstore is both the nexus of social activity – it doubles as the town's bus stop – and the central place of observation. Welles installed signs in his own handwriting, including "Gentlemen! Do Not Deface Walls!" (Potter is less passive-aggressive than the blind shopkeeper in *Touch of Evil*, whose sign warns "If you are mean enough to steal from the blind, help yourself").[44] The script describes Mr Potter as "an immensely fat New Englander, whose philosophy permits but one form of exercise – the punching of a cash register".[45] Potter is so lazy he insists his customers find their own items on the shelves and fill their own coffee cups, a novelty in those days. As portrayed by Billy House, the character enlivens the otherwise dull *dramatis personae* with a spark of Welles's absurdist but homespun humour. Not as crafty as he imagines himself, Potter is the local gossip and 'town clerk', and, as he tells Wilson, "Town clerk runs the town, you might say."[46]

Welles would never again return to so homespun a background as Harper. Political urgencies took him forever away from Main Street, USA.

NOTES

1. Orson Welles, 'Good Neighbor Policy Reconsidered', quoted in Callow, *Orson Welles: Hello Americans*, 186.
2. Welles, 4 December 1944, quoted in Denning, *The Cultural Front*, 395.
3. Denning, *The Cultural Front*, 395.
4. Orson Welles, 'Moral Indebtedness', *Free World*, October 1943, reprinted at http://www.wellesnet.com/orson-welles-debut-as-political-commentator-on-moral-indebtedness/ (accessed 15 July 2015).
5. Welles quoted in McBride, *Whatever Happened to Orson Welles?*, 95–6.
6. Callow, *Orson Welles: Hello Americans*, 184.
7. Patrick Marnham, *Resistance and Betrayal: The Death and Life of the Greatest Hero of the French Resistance* (New York: Random House, 2000), 115.
8. Roland Perry, *Last of the Cold War Spies: The Life of Michael Straight, the Only American in Britain's Cambridge Spy Ring* (Cambridge: Da Capo, 2005), 143.
9. Callow, *Orson Welles: Hello Americans*, 184.
10. To Roland Perry, "The actor was willingly being used as a front for communist propaganda dressed up as liberal international thought" (Perry, *Last of the Cold War Spies*, 144). A less damning judgment of Dolivet's organisation comes from Callow: the International Free World Association was "straightforwardly social democratic with a particularly international bias" (Callow, *Orson Welles: Hello Americans*), 185.
11. François Thomas, 'The Filmorsa Years', lecture at 'Orson Welles: A Centennial Celebration and Symposium', Indiana University, 2 May 2015; streamed online at http://www.indiana.edu/~video/stream/liveflash.html?filename=cinema (accessed 2 May 2015).
12. Barbara Leaming, *Orson Welles: A Biography* (New York: Limelight, 1995), 304.
13. Welles quoted in Leaming, *Orson Welles: A Biography*, 276.
14. Interview with Orson Welles in France (1982), at https://www.youtube.com/watch?v=R15slbtKhLk (accessed 15 July 2015).
15. Welles quoted in Tarbox (ed.), *Orson Welles and Roger Hill*, 102.
16. Welles and Bogdanovich, *This Is Orson Welles*, 108, 376, 380.
17. Dennis Broe says that in the 1945–50 period, "ideas of the left were hegemonic [in film noirs] [...] they formed the core of the genre". Dennis Broe, *Film Noir, American Workers, and Postwar Hollywood* (Gainesville: University Press of Florida, 2009), xxiv–xxv.
18. See Broe, *Film Noir, American Workers, and Postwar Hollywood*, xvii.
19. Broe, *Film Noir, American Workers, and Postwar Hollywood*, xxiv.
20. Agnes Moorehead was Welles's original choice for the role of the Nazi-hunter, but the producers insisted on casting Edward G. Robinson. See Welles and Bogdanovich, *This Is Orson Welles*, 187.
21. Welles quoted in Bazin, Bitsch, and Domarchi, 'Interview with Orson Welles (II)', 63.
22. Andrew Spicer, *Historical Dictionary of Film Noir* (Plymouth: Scarecrow Press, 2010), 45.

23. Slotkin, *Gunfighter Nation*, 233.
24. Berthome and Thomas, *Orson Welles at Work*, 119.
25. Heylin, *Despite the System*, 175.
26. Heylin, *Despite the System*, 175–6; see also Berthome and Thomas, *Orson Welles at Work*, 122.
27. For the first time Welles uses the plot device of an old man released from prison who is then murdered by a former criminal associate. The same premise kick-starts *Mr. Arkadin*, and a shot of Jakob Zouk (Akim Tamiroff) leaving his Munich prison was rumoured to have begun one lost cut (incidentally, actors Konstantin Shayne and Tamiroff were brothers-in-law).
28. The film as produced starred Welles as Kindler, Edward G. Robinson as Wilson, Loretta Young as Mary, Konstantin Shayne as Konrad Meinike, and Billy House as Potter.
29. Benamou, *It's All True*, 247.
30. Welles and Bogdanovich, *This Is Orson Welles*, 388; see also Orson Welles, 'Orson Welles' Almanac', *New York Post*, 30 January 1945, reprinted at http://www.wellesnet.com/orson-welles-almanac-the-new-yorker-ought-to-be-ashamed-of-itself/ (accessed 15 July 2015).
31. Welles quoted in Welles and Bogdanovich, *This Is Orson Welles*, 186.
32. Uncredited [Orson Welles, John Huston, and Anthony Veiller], *The Stranger* (24 September 1945), 6–21 (with some inconsistent numbering). Box 21, folder 14, Lilly Library.
33. Heylin, *Despite the System*, 176–7.
34. Uncredited [Welles, Huston, and Veiller], *The Stranger*, 36–8.
35. Uncredited [Welles, Huston, and Veiller], *The Stranger*, 130.
36. Berthome and Thomas, *Orson Welles at Work*, 124.
37. Uncredited [Welles, Huston, and Veiller], *The Stranger*, 83.
38. Berthome and Thomas, *Orson Welles at Work*, 120.
39. Uncredited [Welles, Huston, and Veiller], *The Stranger*, 36.
40. See Berthome and Thomas, *Orson Welles at Work*, 122. The clocktower action and the dormant clock anticipate elements of Robert Zemickis's *Back to the Future* (1985), which was filmed on the same town square set on the Universal lot.
41. Berthome and Thomas, *Orson Welles at Work*, 122.
42. Uncredited [Welles, Huston, and Veiller], *The Stranger*, 160.
43. Uncredited [Welles, Huston, and Veiller], *The Stranger*, 46.
44. See Naremore, *The Magic World of Orson Welles*, 124.
45. Uncredited [Welles, Huston, and Veiller], *The Stranger*, 42.
46. Uncredited [Welles, Huston, and Veiller], *The Stranger*, 57.

CHAPTER 7

PORT TO PORT
The Lady from Shanghai (1947)

Orson Welles in a publicity still as Mike O'Hara in *The Lady From Shanghai*

The Lady from Shanghai was based on Sherwood King's novel *If I Should Die Before I Wake* (1938). In the spring and summer of 1946, while Welles worked on *Around the World in Eighty Days* in the theatre and the *Mercury Summer Theatre on the Air* for CBS radio, he developed the screenplay with writers William Castle and Fletcher Markle.[1] A 'Third Draft' titled *Black Irish* was finished by 13 August. By then Welles was the sole credited screenwriter. Just four days later he had compiled a 164-page 'Final Draft (for Estimating Purposes)' retitled *Take This Woman*, a tightly conceived noir thriller. Censor Joseph Breen rejected Welles's present conception on 19 August, necessitating revisions to an ending which saw the hero urging the *femme fatale* to suicide.[2]

A mere six weeks before production began, the film was still to be set in New York City and on Long Island. The principal changes made by the time of the 'First Estimating Script' of 20 September were to transfer the action to Cuba, Mexico, and the San Francisco Bay Area, following a set of establishing scenes in New York. Perhaps the international revisions were considered commercially sound after the success of the Rita Hayworth vehicle *Gilda* (Charles Vidor, 1946), set in Argentina but shot in Hollywood.[3] For the first time since *It's All True*, Welles was able work extensively outside the studio, although he later recalled, "In those days there was a deep distrust of all locations,"[4] which he said led to the unit being recalled a few days too early. Whatever the reason for the revisions, the port city settings were more suitable for Welles's political themes.

Shooting began in Hollywood on 2 October. The company moved to Acapulco for a month's work, then on to San Francisco. Hayworth's ill health meant that principal photography dragged on until 27 February 1947. Viola Lawrence's editing began during production and generally worked in antagonism to Welles's aesthetic vision. Many of Welles's carefully choreographed tracking shots were not allowed to stand. He was ordered to make additional shots to allow the scenes to be edited along more conventional lines. Although Welles obliged, he continued to subvert conventionality in other ways, with close-up performances verging on the absurd (particularly Glenn Anders as George Grisby) and sometimes near-surreal back projections.[5]

A record of a provisional cut of *The Lady from Shanghai* survives in a typed document headed 'Scenes as Shot', although a more accurate description would be 'Scenes as Edited'. The document is an adaptation of Welles's shooting script into a shot-by-shot breakdown of the edit as it stood around the end of February. Pages are individually dated from 16 November 1946 – around the time the company returned to California from Mexico – until 25 February 1947, indicating the chronology of Lawrence's work.[6] This provisional editing continuity gives the shape of the film before much of Welles's material was altered or eliminated.

The action begins in New York's Central Park. Irish sailor Mike O'Hara (Welles) approaches a beautiful woman (Hayworth) in her horse-drawn cab, offers her his last cigarette, and later rescues her from a gang of thieves. Her name is Elsa, and she tells him: "You're a bit like Don Quixote yourself, Michael. The age of chivalry's out of business, but I don't think you believe it." They each have international backgrounds. Elsa grew up in China, and Mike was imprisoned in the Spanish Civil War for killing a Franco spy. But when she reveals she is married to Arthur Bannister, "the world's greatest criminal lawyer", he bluntly refuses her offer of a job on Bannister's yacht.

The next day Arthur Bannister (Everett Sloan), who walks with two crutches, personally seeks out Mike at the seaman's hiring hall. Mike again refuses the job, but allows Bannister to buy drinks for him and his sailor chums. Bannister passes out, drunk, and the sailors return him to his yacht. Seeing Elsa again, Mike agrees to take the job. They depart for San Francisco.

Bannister's law partner, Grisby, joins the yacht party in Cuba and immediately makes a distasteful impression, goading Mike by saying that he had been on a "Pro-Franco committee" during the Civil War. Grisby also witnesses Elsa and Mike's first kiss and gleefully lets the couple know they've been caught.

In Acapulco, Grisby tells Mike that he forecasts atomic destruction – "first the big cities, then maybe even this" – and makes a bizarre proposal to pay Mike $5,000 to murder him. Later Elsa argues with her husband at Ciro's nightclub and flees down to the streets to find Mike. Their conversation is interrupted by Bannister's nosy private detective, Broome (Ted de Corsia). Mike knocks him out cold. The party picnics on the coast, and Mike compares the bickering Bannisters and Grisby to a cannibalistic school of sharks he witnessed off the coast of Fortaleza.

Docking in Sausalito in San Francisco Bay, Mike tries to persuade Elsa that they could have a future together. Mike agrees to participate in a bizarre scam to fake Grisby's murder. Without a corpse, Grisby explains, Mike cannot be tried, but with his signed confession Grisby will be legally dead and able to collect his life insurance. Broome has twigged to the scam and tries blackmail. Grisby shoots him. Then Mike and Grisby stage the murder on the Sausalito docks. The plan goes bad. Mike speaks by telephone to the dying Broome, who believes Bannister will be murdered by Grisby. Mike is shocked when Grisby himself is found dead. Now that signed confession is as good as a death sentence.

Bannister represents Mike at a farcical trial, and delights in losing the case so his client will be sentenced to death. Mike causes a disruption of the verdict by swallowing a handful of Bannister's painkillers and then escapes custody. He flees into Chinatown. He passes out in the Mandarin Theatre and is taken by Elsa's Chinese associates to an amusement park. He wakes up in a semi-coherent state inside the bewildering crazy house. Outside he encounters the Bannister maid, Bessy (Evelyn Ellis), who leads him to Elsa. Bessy refuses to call the police on Mike's behalf. Mike and Elsa step into the hall of mirrors to talk. Bannister appears and the unhappily married couple shoot each other. Mike survives, leaves Elsa to die, and walks out in solitude.

* * *

Welles claimed to have previewed one version of the film in Santa Barbara with a temporary track of incidental music. After late February, Cohn imposed large deletions, a narration, and a schmaltzy music score by Heinz Roemheld to which Welles emphatically objected. He wrote to Cohn: "If the lab had scratched initials and phone numbers over the negative, I couldn't be unhappier about the results."[7] Perhaps tellingly, Welles's credit reads for screenplay and production, but not direction.

The Lady from Shanghai was one of the first Hollywood thrillers to be shot substantially on location, although other thrillers of this period, such as Jules Dassin's *The Naked City* (1948), made a point of their semi-documentary realism.[8] By contrast, Welles was moving further away from anything resembling realism to embrace the carnivalesque, the absurd, the obviously artificial. James Naremore describes *Shanghai* as a film "characterized by a sort of inspired silliness, a grotesquely comic stylization that has moved beyond expressionism towards absurdity".[9]

* * *

The Lady from Shanghai is a tale of three port cities. Most of the exterior shots of Acapulco and San Francisco were made on location, with some studio-made insert shots using back projection. The exteriors of New York were largely created at Columbia's Hollywood studios.

The provisional editing continuity preserves Welles's original scripted conception of a pre-title sequence in New York:

It's late August – very early morning … the city, fretfully awake, in the stuffy atmosphere of a closet, gasps for its breath. Spires and tenements seem to sweat in the dizzying heat like the New Yorkers living in them. It's been a heavy summer, the whole weight of it seems congealed into one oven of a night.[10]

Although gestural rather than indicative of any specific approach Welles might have taken to filming this palpably hot summer dawn, the sketch recalls the Manhattan city symphony concept that opened the *Heart of Darkness* screenplay. There is no pre-title sequence in the final cut of *Shanghai*. A shot of waves plays behind the titles, followed by generic on-location establishing shots of the Brooklyn Bridge and Central Park:

The Brooklyn Bridge and Central Park, New York City

The rest of Central Park was recreated at the Columbia Ranch in Burbank, California.[11] The long sequence was hacked down for the final cut, eliminating its central theme of urban surveillance, which butts against Mike's anti-police stance and Elsa's desire for freedom from her husband.

As laid out in the provisional editing continuity, we first see Elsa outside the park being followed by Broome. Meanwhile, Grisby fruitlessly awaits a call from Elsa at the El Morocco nightclub. Broome reports to Bannister by telephone that he abandoned Elsa's trail when she entered the park in a horse-drawn cab. All of these preliminaries were deleted.

The park itself is under the surveillance of police squad cars (aided by police radio). The first tracking shot inside the park was to have shown a police car overtaking Elsa's horse-drawn cab as Mike walks on foot. As the cab and the police car are stopped side by side at a red light, Mike speaks to the cabby and makes an intentionally provocative comment in earshot of the police about the particular pointlessness of a traffic light inside the park, if indeed "there's ever a point in a traffic light at all". The unfriendly cabby says his is a "law abiding horse", to which Mike responds, "Sure, there's nobody obeys a law unless he's afraid of something." When Mike calls the horse Rosinante, after Don Quixote's nag, the cabby warns, "Don't be callin' her names."[12]

Mike offers Elsa his last cigarette, and as the squad car moves off, one of the cops warns Elsa about being out alone in the park. After she accepts the cigarette, her cab drives away, too, leaving Mike alone. When he sings an old Irish song, the squad car returns to question why he's singing. He provocatively explains, "to keep [myself] from remembering that the world is full of cops".[13] An altercation is avoided when the police radio calls the squad car to an emergency in another part of the park. The scene was reedited to remove the police presence and the cabby's dialogue, completely altering its drama and Mike's behaviour. All that survive are a few glimpses of what is probably the squad car behind Elsa's horse-drawn cab:

Later, after Mike rescues Elsa from three bandits, he spirits her away in the cab. The final cut's narration glosses over Mike's treatment of the cabby, who had also been attacked: in the provisional editing continuity he abandons the unconscious man in the park with nothing but a robe to cover him and steals his horse and cab, rather excessive revenge for gruff unfriendliness. That excised action would have further explained why Mike is so particularly eager to avoid the police squad car they spot.

Mike's subsequent admissions to Elsa that he does not like the police survive in the final cut, although his aversion now appears to be due mostly to his unpleasant experience in a Spanish jail rather than to the ideological opposition to police authority suggested by his behaviour in the provisional edit. This

Mike spots a police car

is a loss of valuable nuance. Welles had spent a season publicly campaigning for justice in the Isaac Woodard assault case. It coincided with a radicalised attitude to police, and shifted his anti-fascism towards interrogation of the abuse of institutional power. The "aristocratic" Mike, for all his chivalric naivety, voices Welles's own anti-police attitudes. In a UK television interview from 1955, Welles was asked how he would make use of a fortune. Rather than pitch a film concept, as expected of him, he answered, "I would start a foundation and hire a great number of constitutional lawyers and study the encroachment of the police on civil liberties all over the world in every country."[14]

In *The Lady from Shanghai*, Mike's fellow veteran of the International Brigades, Jake Bejornson, puts a cop in the same category as any other 'tough guy', with just as little moral authority.

> What's a tough guy? A guy with an edge. ... A gun or a knife, a night stick or a razor, something the other guy ain't got, a little extra reach on a punch, a set of brass knuckles, a stripe on his sleeve, a badge that says 'Cop' on it, or a rock in your hand, or a bankroll in your pocket. That's an edge, brother. Without no edge, they ain't no tough guy.[15]

* * *

The pre-international draft of the script (17 August 1946) contains two noteworthy and unique New York City scenes. One was eliminated by the time of the shooting script, and the other was revised for a San Francisco setting. In the 17 August draft, Grisby's assassination occurs on screen in the vicinity of Wall Street. He is killed in a distant shot, presumably to render his identity ambiguous, from the point of view of Bannister's office window while the phone buzzes. The caller is the wounded Broome, who is attempting to warn Bannister of Grisby's imminent attempt on his life. Welles sketches another of his never-realised sound schemes to provide a fuller dimension to urban space, this time in the isolated concrete canyons of the city's financial centre:

> The tiny figure of the man can be just made out on the black pavement… Suddenly, with the sound perspective matching this distance, there is heard a faint but sharp textured gunshot! The noise ricochets off the granite faces of the empty buildings echoing remotely. This during a silent phase of one of the measured pauses between the exclamations of the phone buzzer… Precisely on the instant of the gunshot, the moving CAMERA had pulled up and locked its focus in a fixed stare at the street below… The miniscule shape of the man is seen to fall… The phone bell clatters… The man lies motionless.[16]

For the shooting script, Welles chose to cut this scene rather than transfer the action to Bannister's office in Montgomery Street, San Francisco.

When Mike escapes from court in the 17 August New York-based draft, he takes the subway uptown. The script leaps into Mike's subjectivity. Having swallowed Bannister's pills, he hallucinates while examining advertisements inside the subway car:

> Through Mike's eyes, the posters seem to change. A girl in a bathing suit suddenly becomes Elsa, the man next to her advertising the razor becomes Bannister. The man in the speedboat becomes Grisby. Each ad becomes some incident in Mike's mind, leading up to the murder. A subway sign streaks over the scene with a roar, then stops, vibrating queerly.

A conductor's offscreen voice orders Mike out of the car at 205th Street, but Mike hallucinates that Bannister – whose "face bolts into the aperture", shot with a distortion lens – is speaking to him. We see money swirling; it becomes a whirling telephone dial.[17] Elsa's voice also intrudes into the subjective soundscape as she tries to spirit him away. Mike also hears the echoing voices of two dead men, Grisby and Broome. He passes out and wakes up in the crazy house at the Palisades Amusement Park in New Jersey.[18]

The shooting script for *The Stranger* had featured a similar subjective sequence – as Welles called it, an "impressionistic montage" – of Mary Longstreet's psychological breakdown (it also did not make the final cut). The New York subway ride in this early draft of *Shanghai* was rewritten as Mike's flight into San Francisco's Chinatown, although the final cut does not attempt to represent Mike's subjective experience of the city while under the influence of the overdose of pills. Only what remains of the crazy house sequence gestures towards Mike's bewildered subjectivity.

Acapulco proved an ideal setting to depict the greed of the postwar wealthy. *The Lady from Shanghai* delivers contrasting images of the resort city – glamorous spectacle from above, squalor down below. Although Welles recalled, "We didn't build a thing. We used Acapulco as we found it,"[19] the market street of the city was actually shot in a studio.

Grisby's mysterious proposition to Mike is delivered in a series of impressively choreographed tracking and panning shots in the bustling sun-soaked hills. The Mexican locals serve as fishermen, load-bearers, washerwomen, and gigolos; wealthy tourists sunbake, flirt, and bicker. The sequence was abridged and altered after late February. Insert shots were added featuring obviously

Moving shots through the Acapulco Hills

Inserted close-ups filmed in front of a process screen

projected backgrounds that interrupted the virtuoso camera movements. Intentionally or not, the film's political radicalism was blunted by the changes. Some dialogue was cut, silenced, or smothered with music, including most of the clever string of fragmented conversations of various tourists, all of whose petty comments concern money. This was surely the principal inspiration for Mike's world-weary demurral in response to Grisby's comment on the beauty of "everything": "You mean the whole of the world? There's a fair face to the land but you can't hide the hunger and the guilt. Sure, it's a bright, guilty world."[20]

Later, Elsa flees the luxurious rooftop nightclub to find Mike down in the Calle del Mercado. The realisation of working-class Acapulco is more elaborate than what was sketched in the 20 September shooting script, which simply staged Broome's confrontation with Elsa and Mike around a crumbling adobe wall.[21] This noirish side of Acapulco was filmed at the Twentieth Century Fox ranch in Hollywood.[22] Welles and presumably art directors Sturges Carne and Stephen Goosson create a palpable early evening atmosphere of tranquillity interrupted by Broome's menace. A tracking shot follows Mike and Elsa between colonnades and archways, past busy open-air eateries and a well-lit cantina, giving a stunning impression of a living city populated by working-class people.²³ The physical structures of the street seem almost in ruins. The griminess of the building exteriors and the use of paper detritus anticipate the border town in *Touch of Evil*, which would be, by contrast, shot in a real urban location. The walls and columns are plastered with torn and overlapping film posters. Among these exotic images of romance is a stereotypical Polynesian *wahine*, perhaps an ironic foreshadowing of Grisby's purported plan to escape the world of cities for the smallest Pacific island. That was a popular atomic age fantasy that explains the popularity of James A. Michener's *Tales of the South Pacific* (1947) and the fad for pseudo-Polynesian tiki kitsch.

Of course, Grisby's fantasy of island escape is just a ploy; Mike is the real romantic dreamer. In a cantina, Mike suggests to Elsa they escape to "one of the far places". She tells him, "we're in one of them now – running away doesn't work … you're such a foolish knight errant, Mike."²⁴

Welles would briefly return to sun-drenched Acapulco in *Mr. Arkadin*, although in that case the setting was recreated in Spain.

The action of *The Lady from Shanghai* culminates violently in a final port city, San Francisco, where Welles had reported on the birth of the United Nations in 1945. Welles used a variety of the city's locations: Nob Hill, Portsmouth Square, the Steinhart Aquarium, and Whitney's Playland-at-the-

The streets of Acapulco created at the 20th Century Fox Ranch

Beach for the exteriors of the amusement park.²⁵ Sausalito is described in the script as a "Saroyanesquely ramshackle litter of old buildings"; it appears on screen as a quaint marine outpost across the bay from the big city. It is there that Grisby, in his unconvincing guise of pre-emptive atomic refugee, says: "I don't want to be within a thousand miles of that city, or any other city, when they start dropping those bombs."²⁶

San Francisco had already been mooted as the setting of at least two prior unfilmed Welles projects: John Fante's weak 1941 'Love Story' script from *It's All True*, and Welles's little-known attempt to adapt a novel by Mike Fessier, *Fully Dressed and In His Right Mind* (1934). The latter, a psychological drama with supernatural elements, is possibly the only one of Welles's 1940s thriller projects without a political dimension. It is difficult to establish exactly when Welles worked on the *Fully Dressed* project, or if other writers were involved, but it provides a few insights into Welles's unrealised sketches for putting San Francisco on screen.²⁷

The story centres on a 'Little Old Man' (LOM) who freely admits to the protagonist, Johnny Price, that he has murdered the editor of the *San Francisco*

The Lady From Shanghai's San Francisco panoramas

Herald; he also reveals he once cannibalised a British Colonial Officer in Africa. The LOM stalks Price around the city. After reporting the man to the police, who dismissively eject him from the station, Price takes a crowded street car.

> His attention is drawn to the windows of the car in which he sees 2 or 3 reflections (all different) of the LOM. He looks apprehensively around in back of him, but sees only the regular passengers standing. He turns quickly and looks at the windows, but the reflections have vanished.[28]

Welles's visual interest in multiple reflections was most spectacularly expressed in *The Lady from Shanghai*'s hall-of-mirrors conclusion. Years later he would use reflecting windows in a stunning film-within-a-film sequence in *The Other Side of the Wind* shot in Century City, Los Angeles. *Fully Dressed and In His Right Mind*, however, was never realised. One of the few scholars to have researched the project, Bret Wood, compares it to *The Trial* for its "themes of guilt, injustice and sexual uncertainty".[29]

The San Francisco of *The Lady from Shanghai* is a similar cocktail. Mike is framed for Grisby's murder and falls victim to a farcically unjust court that is the province of exhibitionists and voyeurs. The judge, as played by Erskine Sanford, is a flustered buffoon. There were very few images of Mike in the trial scene as it stood in late February, the better to emphasise his lack of agency under the law.[30] A number of additional reaction shots of Mike were inserted into the final cut to push the scene back towards conventionality. Welles later acknowledged that the shot of the judge playing chess in front of the San Francisco cityscape, which is juxtaposed with an extreme high angle of the chessboard of the court, was "right on the jagged edge of symbolism".[31]

Mike's escape into Chinatown does not seek to represent his drugged subjectivity as did its earlier incarnation as the New York subway hallucination. The editing of the chase in the final cut represents the neighbourhood's geography with reasonable spatial coherence. The continuity notes that the location shots had been made with hidden cameras and lays out plans for the special-effects shots still to be interpolated. Some of these shots were filmed from inside plate-glass shop windows looking onto process plates of the Chinatown streets.[32]

Chinatown location shots

Elsa's knowledge of Chinese allows her to successfully navigate the neighbourhood in pursuit of Mike, although in the release version of the film her early Chinese background has only been cursorily established. Mike hides out in the audience of a musical play at the Mandarin Theatre, shot in its location and featuring an unusually authentic musical performance for a Hollywood film of the era. Elsa goes backstage to phone her servant Li, whose apartment improbably shares the same panoramic view of San Francisco as the judge's chambers (both were really the view from the Fairmont Hotel). We are given a

Special effects shots

brief glimpse of the communication network binding the Chinese community of San Francisco: the Chinese Telephone Exchange, shot inside its real location at 743 Washington Street.[33] Li's men mobilise to remove Mike from the theatre, killing the lights to flummox the police.

Harry Cohn insisted on cutting Elsa and Mike's discussion of the supposed plot of the Chinese play, which they use as an allegory of their own drama.[34]

The Chinese Telephone Exchange and Li's Apartment

* * *

The Lady from Shanghai as it survives represents Columbia's comprehensive rejection of Welles's visual and aural aesthetics in favour of the conventional. Making *Shanghai* resembled his experience making *The Stranger* the previous year – unavoidable compromises throughout the process of production from scripting to editing. Nevertheless, making *Shanghai* on location allowed some breakthroughs in Welles's work as an urban filmmaker, at least in his use of extended moving takes, even as he was about to return to Hollywood to make an entirely studio-bound film.

Welles's low-budget adaptation of Shakespeare's *Macbeth*, a brilliantly expressionist film set in an eleventh-century Scottish landscape, was a departure from the modern world into the theatrically medieval. The filming took a mere twenty-three days in the summer of 1947, but post-production was prolonged into 1948, by which time Welles was no longer living in the United States. He returned briefly to Hollywood to finalise the editing, scoring, and sound mixing. A Welles-authorised 107-minute version premiered at the 1948 Venice Film Festival and was briefly distributed in the United States. In 1950 Welles was asked to reedit and redub the film for rerelease. This 86-minute version also survives.

Welles had left the United States in November 1947. There were many reasons to leave. He had hopes for independent control over the production of his films in Italy. His recent divorce from Rita Hayworth may have contributed to the desire for a fresh start. There were tax problems due to *Around the World in Eighty Days*.[35] Nevertheless, the anti-leftist purge of Hollywood, which began with the House Un-American Activities Committee's hearings in October 1947, cannot be ignored. Louis Dolivet was named an agent of the Comintern in 1947 by the *Washington Evening Star*, was denounced by the House Un-American Activities Committee in 1949, and was thereafter unable to re-enter the United States, even on the occasion of the drowning of his daughter in 1952.[36]

Joseph McBride makes a strong case for Welles as a victim of the blacklist,[37] although Welles refused to take on the role of ideological martyr. His fearless anti-fascism and cosmopolitan one-worldism, useful to his role as Good Will Ambassador during wartime, would have made him a problem figure amid the McCarthyist hysteria and revived provincialism of the Cold War. The very forces of ideological persecution that made the United States uncongenial to Welles's political activism pushed him towards the fulfilment of what would become his emblematic self: Orson Welles the endlessly wandering player, cosmopolitan citizen of the world, rumoured rather than known, everywhere-at-once and nowhere-to-be-found.

NOTES

1. Welles and Bogdanovich, *This Is Orson Welles*, 508–9.
2. Heylin, *Despite the System*, 205–6.
3. Spicer, *Historical Dictionary of Film Noir*, 238.
4. Welles quoted in Welles and Bogdanovich, *This Is Orson Welles*, 191.
5. Berthome and Thomas, *Orson Welles at Work*, 131, 137, 141.
6. Uncredited [Orson Welles], *Lady from Shanghai* 'Scenes as Shot' (provisional editing continuity) (16 November 1946 – 25 February 1947). Box 22, folder 4, Lilly Library.
7. Welles quoted in Welles and Bogdanovich, *This Is Orson Welles*, 194–6.
8. Berthome and Thomas, *Orson Welles at Work*, 142.
9. Naremore, *The Magic World of Orson Welles*, 133.
10. Uncredited [Welles], *Lady from Shanghai* 'Scenes as Shot', unpaginated (cover page).
11. Berthome and Thomas, *Orson Welles at Work*, 135.
12. Uncredited [Welles], *Lady from Shanghai* 'Scenes as Shot', 4.
13. Uncredited [Welles], *Lady from Shanghai* 'Scenes as Shot', 8.
14. Interview with Orson Welles on *Press Conference* (UK: BBC TV, 1955), part I at https://www.youtube.com/watch?v=kOmhLouJVuw; part II at https://www.youtube.com/watch?v=YQDStxPSaWU (accessed 8 August 2015).
15. Uncredited [Welles], *Lady from Shanghai* 'Scenes as Shot', 27A.
16. Orson Welles, *Take This Woman* 'Final Draft (for Estimating Purposes)' (17 August 1946), 102–3. American Film Scripts Online (database) (Alexandria, VA: Alexander Street Press), at http://alexanderstreet.com/products/american-film-scripts (accessed 30 September 2013).
17. The cash is Broome's; in this draft, Mike's early comment about thinking it "very sanitary to be broke" is given an ironic payoff. The dying Broome had demanded five thousand dollars in cash for handing over Mike's confession letter. Mike pays him then takes back the "precious garbage", "moist and dripping" with blood, seconds later when Broome is dead. Welles, *Take This Woman* 'Final Draft (for Estimating Purposes)', 109.
18. Welles, *Take This Woman* 'Final Draft (for Estimating Purposes)', 151.
19. Welles quoted in Welles and Bogdanovich, *This Is Orson Welles*, 198.
20. Uncredited [Welles], *Lady from Shanghai* 'Scenes as Shot', 47b.
21. Studio synopsis of the 20 September 'First Estimating Script', 3. Box 22, folder 6, Lilly Library.

22 Adrienne L. McLean, *Being Rita Hayworth: Labor, Identity, and Hollywood Stardom* (Piscataway: Rutgers University Press, 2004), 154.
23 Berthome and Thomas, *Orson Welles at Work*, 131.
24 Uncredited [Welles], *Lady from Shanghai* 'Scenes as Shot', 53–7 (a single page numbered as such).
25 Berthome and Thomas, *Orson Welles at Work*, 135.
26 Uncredited [Welles], *Lady from Shanghai* 'Scenes as Shot', 72–4.
27 No complete script survives in the Welles archive at the Lilly Library. A composite typed text of about sixty pages contains pencilled annotations probably in Welles's own handwriting. There are redundancies and repetitions, and the structure is not fully worked out. Some of the text is in treatment form.
28 Uncredited, *Fully Dressed and In His Right Mind*, 18. Box 22, folder 22, Lilly Library.
29 Wood, *Orson Welles: A Bio-Bibliography*, 242.
30 See Wood, *Orson Welles: A Bio-Bibliography*, 209; the provisional editing continuity records a single close-up of Mike. Uncredited [Welles], *Lady from Shanghai* 'Scenes as Shot', 108–24.
31 Welles quoted in Welles and Bogdanovich, *This Is Orson Welles*, 198.
32 Uncredited [Welles], *Lady from Shanghai* 'Scenes as Shot', 132A.
33 See CitySleuth, 'The Lady from Shanghai', *Reel SF*, at http://reelsf.com/the-lady-from-shanghai-1947 (accessed 30 August 2015).
34 Memo by Harry Cohn reproduced in Berthome and Thomas, *Orson Welles at Work*, 140; see also Uncredited [Welles], *Lady from Shanghai* 'Scenes as Shot', 135–8.
35 Alberto Anile (translated by Marcus Perryman), *Orson Welles in Italy* (Bloomington: Indiana University Press, 2013), 10.
36 Callow, *Orson Welles: Hello Americans*, 184.
37 See McBride, *Whatever Happened to Orson Welles?*, 99–104.

CHAPTER 8

THE BORDER
Touch of Evil (1958)

There was no attempt to approximate reality; the film's entire 'world' being the director's invention.

– Orson Welles, 1958¹

Quinlan's entourage: Representatives of U.S. law in Mexican territory

Touch of Evil, made during Welles's two-year return to the United States after nearly a decade in Europe, was the (almost) triumphant culmination of Welles's anti-fascist Pan-American thrillers. After two independent Pan-European films (*Othello* and *Mr. Arkadin*) and various British and American television projects, all of which demanded the invention of radical low-budget methods, Welles returned one final time to the relatively ample financial and technical facilities of a Hollywood studio. He exploited these resources to create 'Los Robles', a stunning noir city filmed in the streets of Venice Beach, Los Angeles.

Touch of Evil expresses a number of Welles's political concerns, most obviously the racial discrimination against Mexicans inside the American policing and legal system. It was a long-term concern: back in 1942 Welles had joined the Sleepy Lagoon Defense Committee to defend falsely accused Mexican-American youths in a notorious California trial.[2] Mike O'Hara's dislike of the police in *The Lady from Shanghai* had been a stance of revolutionary anti-authoritarianism; *Touch of Evil* centred its drama on the racism, corruption, and violence of a police captain and his entrenched position within the legal bureaucracy.

Another palpable political context of *Touch of Evil* is Welles's hostility not just to nationalism, which he had long argued was the seed of fascism, but more radically to the bureaucratic accoutrements of the modern nation state (which included the police). In 1955 Welles had filmed a monologue for the UK's BBC television on the subject of 'The Police'. He began by recalling his involvement in the Isaac Woodard case, and went on to say:

> I'm willing to admit that the policeman has a difficult job … but it's the essence of our society that the policeman's job should be hard. He's there to protect the free citizen, not to chase criminals. That's an incidental part of his job. The free citizen is always more of a nuisance to the police than the criminal. He knows what to do about the criminal.

Welles also denounced customs officials, the necessity of passports, "red tapism and bureaucracy, particularly as it applies to freedom of movement". "[Travel is not what it was in] our fathers' day", before passports, because now "we're treated like demented or delinquent children and the eyes are always on us." He told an anecdote about a European experience in which he sarcastically informed humourless police inspectors he was carrying an atomic bomb in his bag.

Welles lumped police and bureaucrats together as "one great big monstrous thing" and said

> the bureaucrat is really like a blackmailer. You can never pay him off. The more you give him, the more he'll demand… I'm not an anarchist, I don't

Welles's sketches of his European police encounter in *Orson Welles' Sketchbook* (1955)

want to overthrow the rule of law. On the contrary, I want to bring the policeman to law.

Welles suggested the formation of the International Association for the Protection of the Individual Against Officialdom. "If any such outfit is ever organized, you can put me down as a charter member."[3]

In his 1950s work Welles frequently mocked the modern nation state itself as a political fiction. *Mr. Arkadin* and his television documentaries frequently expressed *saudade* for antiquated cultural unities – the Austro-Hungarian Empire and interwar Eastern Europe – now obliterated and divided by the postwar political order. In his television series *Around the World with Orson Welles*, he celebrated Pentecost because it was the one day of the year when the border dividing the ancient Basque country between Spain and France was open to free human passage. Welles goes on to say:

> It's not only the Basques. Nobody really likes an international border. The nations it divides always want to push the border back a bit in their favor, and I rather think the people it divides would just as soon do away with it altogether.[4]

Touch of Evil provided Welles with the opportunity to explore the cinematic possibilities of a border setting in the Americas after reimagining the American small town and the Pan-American port city in his mid-1940s noirs. Only a few contemporary thrillers had used the border setting, including Anthony Mann's *Border Incident* (1948). *Touch of Evil* particularises Welles's political insights into the operation of power on the border, and illustrates the ways racism thrives in such an ideologically divided space. A racist American detective's long-term abuse of his position has been protected by a network of institutional, personal, and criminal associates on both sides of arbitrarily divided Los Robles, as well as by the myths of his investigative 'intuition' and self-sacrifice for the law. The arrival of a conflicting liberal and international vision of law leads to the detective's downfall. The film frequently upsets the clichés of the 1950s police procedural.

In any of the several versions of *Touch of Evil*, Los Robles is Welles's most palpably realised cinematic city; in his original conception, it would have been the culmination of the director's career-long innovations in *mise-en-scène*, mobile tracking shots, editing, and sound. Moreover, Welles uses the spaces of the cinematic city itself to illustrate his ideas.

In the tradition of leftist spatial theory, Iván Zatz offers a political reading of how power is enforced in the "abstract space" of Welles's Los Robles, which is "not broken by any natural or physically obvious obstacle, [but] by the sheer presence of authority". He writes:

> Inequality would be a lot harder to maintain without the protected and policed exclusivity of fenced communities – borders, as this film makes clear […] Space, at this level, can be said to be abstracted precisely because there is no reason, other than an ideologically constructed one, to divide this space [with the border except] in order to prevent a natural movement of human beings through it.[5]

* * *

There are several contradictory accounts of how Welles was promoted from supporting actor to the job of rewriting and directing *Touch of Evil*, which was produced by Albert Zugsmith for Universal Pictures. The lead actor, Charlton Heston, supported Welles's employment as director. Welles had performed a supporting role in Zugsmith's similarly themed contemporary western *The Man in the Shadow* (Jack Arnold, 1957), and Zugsmith later claimed that Welles had offered to rewrite and direct Zugsmith's worst story property.[6]

The source was the 1956 novel *Badge of Evil* by 'Whit Masterson', a joint pseudonym for Robert Wade and William Miller. A first-draft screenplay was written by Paul Monash before Welles signed on. In a short time Welles completely rewrote the Monash script and drew additional material from the source novel. Welles's shooting script is further proof of his exemplary talent at reconceiving and personalising existing material. He altered the setting and the races of various characters to upset conventions, and reset the film on the tense American-Mexican border.[7]

Touch of Evil dramatises the exposure and death of Hank Quinlan (Welles), the corrupt Los Robles police detective. The trigger for his downfall is the investigation of the assassination by car bomb of local businessman Rudy Linnekar and a striptease dancer, Zita. Quinlan is discovered planting evidence in a suspect's apartment by Ramon Miguel 'Mike' Vargas (Charlton Heston), a high-ranking Mexican narcotics official engaged in the prosecution of the criminal Grandi family in Mexico City. Vargas attempts to find evidence that will convince the local American authorities to bring Quinlan to justice. Meanwhile Quinlan, slipping back into alcoholism, agrees to conspire with the local Grandi boss, 'Uncle Joe' (Akim Tamiroff), to smear the reputation of Vargas and his American wife, Susan (Janet Leigh), by framing them in a drug conspiracy. The Grandi gang attack Susan at the Mirador Motel in the desert, (probably) sexually assault her, and leave her drugged in a skid row hotel room as a gift to the vice squad. Quinlan murders Uncle Joe at the skid row hotel to cover his tracks and sits out an alcoholic bender at a brothel run by a woman called Tana (Marlene Dietrich) on the Mexican side of the border. When Quinlan's partner, Menzies (Joseph Calleia), discovers Quinlan's cane at the Grandi murder scene, he goes to Vargas, who convinces him to secretly record Quinlan's confession. Discovering the wire, Quinlan shoots Menzies; ailing, Menzies shoots Quinlan to protect Vargas. Quinlan falls into the river and dies.

Once again, the studio removed Welles from oversight of the editing and sound mix. After his departure in July 1957, additional expository or replacement scenes were directed by Harry Keller; they are inferior in every way to Welles's material. Welles was shown a rough cut in early December, and immediately wrote a long memo to studio executive Edward Muhl suggesting improvements in editing and sound.[8] Only some of his suggestions were adopted for a version of 108 minutes that was previewed in January 1958.[9] The 95-minute film as released in February was an abridged version of that preview cut and lost several dramatically essential scenes, rendering other parts confusing.[10]

* * *

Los Robles is improbably advertised within the film on a billboard as the 'Paris of the Border'. Much of the film was actually shot around the intersection of Windward Avenue and Pacific Street in Venice Beach, a suburb of Los Angeles that had been originally designed to evoke the Italian namesake.[11] Venice was distinguished by streets lined by colonnades; Welles would use them as the architectural centrepiece of his invented border town. In addition to an installed border post, there are numerous shop signs in both English and Spanish, as well as masses of paper detritus, particularly in the area surrounding Grandi's Rancho Grande, the striptease nightclub: frayed bilingual bill posters for stripteases, fights, and *corridas*; cardboard cut-outs of strippers; garbage and old newssheets billowing around the streets.

Touch of Evil revives the ambulatory mobility Welles had featured in *The Stranger* and *The Lady from Shanghai*. Propelling characters around the streets by foot, Welles maps this border area with his roving camera. In the 1960s Welles said, "I believe, thinking about my films, that they are based not so much on pursuit as on a search. If we are looking for something, the labyrinth is the most favorable location for the search."[12] Welles had intentionally created labyrinthine spaces in *The Lady from Shanghai*'s hall-of-mirrors sequence, and would later do the same for the dreamlike city of *The Trial*. It's also true that as early as *Othello* he had ceased to prioritise the spatial continuity expected by Hollywood and enforced by conventional filming and editing practices. Close study of Welles's editing – in those few films up to this point whose final form he was able to control – shows how frequently he flouted those conventions. Nevertheless, it is a simplification to categorise the spatiality of Los Robles as another noirish labyrinth, as have many past critical studies of *Touch of Evil*.

Although the cities of classic film noir are varied, they are nevertheless frequently described as labyrinthine cityscapes that mirror the unfathomable interpersonal relations of the population as well as the protagonist's psychological disorientation and confusion.[13] The interpretation puts the film noir firmly in the tradition of the classic German Expressionist film, examples including Robert Weine's *The Cabinet of Dr. Caligari* (1920) and F. W. Murnau's *Nosferatu* (1922). Clearly that tradition was important to the development of the visual language of film noir, not least due to the flight of directors such as Fritz Lang, Billy Wilder, and Robert Siodmak from Nazi Germany to Hollywood. And yet the typically supernatural or fantastic settings of the German Expressionist films of the early 1920s differ from the settings typical of film noir, which has much more in common with the slightly later German *Kammerspiel* ('chamber drama') and street film.[14] As Siegfried Kracauer defined it, this hybrid movement, like traditional Expressionism, "manages to transform 'material objects into emotional ornaments,' illuminate 'interior landscapes,' and emphasize 'the irrational events of instinctive life'" while staying within a "plausibly realistic representational format".[15] Examples of the *Kammerspiel* include *Der letzte Mann* (*The Last Laugh*, F. W. Murnau, 1924), *Varieté* (*Variety*, Ewald André Dupont, 1925), and *Der blaue Engel* (*The Blue Angel*, Josef von Sternberg, 1930). The street films include *Die Straße* (*The Street*, Karl Grune, 1923) and *Asphalt* (Joe May, 1929). This approach was defined as 'functional expressionism' by critic John D. Barlow.[16]

Film noir's varied attempts to reconcile expressionism with street-bound realism make the labyrinth a too-reductive spatial model for many cities in the noir canon. The early private-detective-centred noirs, adaptations from the hardboiled genre for which Dashiell Hammett had set the template, are really narratives about mastering the city through the successful navigation of public and private spaces, and the discovery and exposure of its complicated hierarchies of legal and criminal power. Sam Spade and Philip Marlowe, the street-smart protagonists of *The Maltese Falcon* (John Huston, 1941) and *Murder, My Sweet* (Edward Dmytryk, 1944) serve as cartographers of the city's secret spaces. Even if the plot of *The Big Sleep* (Howard Hawks, 1946) is notoriously difficult to follow – even labyrinthine – Philip Marlowe does not have trouble finding his way around Los Angeles.

Then there are the cinematic cities of pseudo-documentary police procedurals like *The Naked City* (Jules Dassin, 1948), *He Walked by Night* (Alfred L. Werker, 1948), *The Street with No Name* (William Keighley, 1948), and *Side Street* (Anthony Mann, 1950). In these films, innovative 'scientific' methods of crime fighting allow the police to resume control over a wayward city. These films regularly attempt synoptic overviews of urban space. A typical component of the opening sequences are aerial shots of the cityscape. *The Street with No Name* features maps that monitor and pin down the routine movements of a criminal suspect.[17] The opening narration by a police officer in *Side Street* brings narrative order to the diversity of human activity presented on screen and moreover instructs the audience to interpret those images in a fundamentally reactionary way.[18]

The labyrinth model is most applicable to the cities of those noirs of the immediate postwar period, which, in Dennis Broe's expression, centred on an 'outside-the-law fugitive protagonist'. Only the fun house and hall of mirrors really qualify as labyrinthine spaces in Welles's *The Lady from Shanghai*, but many other film noirs of that period reimagine the city as a bewildering maze-like space for ensnared everyman protagonists, and adopt the protagonist's point of view as he is persecuted by duplicitous women, criminals, the rich, or the authorities. Whereas Dassin's *Naked City* emphasises the police's synoptic mastery of New York City, his *Night and the City* (1950), set in postwar London, has been described as its "flipside … with overheated lighting patterns, bizarre angles, and claustrophobic compositions replacing the more methodical, unhurried organization of the earlier film".[19]

Los Robles has been consistently lumped in with other noir labyrinths as a spatially incoherent, disorientating space. A key influence on this interpretation seems to have been the film's mobile deep-focus cinematography. Welles and Russell Metty used lenses with focal lengths as short as 18.5mm; certainly the wide-angle distortion in some facial close-ups allowed the intrusion of the grotesque.[20] Although Welles's long opening crane shot fluidly tracks the passage of its characters through the border zone from Mexico into the United States, its cinematography and the busy choreography of the human crowd have often been categorised as disorientating. The frequently republished essay of one critic deems the mobile opening shot "less concerned with monitoring the events on screen than in disorientating the spectator"; it is a shot with "no mimetic function"; there is "too much information to pick and sort into stable hierarchies of attention"; the long shot is "a dance in which we lose our bearings … a whirling labyrinth" that produces "anxiety" born of "too much freedom".[21] The distortions of wide-angle photography notwithstanding, this reading seems a bizarre over-reach for a smoothly executed crane shot moving along two streets that form a right angle towards the clear destination of the border post.

Another factor in the designation of Los Robles as a labyrinth was the editing of the 1958 release version and the longer preview version rediscovered and screened from 1975. Early critics criticised the confusing editing, citing the difficulties in following the spatial position of characters on either side of the border.[22]

But much of the famous December 1957 memo of fifty-eight pages in response to the studio's rough cut supports the theory that Welles intended to present the border city not as a disorientating labyrinth at all but as a geographically coherent space – expressionist, baroque, and grotesque though it may have been. The release and preview versions muddied Welles's editing preferences, and blunted the effectiveness of his attempt to illustrate the networks of power that thrive in the spaces of the politically divided city, as well as the social networks and legal institutions that have allowed the corrupt Quinlan to thrive.

* * *

The opening shot brilliantly establishes the film's key staging location on the Mexican side of the border. It is a deep-focus tracking shot of three minutes and twenty seconds. The shot follows the planting of a time bomb in a convertible before it moves from the parking lot of a Mexican strip club to its obliteration just inside the United States. The first half-hour of the film is set in this vicinity, on both sides of the border, from late night until dawn.

The shot begins with an assassin setting the time bomb on a main street lined with colonnades. From a distance the assassin watches Linnekar and Zita leave the front door of a nightclub. We later discover the club is owned by 'Uncle Joe' Grandi and is called Grandi's Rancho Grande. "Kind of a joke," Uncle Joe later explains to Susan (the Grandis are apparently ancestrally Italian, not Mexican, and live on both sides of the border). The assassin runs to plant the bomb in the trunk of Linnekar's convertible, parked near the side entrance of the nightclub, behind the Clarence liquor store.

Planting the bomb

THE BORDER

Almost opposite the Clarence liquor store is the St Marks Hotel, honeymoon rendezvous for Mike and Susan Vargas. We later discover that the Vargases are staying in a first-floor room above the intersection of the main street with a narrow one-way lane.

Linnekar drives off with Zita. The camera tracks backwards ahead of the car as it drives along the main street for one block in a westerly direction. The car crawls through police-directed pedestrian traffic (and past such oddities as a cart selling sombreros) and makes a perpendicular right-hand turn onto another street that leads directly to the border checkpoint. At the corner the camera switches allegiance to anticipate the path of the Vargases, who are making a leisurely ambulatory passage towards the border, "hot on the trail of a chocolate soda".

The doomed car comes within the Vargas's vicinity several times as it weaves through the pedestrian, automobile, and livestock traffic. It moves away as the

Movement to the border checkpoint

Vargases cross the border into the United States. Their kiss on Susan's side of the border is interrupted by the sound of the car exploding.

The soundtrack on the original 1958 release print was not approved by Welles. He planned another version of the sound scheme which went back to *Heart of Darkness*.[23] The December memo explains:

> As the camera moves through the streets of the Mexican border town, the plan was to feature a succession of different and contrasting Latin American musical numbers – the effect, that is, of our passing one cabaret orchestra after another. In honky-tonk districts on the border, loudspeakers are over the entrance of every joint, large or small, each blasting out its own tune by way of a 'come-on' or 'pitch' for the tourists. The fact that the streets are invariably loud with this music was planned as a basic device throughout the entire picture.[24]

The soundtrack of this sequence in *Touch of Evil* was remixed for the 1998 restoration along these lines.[25] It is dramatically effective in several ways. It emphasises the suspense of the scene; the distinctive rock and roll from the convertible's radio fades in and out as the rigged car approaches and moves away from the Vargas couple. The soundtrack as mixed in the preview and theatrical release versions, with its excellent but overwhelming Henry Mancini non-diegetic score and superimposed title credits, makes it easier to forget about the bomb in the Linnekar car.[26] Welles's sound scheme complements the roving crane shot with a matching aural component. Each element is designed to envelop the audience in the space of the border city.

The opening shot ends with the sound of the explosion of the Linnekar car just inside US territory, followed by a cut to the flaming car leaping in the air. The next shot is slightly spatially inconsistent, because the Vargases are now further away from the border checkpoint, in the area in front of the Paradise Dance Hall.

At Mike's request, Susie re-crosses into Mexico to wait at the St Marks Hotel. She is followed across the border by the young Mexican she will come to nickname 'Pancho' (Valentin de Vargas); however, an abrupt cut from the entrance of the Paradise Dance Hall in the United States to a Mexican street skips any depiction of Susan and Pancho's actual border-crossing, which no doubt adds to the spatial confusion. However, responsibility for this particular cut cannot necessarily be attributed to Welles; it may well have been part of the studio's reworking of the separate adventures of Mike and Susie after the explosion, a section of the film with which Welles was particularly unhappy because the studio altered his pattern of crosscutting. Susie is accosted by Pancho and invited to receive something for her husband. Pancho leads her back into the United States. "Across the border again?" she asks.

The next time we see Susan she arrives with Pancho at another key staging location in the film's geography, a skid row hotel named the Ritz, an American counterpart to the Mexican Grandi's Rancho Grande/St Marks Hotel intersection. The Ritz is a few doors up from a neon crucifix ("Jesus Saves") and across the street from the Grande Hotel – Grande and Grandi are everywhere on both sides of the border. Uncle Joe has a kind of headquarters in the ground floor lobby of the Ritz. An upstairs room of the hotel is later the scene of Grandi's murder by Quinlan.

When the grotesquely obese Quinlan arrives at the bomb site, he exercises complete authority over the investigation. Police Chief Gould (Harry Shannon) seems totally at Quinlan's command, confused perhaps by Quinlan's methods ("you don't even want to question the daughter?") but always acquiescent. This sequence, built out of a series of close-ups and medium shots around the smoking and flaming car, expertly establishes Quinlan's entrenched and protected position in the legal and investigative network of Los Robles. Quinlan has protected his position by promoting his own myth as a crime solver. The district attorney, Adair (Ray Collins), refers to Quinlan as "our local police celebrity" and later "one of the most respected police officers in the country". Quinlan demonstrates a joking and even condescending acquaintance with Adair, who is dressed up in a "monkey suit" for a banquet.

Quinlan's fraudulent success as a detective is sustained by the broad acceptance of his myth by the legal authorities of Los Robles.[27] Vargas is quickly introduced to the myth of Quinlan's 'intuition'. Quinlan senses immediately the bomb was dynamite because of his "game leg". "Sometimes he gets a kind of twinge," says Menzies with an admiring grin, "like folks do for a change of weather. 'Intuition', he calls it." Quinlan smiles benevolently at the propagation of the myth. Menzies later confides to Vargas that Quinlan's leg was wounded by a bullet meant for him; it makes Menzies's final betrayal of Quinlan all the more emotionally difficult.

Hobbling on his cane, Quinlan leads Menzies and an entourage of American legal representatives across the border into Mexican territory, retracing in reverse the path of the rigged convertible back to Grandi's Rancho Grande.

The entourage consists of District Attorney Adair, Al Schwartz (Mort Mills) (from the DA's office), Chief Gould, and Blaine (some kind of American official who already knows Vargas). This flouting of police procedure, an investigation outside American jurisdiction, continues despite the DA's weak protests. The sequence also reaffirms the Grandi's Rancho Grande/St Marks Hotel intersection as a key area in the city's geography.

Vargas is momentarily distracted at the hotel by his reunion with Susie and her tale of near-abduction by Pancho (the weak expository scene in the preview and release versions was actually directed by Harry Keller). He lags behind Quinlan's entourage as they head into the side entrance of Grandi's Rancho Grande to question the strippers. Risto (Lalo Rios), a young member of the Grandi family, trails Vargas from the St Marks. Vargas strides purposefully and Risto's distorted shadow leaps across the poster-papered exterior walls of the nightclub – the same expressionism-within-realism lighting technique cinematographer Russell Metty and Welles had pursued more than ten years earlier in the Puerto Indio sequence of *The Stranger* (Welles had also used a similar technique in *Othello* and *Mr. Arkadin*).

Expressionist wall shadows in *The Stranger* (L) and *Touch of Evil* (R)

Risto hisses Vargas's name and attempts to hurl a glass bottle of acid into his face; the acid misses Vargas and destroys a poster advertising performances by the ever-unfortunate Zita. This acid attack occurs approximately at the site of the bomb planting.

After Quinlan and his entourage fruitlessly question Zita's co-workers, they emerge from the nightclub's back entrance. Oil derricks tower in the dawning sky. The space is filled with the paper detritus of newspapers and garbage.

Early critic Eric M. Krueger described Los Robles as "a world where filth, garbage, and disarray become metaphors for evil – swirling in the funhouse, the dream, and the delirium".[28] The transformed Venice Beach, filled with the

Garbage around Grandi's Rancho Grande and Tana's brothel

realistic detritus of daily urban human activity, allows Welles to again introduce expressionism into an ostensibly realistic setting.

Quinlan finds himself near a brothel and its siren call of pianola music. Quinlan goes inside to renew his old acquaintance with the madam, Tana, who doesn't recognise him in his obese state. Quinlan jokes about returning to sample Tana's chilli – "maybe too hot for you", she warns. This echoes a jokey comment made by the district attorney cut from the theatrical release version. Quinlan's past patronage of the brothel seems to be an agreeable part of his personal mythology in the legal hierarchy.

Again outside Tana's brothel, confronted by Vargas's earnest distress over his wife's near-abduction by the Grandis, Quinlan makes insinuations about Mrs Vargas's sexual morals; at Adair's defensive and uneasy joke that Quinlan is a "born lawyer", the detective insists: "Lawyer! I'm no lawyer. All a lawyer cares about is the law." In response to Vargas's earnest insistence about law enforcement – "A policeman's job is only easy in a police state. That's the whole point, captain. Who's the boss, the cop or the law?" – Quinlan defines his job bluntly: "When a murderer's loose, I'm supposed to catch him."

To Iván Zatz, the Mexican Vargas and American Jew Schwartz are "transnational technocrats" who overcome the jurisdictional challenges of an ideologically divided space to impose international, United Nations-style justice and defeat Quinlan's corruption.[29] Vargas introduces himself to Quinlan as "what the United Nations would merely call an observer", but he quickly angles for a stronger role on US soil in the name of justice. International governance remained Welles's preferred antidote to fascism.

As the night wears on towards a grim dawn, Pancho harasses Susie in her hotel room by shining a flashlight on her from a window across the way. Soon Risto, who threw acid at Vargas on his own initiative, is chased by Uncle Joe and Sal (another Grandi nephew) from the intersection outside the St Marks across the street to the parking lot beside and behind Grandi's Rancho Grande. During this chase the camera angles are canted, and spatial coherence is momentarily disjointed; also, improbably, the sands of Venice Beach seem to be glimpsed for a moment during the scuffle.

By the conclusion of the film's opening act, Quinlan's deeply entrenched position in the legal and social structure of Los Robles is established. Quinlan's habit of planting evidence will soon be discovered by Vargas during the investigation of the car bomb, but Vargas's insistent attempts to bring Quinlan to justice have to break through the defensive clique of local legal and police authorities, with their mythical narratives of Quinlan's past exploits, and finally Quinlan's employment of his criminal associate Uncle Joe Grandi. In the best version, the 1998 edition, *Touch of Evil* is a stunning product of Welles's career-long cinematic innovations in service of his mature insights into the operation of power in an American border city.

NOTES

1. Orson Welles letter to New Statesman (24 May 1958), reprinted at http://wellesnet.com/touch_memo2.htm (accessed 1 September 2015).
2. Benamou, *It's All True*, 261.
3. 'The Police', *Orson Welles' Sketchbook* (Orson Welles, 1955). Original broadcast: 7 May (UK: BBC TV).
4. 'Pays Basque I (The Basque Countries)', *Around the World with Orson Welles* (Orson Welles, 1955). Original broadcast: 7 October.
5. Iván Zatz, 'Tan lejos de Dios: The Production of Space and the Meaning of Power in Orson Welles' *Touch of Evil*', *Found Object*, No. 10, spring 2001, 65–6.
6. John C. Stubbs, 'The Evolution of Orson Welles's *Touch of Evil* from Novel to Film', *Cinema Journal*, Vol. 24, No. 2, winter 1985, 20.
7. See Stubbs, 'The Evolution of Orson Welles's *Touch of Evil* from Novel to Film', for an

analysis of the step-by-step process of the novel's screen adaptation.
8   The 1998 reedited version of *Touch of Evil* attempted to incorporate Welles's requests. The restored version does not feature previously unseen footage, but instead restructures some sequences and remixes the soundtrack of the opening shot.
9   This version was rediscovered in 1975.
10 Berthome and Thomas, *Orson Welles at Work*, 219.
11 Berthome and Thomas, *Orson Welles at Work*, 211; Laurent Bouzereau, *Bringing Evil to Life* (documentary), included in *Touch of Evil: 50th Anniversary Edition* (USA: Universal Studios Home Video, 2008).
12 Welles quoted in Terry Comito, 'Welles's Labyrinths: An Introduction to *Touch of Evil*', in Comito (ed.), *Touch of Evil: Orson Welles, Director* (New Brunswick: Rutgers University Press, 1985), 10.
13 This definition is from Nicholas Christopher, *Somewhere in the Night: Film Noir and the American City* (New York: Owl Books, 1997), 16–17.
14 Vincent Brook, *Driven to Darkness: Jewish Émigré Directors and the Rise of Film Noir* (New Brunswick: Rutgers University Press, 2009), 53.
15 Siegfried Kracauer summarised in Brook, *Driven to Darkness*, 54.
16 Brook, *Driven to Darkness* 53–4.
17 See Edward Dimendberg, *Film Noir and the Spaces of Modernity* (Cambridge: Harvard University Press, 2004), 29.
18 See Love, '"Architectural jungle" or the "sum of its people"?'
19 Paul Arthur, 'In the Labyrinth' (DVD notes), *Night and the City* (New York: Criterion Collection, 2005).
20 Berthome and Thomas, *Orson Welles at Work*, 115.
21 Comito, 'Welles's Labyrinths: An Introduction to *Touch of Evil*', 9–11.
22 For example, in 1972 Eric M. Kruger wrote that "the constant criss-crossing of the border by most of the major characters in the film tends to confuse one's sense of location. This only adds to the ambiguous, crazed atmosphere of the film by heightening a certain feeling of dislocation and by undermining any search for surety." Consequently, "the film viewed once is a manic vortex of time, space, and energy; no structure or logic of any type appears until it is seen three or four times." Krueger, '"Touch of Evil": Style Expressing Content', *Cinema Journal*, Vol. 12, No. 1, autumn 1972, 58.
23 See Rosenbaum, 'The Voice and the Eye: A Commentary on the *Heart of Darkness* Script', in *Discovering Orson Welles*, 33; and Heylin, *Despite the System*, 127.
24 Lawrence French, 'Orson Welles' Memo on *Touch of Evil*', *Wellesnet*, n.d., at http://wellesnet.com/touch_memo1.htm (accessed 1 August 2015).
25 Walter Murch, who was responsible for remixing and reediting the 1998 version, claims that Welles's intended sound scheme anticipates a technique he pioneered working on George Lucas's *American Graffiti* (1973). Murch named the technique 'worldizing'. To remix the soundtrack to Welles's specifications, Murch replaced Henry Mancini's original main title cue with a succession of other Mancini tracks (from the original scoring sessions) replayed

through various low-quality car and nightclub loudspeakers to simulate movement through the ambient environment of the Los Robles streets. The original location sound elements were also integrated back into the mix. See Michael Jarrett, 'Sound Doctrine: An Interview with Walter Murch', *Film Quarterly*, Vol. 53, No. 3, spring 2000, 2–11; and Rick Schmidlin's second commentary track on *Touch of Evil: 50th Anniversary Edition*.

26 Although the producers of the 1998 version chose not to run the credits over the opening shot, the Welles memo merely questions rather than specifically rules out using them at this point; indeed, his shooting script positions the credits at this point. See Orson Welles, *Badge of Evil* 'Revised Final Screenplay' (5 February 1957), 1, at http://www.scribd.com/doc/201288667/Touch-of-Evil (accessed 1 August 2015).

27 Krueger says in Los Robles "the truth is what people believe to be true. Quinlan had the power to create truth – the power to fashion his own reality and have others make it theirs as well. It is precisely this power of Quinlan's that had contributed so much to his identity and had enabled his workable compromise with the evil of Welles's world." Krueger, '"Touch of Evil": Style Expressing Content', 62.

28 Krueger, '"Touch of Evil": Style Expressing Content', 57.

29 Zatz, 'Tan lejos de Dios', 75, 80.

CHAPTER 9

RETURN TO THE PERIPHERY
The Other Man (unproduced, 1977)

> America has missed absolutely no opportunity, not only during the Reagan administration, but in my lifetime, to render it impossible for us to be anything but the deathly enemy of all Arabs, and, of course, all Latin Americans. We can never polish that image. I don't care how much money we pour into it.
> – Orson Welles in conversation, circa 1984–85[1]

A final project to consider in this survey of Welles's Pan-American cities is *The Other Man*, an unmade thriller based on Graham Greene's novel *The Honorary Consul* (1973). The screenplay was written in 1977, around the time Welles permanently relocated his filmmaking operations back to the United States.

From the late 1960s until his death Welles worked in frequent collaboration with the Croatian actress Oja Kodar. They worked together scripting *The Other Side of the Wind*, which Welles shot in the United States between 1970 and 1976 but was never able to finish editing. Kodar was a featured actress and the uncredited source for a tall tale about Picasso in *F for Fake*. In the 1970s the pair wrote other unmade projects including the supernatural Spanish period piece *Mercedes* (based on a story by Kodar called *Blind Window*; the script was also known as *House Party* and, in a later American version, *Mercy*) and the Spanish bullfighting drama *Crazy Weather* (circa late 1973).[2]

In 1975 Welles was approached to act in a film that would dramatise a supposed conspiracy behind the assassination of Robert F. Kennedy. He and Kodar quickly reconceived *Sirhan Sirhan*, the original script by Donald Freed, into a joint starring vehicle called *Assassin*. The Welles-Kodar changes amount to about one half of the script. The pair did not much tamper with Freed's urban conspiracy plot set in various cities of the United States; their work was restricted to an original narrative about the sexually tense relationship of a wheelchair-bound intelligence conspirator and the mysterious 'girl in the polka dot dress' inside a 'safe house'. Welles became deeply involved in the film's pre-production, obtaining cast, script, and director approval, but the independent producers were unable to complete financing of this radical project.[3]

The Other Man screenplay gives joint credit to Kodar, who about that project recalled, "I really was fifty percent his partner."[4] The principal reason Welles never brought his version to production was financial: although he purchased a two-month option from Greene's agent in April 1977 for $1,000, and immediately co-wrote a script with Kodar, he was unable to buy the rights to the property outright for its price of $150,000 (including $100,000 upfront).[5] Despite the lapse of the option, Welles continued to seek investors for the project at least as late as October 1977.[6] Screen rights to the novel were bought by British producer John Heyman, and although Welles remained hopeful that Heyman's rights would lapse, it was not to be.[7] Heyman's wife, Norma, ultimately produced the film, directed by John Mackenzie, from a screenplay by Christopher Hampton. That 1983 production, also known as *Beyond the Limit*, was poorly received – and a sadly wasted opportunity, because the unmade Welles-Kodar adaptation is superb and illustrates Welles's enduring interest in Latin American politics.

Greene's novel, set in contemporary Argentina, concerns the love affair between Doctor Eduardo Plarr and Clara, a former prostitute and the wife of Charley Fortnum, an alcoholic 'honorary' British consul. Marxist revolutionaries led by a former priest, Leon Rivas, plan to kidnap the US ambassador in a bid to force the release of political prisoners in Paraguay. Because Plarr's father is said to be among those prisoners, Plarr cooperates with the revolutionaries. They mistakenly kidnap Fortnum and hold him in a shantytown outside the city. The British refuse to negotiate for a mere honorary consul, and Plarr's efforts to convince Rivas to free Fortnum are frustrated. Finally Plarr and the kidnappers are killed as the police storm the shantytown. Fortnum survives.

Apart from the usual caveats regarding the provisional nature of Welles's screenplays, *The Other Man* warrants another type of critical caution. Professionally typed and billed as "based on the best-selling novel", the Welles-Kodar script was clearly designed to attract investors. That said, the script indicates that had the film been made it would have avoided the carnivalesque qualities of Welles's previous thrillers.[8]

Welles prefaces the script with a note stating that "all technical verbiage including indications for camera have been avoided in this script". There are only occasional indications of a shadowy, noirish *mise-en-scène*: next to the city's Italian Club is a "dark side street … where the shadows are deepest, a car. The headlights flick on and off" over the figure of the doctor.[9] The consul's wife, standing outside her house, "seems a melancholy little ghost there in the shadows".[10] Later, during the stand-off in the shantytown, "the doctor's shadow shoots back into the hut and lies stretched out there like a dead man on the floor".[11]

The new title, *The Other Man*, alludes to both the love triangle at the centre of the drama and Welles's previous, very successful project associated with Graham Greene, *The Third Man*. It seems fitting that Welles would finally turn to adapting the fiction of Greene, decades after he had adapted *Journey into Fear* by Eric Ambler, the other important writer in the establishment of the left-wing serious thriller back in the 1930s. Moreover, *The Honorary Consul* was strikingly relevant to international progressive concerns of the 1970s, set in the context of the United States' disastrous long-term interference in Latin American politics. The fictional British ambassador, Sir Henry Belfrage, makes fun of his US counterpart's bragging about the popularity of the USA in Paraguay – "Nelson Rockefeller's tour proved that. No one threw stones in Paraguay or set fire to any offices. It was as quiet as it was in Haiti."[12] Rockefeller's 1969 tours of Latin America at the request of President Nixon had been met by mass protests against US influence in Latin American affairs.[13] Present Governor of New York State and former Coordinator of Inter-American Affairs – the very man who had sent Welles south of the equator as a Good Will Ambassador in 1942 – Nelson Rockefeller is not mentioned in the Welles-Kodar script.

Another possibly appealing theme was Greene's very British rejection of the idiocies of Latin machismo. In his novel, Doctor Plarr asks rhetorically: "Who invented *machismo*? A gang of ruffians like Pizarro and Cortés. Can't any of you for a moment escape your bloody history? You haven't learned a thing, have you, from Cervantes. He had his fill of *machismo* at Lepanto."[14]

The ultimate invisibility of most of Welles's work in his later years has obscured his late critical interest in the theme. Greene's novel provides satire in the ridiculous figure of Jorge Julio Saavedra, fictitious author of *The Taciturn Heart*, which was "full of the spirit of machismo".[15] Welles and Kodar eliminated the Saavedra subplot from their adaptation, but Greene's theme endures in other places. Colonel Perez, the local police authority, insists: "When there is no machismo, doctor, a man is dead."[16] The kidnappers refuse to release the consul, even when all is lost, because to Aquino it would be an admission of failure. "It isn't macho enough for you, is that it?" suggests the doctor.[17]

One of Welles and Kodar's major changes to the novel is an intentional blurring of the setting. The international settings of Greene's novels had become known collectively as Greeneland. One critic had described it as "a seedy world of relics of happier times, of thin men in frayed shirts, of hungers that cannot be blunted, of bad beds and drinks made of pink gin, doomed departures, tyrants and bullies – and, always, victims."[18] Greene prefaced *The Honorary Consul* with the disclaimer:

> The province and the city in Argentina where the scene is principally set bear, of course, resemblance to a real city and a real province. I have left them nameless because I wished to take certain liberties and not to be tied down to the street plan of a particular city or the map of a particular province.[19]

Greene's lightly fictionalised and unnamed city is based on Corrientes, close to the Rio Paraná, which separates Argentina from Paraguay.[20] The river is an important element in Greene's novel, symbolic of Plarr's division from his missing father. In his previous Pan-American thrillers Welles had shown how powerfully he could use both port cities and border towns, but in this screenplay the river border dividing the two countries is not featured. Welles and Kodar chose to set their drama in the fictional 'Santa Cruz', "only the third largest city in one of the dimmest and most poverty stricken of all the dictatorships in Latin America". Traces of Corrientes remain: Clara listens to the same "sad Guaraní song"[21] heard on the radio in Greene's novel, leaving no doubt as to the city's proximity to Paraguay. But late in the script one of the kidnappers says, "we lost the football game today with Argentina",[22] which seems to be the same sort of intentional obfuscation as *Citizen Kane*'s newsreel director wondering why the life of Charles Foster Kane was different to William Randolph Hearst's – or Shakespeare disclaiming Falstaff's debt to the historical John Oldcastle: "for Oldcastle died a martyr, and this is not the man".

Although the relative geographical relation of the provincial city to the capital is retained – Santa Cruz is "up there" – Welles and Kodar are careful not to identify the capital as Buenos Aires, which Greene describes as "the great sprawling muddled capital with its *fantástica arquitectura* of skyscrapers in mean streets rising haphazardly and covered for twenty floors by Pepsi-Cola advertisements".[23] Welles and Kodar's unnamed capital is an apparently smaller city where "the international wire services maintained no full-time representatives".[24] They also changed the famous Confitería Richmond in Bueno Aires's Calle Florida – where the doctor's mother gorges on éclairs – to 'Dressler's Tea Shop & Patiserie'.

These changes were necessary to reflect the developments in Argentina in the four years since the publication of Greene's novel: Juan Peron's return from exile to assume the presidency in 1973–74 and then the onset of the 'Dirty War'. The aim of these practical changes was probably to make it possible for Welles to shoot a contemporary thriller, rather than make a period piece set earlier in the decade. Several years later, when pitching a doomed drama about a Central American resort to an HBO television producer, Welles insisted,

> I'm not interested in real history, because I know Latin American politics to an unbelievable degree. I'm an expert on it. And you cannot tell that story using any individual country. You must combine them to do it properly, and it must be fictional.[25]

Welles and Kodar also made changes to the ethnic backgrounds of the principal characters. As with Welles's changes to *Touch of Evil*, the shifted ethnicities create different dramatic nuances. Doctor Plarr becomes Doctor Farrel. The name change is for cinematic reasons. The script explains:

> The emphasis in this country is on the last syllable. In England where – until his father's imprisonment (and the collapse of the family fortune) Farrel was educated – the accent is on the first part of the name. We'll hear both versions and see both sides of a personality at once Latin American and Anglo-Saxon.

Farrel has an English mother and a Spanish father, "for long years a political prisoner", who "broods over his life like a ghost"[26] (in Greene's novel the nationalities of the doctor's parents are reversed). Farrel's father, who is presumed still in prison in a neighbouring country, was once a "distinguished governor" – and also "a direct descendent" of "the Farrel who was the Liberator",[27] embedding Doctor Farrel rather murkily in this fictional nation's history.

The "old estancia" of the family, vanished in Greene's novel, is still standing for a scene in Welles's Santa Cruz, albeit "deserted and boarded-up … in a state of grandiose and melancholy decay. The garden is a jungle."[28] Decayed buildings, reminders of a long-vanished grandeur, are the rule: the Italian Club, where Farrel dines with the elderly English expatriate Humphries, has "a crumbling 19th Century facade … and a few tables where one can eat cheaply without paying a subscription".[29] Likewise described is the British embassy in the unnamed capital, its "old Imperial pretensions gone to seed".[30]

Greene's honorary consul, Charlie Fortnum, becomes Charlie Fineman, a British Jew, in the Welles-Kodar revision. Joseph McBride notes that this change "heightens [the consul's] outsider status",[31] which is certainly one consequence. Lady Belfrage at the British embassy in the capital mistakenly refers to him as "poor Mr. Fineburg",[32] and there seems even less chance of official intervention on his behalf. But the effect is also to add nuance to the claustrophobic Catholic drama of Greene's novel, which in its later stages becomes bogged down in theological discussions between the doctor and the priest-turned-revolutionary Father Rivas. Fineman tells Jewish-themed jokes to lighten the mood throughout Welles and Kodar's script, including one to his kidnappers about a priest delivering the last rites to a Jewish man dying in an Irish boarding house: "The priest says, 'Do you believe in the Father, the Son, and the Holy Ghost?'… The old guy turns around. 'I'm a dying man!' he says, 'and he asks me riddles.'"[33]

This is not only a weak joke from Welles's own repertoire,[34] but also an eerie foreshadowing of what will actually happen in the script's climactic sequence, transported directly from Greene's novel but disturbingly altered by the fact of Fineman's Jewishness. Rivas comes across as a different kind of monster when he proposes the blameless Jew confess his sins to him, an act of "contrition", before this ideologically warped former priest proceeds to murder the man for mere political expediency.[35]

Another Welles-Kodar addition is the character of Asunta, one of the revolutionary kidnappers, who would likely have been played by Oja Kodar herself. Asunta wounds the consul as he tries to escape (in the novel, it is the revolutionary Aquino who shoots the consul). Asunta has a dramatic role in one long sequence and comes to a violent end.

In this collaborative script Welles returns to the impoverished periphery of a Latin American city thirty-five years after his botched attempt to put Rio de Janeiro's favelas on screen in *It's All True*. As in the novel, the consul is held hostage in a shantytown on the outskirts of the city. Throughout the script Welles and Kodar adopt the French term *bidonville*, used only once by Greene. Greene describes the bidonville lying "between the city and the bend in the river". Welles and Kodar rework this evocatively as "beyond the bend in the river and the Coca-Cola bottling works … a place where the land sinks into a small valley mostly filled with stagnant water". They recast Greene's description of the landscape as dialogue by Father Rivas: "The mud is permanent. There's no place for anything to drain, yet the people who live here have to walk more than a mile for their water."[36]

Significantly, the revolutionaries have not emerged from the underclass. The bidonville market, Aquino tells Asunta, is "a market for the poor, beautiful – the *very* poor. You've only read about that kind of poor."[37]

Greene's novel features a tense scene in which an old blind villager, José, having heard rumours of the presence of a priest, comes to the hut of the kidnappers to ask Father Rivas to bless the body of his dead wife. José is suspicious when he hears the foreign voice of the consul, but he is distracted by the novelty of a radio. Although the old man seems persuaded that Rivas is not, in fact, a priest, the kidnappers worry the old man is a spy or may blow their cover. They contemplate murdering him but do not follow through with the task.

Welles and Kodar expand this germ of a situation into a violently macabre sequence that marries the shantytown setting with the kind of murderous chase sequences through claustrophobic urban environments seen in *The Lady from Shanghai*'s Chinatown, the Naples docks in *Mr. Arkadin*, and the oil derricks and river in *Touch of Evil*.

The old blind man, unnamed in the script, is given the distracting radio as a present. Asunta trails the man through the bidonville as "the day is fading and the sky, under heavy clouds, is blood red".[38] She wears a shawl to blend in with the villagers; underneath she conceals a revolver. She intends to kill the old man, who is accompanied by two dogs and seems to suspect being followed. Asunta removes her shoes to muffle her approach.

Aquino tries to follow Asunta, but is lost in the bidonville, disorientated amid the maze of poverty:

> He runs frantically through the maze of narrow alleys winding between the shacks… Faces peer out at him from doorways and windows… Realizing that he's attracting undue attention, he forces himself to slow up. The trouble

is, he has no idea in what direction he should be heading. He is deep in the shantytown and Asunta is following the old man through what amounts to open country.[39]

The sound of a radio momentarily promises spatial reorientation. As it turns out, Aquino has discovered not the old man but instead a policeman's radio mounted on a bicycle outside a cantina. He steals it.

The "city-bred" Asunta is now on the rural edge of the bidonville. She is close to killing the old man either by gunshot or by bashing a stone against his head, but the old man temporarily eludes death by hiding on the back of a passing truck.

The dogs of the old man linger, and one savages Asunta's shoes. Darkness is coming. Asunta watches one of the dogs walk to a hut, clearly the old man's home. A police helicopter appears and noisily surveys the bidonville from above. Aquino, hiding behind an automobile in another part of the shantytown, seizes on the moment of confusion to rush back through the "maze of narrow alleys". Asunta enters the old man's hut, which has "scarcely nothing in it except an old wooden bench and a few dishes stuck in holes meant to serve as cupboards in the mud wall". She sees the dead body of his wife, "very thin and looking more like a wrinkled little child". A scarf is tied around the woman's head to keep her mouth closed, and a candle burns between her dead hands. A truck pulls up outside the hut, and Asunta in panic inadvertently moves another candle dangerously near to the ceiling, with its "hanging wisps of straw".

The old man enters his hut and "the candle in the dead woman's hand goes out". As he lights a new candle, he is attacked by Asunta, who strangles him with a "thin leather rope" in a horrifying and animalistic fight to the death. In the struggle the door is flung open and one of the dogs enters and "immediately leaps on Asunta, tearing at her blouse and shoulder". She fights off the dog, finally by shooting the animal "at close range between the eyes". The dead dog is left on top of the corpse of the old man. Asunta is wounded, and strips off her ruined blouse. She is now "naked to the waist; even her trousers aren't much like trousers anymore". She uses the scarf clamping the dead woman's jaw to bandage her own arm; crouching, "almost on all fours", she strips the corpse's clothes for her own use, and "close under her face she sees the gaping toothless mouth yawning at her" – a moment of horror that may have played like the distorted dead face of 'Uncle Joe' Grandi in a flash of neon in *Touch of*

Evil. Asunta now "forces herself to her feet and starts putting on the blouse. It's too small and she can hardly button it across her breasts." The hut has caught fire; outside, "it seems that all the dogs from the barrio are there". With her bare hands she retrieves her revolver from the flames and runs out as the hut incinerates. She momentarily holds off the dogs with gunshots, but the scene ends as "the dogs leap forward looking to her as though they were on fire themselves".[40]

This sequence recalls the previously discussed offscreen killing of Señora Marvales by vicious dogs in scenes cut from Welles's Puerto Indio sequence in *The Stranger*. There were thirty years between the two projects, but the motif is remarkably consistent – a fictionalised city not officially in Argentina; the vicious killing of a beautiful woman by wild dogs.

Welles and Kodar invented other violent scenes that were not in the Greene novel. The script's opening sequence shows the massacre by guards of escaping political prisoners as well as innocents in a wedding procession. And Welles and Kodar apparently intended a much more violent end to the siege in the bidonville. Paramilitary police, who the novel reveals are trained by the United States in Panama, close in on the revolutionaries with automatic rifles: "The carnage is terrible … they finish only when nothing moves."[41]

The Other Man would have made a disillusioned counterpart to *It's All True*'s propagandist approach to Pan-American solidarity and its optimism about progressive urban development to erase the property of the slums. The never-made script takes us to the seemingly eternal favela on the periphery of another noirish Puerto Indio, to a "wasteland of garbage" with a view to the "distant skyline of tin shacks",[42] to another Latin American city gone to the dogs.

NOTES

1. Welles quoted in Peter Biskind (ed.), *My Lunches with Orson: Conversations Between Henry Jaglom and Orson Welles* (New York: Metropolitan Books, 2013), 214.
2. See Stefan Drössler, 'Oja as a Gift: An Interview with Oja Kodar', in Drössler (ed.), *The Unknown Orson Welles* (Munich: Belleville Verlag/Filmmuseum München, 2004), 22–44; the approximate date for *Crazy Weather* is based on textual evidence within the treatment:

Uncredited [Orson Welles and Oja Kodar], *Crazy Weather*, Draft (1972?) (photocopy of annotated typescript, 143 pages, n.d.) (3 folders), 44. Box 7, Orson Welles–Oja Kodar Papers, Special Collections Library, University of Michigan.

3   See my two-part history of this project: Matthew Asprey Gear, 'Orson Welles and the Death of *Sirhan Sirhan*: Part I: The Conspirators', *Bright Lights Film Journal*, 20 February 2015, at http://brightlightsfilm.com/orson-welles-and-the-death-of-sirhan-sirhan-part-i-the-conspirators; and 'Orson Welles and the Death of *Sirhan Sirhan*: Part II: The Safe House', *Bright Lights Film Journal*, 26 February 2015, at http://brightlightsfilm.com/orson-welles-and-the-death-of-sirhan-sirhan-part-ii-the-safe-house (accessed 26 February 2015).

4   Drössler, 'Oja as a Gift', 43.

5   Welles's lawyer Arnold Weissberger sent a $1,000 cheque to Greene's agent Monica McCall covering a two-month option commencing 11 April 1977. Greene's editor at Simon & Schuster, Michael Korda, claims Greene expressed his pleasure that Welles had optioned the novel because "there was no danger of him actually making the film". At least one draft had already been completed by Welles and Kodar by mid-May 1977, the speed of which "certainly startled" Greene's agent Monica McCall. See Arnold Weissberger, letter to Monica McCall, 26 April 1977, in *The Other Man / Honorary Consul* (1977) 'Development Materials, 1977', Box 11, Orson Welles–Oja Kodar Papers, Special Collections Library, University of Michigan; Michael Korda, *Another Life: A Memoir of Other People* (New York: Delta, 2000), 321; Monica McCall, letter to Arnold Weissberger, 20 May 1977, in *The Other Man / Honorary Consul* (1977) 'Development materials, 1977'.

6   See Donald W. Brodsky, letter to Orson Welles, 29 December 1977, in *The Other Man / Honorary Consul* (1977) 'Development materials, 1977'.

7   Arnold Weissberger, letter to Orson Welles, 20 August 1979, in *The Other Man / Honorary Consul* (1977) 'Development materials, 1977'.

8   Orson Welles and Oja Kodar, *The Other Man* [Final?] Draft (photocopy of typescript, copy 1, n.d.) (4 folders). Box 10, Orson Welles–Oja Kodar Papers, Special Collections Library, University of Michigan.

9   Welles and Kodar, *The Other Man*, 20.

10   Welles and Kodar, *The Other Man*, 54.

11   Welles and Kodar, *The Other Man*, 141.

12   Graham Greene, *The Honorary Consul* (London: Vintage, 2004 [1973]), 127.

13   See Ernesto Capello, 'Latin America Encounters Nelson Rockefeller: Imagining the *Gringo Patrón* in 1969', in Jessica Stites Mor (ed.), *Human Rights and Transnational Solidarity in Cold War Latin America* (Madison: University of Wisconsin Press, 2013), 48–73.

14   Greene, *The Honorary Consul*, 219.

15   Greene, *The Honorary Consul*, 5.

16   Welles and Kodar, *The Other Man*, 94.

17   Welles and Kodar, *The Other Man*, 133.

18   Gloria Emerson, 'Our Man in Antibes: Graham Greene', in Graham Greene, *Conversations with Graham Greene*, ed. Henry J. Donaghy (Jackson; London: University Press of Miss-

issippi, 1992), 129.
19. Greene, *The Honorary Consul*, xxii.
20. Graham Greene, *Ways of Escape* (London: Vintage, 1999 [1980]), 292.
21. Welles and Kodar, *The Other Man*, 40.
22. Welles and Kodar, *The Other Man*, 133.
23. Greene, *The Honorary Consul*, 4.
24. Welles and Kodar, *The Other Man*, 60.
25. Welles quoted in Biskind (ed.), *My Lunches with Orson*, 264.
26. Welles and Kodar, *The Other Man*, 14.
27. Welles and Kodar, *The Other Man*, 64.
28. Welles and Kodar, *The Other Man*, 11.
29. Welles and Kodar, *The Other Man*, 15.
30. Welles and Kodar, *The Other Man*, 60.
31. McBride, *Whatever Happened to Orson Welles?*, 271.
32. Welles and Kodar, *The Other Man*, 63.
33. Welles and Kodar, *The Other Man*, 57.
34. See Welles and Bogdanovich, *This Is Orson Welles*, 278.
35. This change is all the more interesting as Welles was himself raised Catholic, a fact not revealed, as Rosenbaum notes, until the Bogdanovich interviews published as *This Is Orson Welles*. See Rosenbaum, *Discovering Orson Welles*, 183.
36. Welles and Kodar, *The Other Man*, 23–4.
37. Welles and Kodar, *The Other Man*, 73.
38. Welles and Kodar, *The Other Man*, 117.
39. Welles and Kodar, *The Other Man*, 119.
40. Welles and Kodar, *The Other Man*, 129–31.
41. Welles and Kodar, *The Other Man*, 163.
42. Welles and Kodar, *The Other Man*, 29.

INTERLUDE

A FREE MAN IS EVERYWHERE[1]
Europe & Beyond: 1947–55, 1958–85

In the 1950s Orson Welles described Europe as "a kind of frontier for us in films… It's a less organised, more anarchistic, and freer atmosphere because it isn't organised on an industrial basis." He said he favoured

> a touch of anarchy in a business which is as difficult and as complicated as the films … the kind of freedom that can't go with a really superb organisation, an assembly line. I don't happen to be a good assembly line filmmaker – but it's possible to make very good films on the assembly line. I'm not temperamentally adapted to it.[2]

From late 1947 Welles attempted to direct his projects in Europe under conditions of editorial authority previously available to him only on *Citizen Kane*. After Italian film producer Michele Scalera went bankrupt, the already in-progress *Othello* was largely funded by Welles himself through fees earned for appearances in *The Third Man* (Carol Reed, 1949), *Prince of Foxes* (Henry King, 1949), and *The Black Rose* (Henry Hathaway, 1950). The production was unable to afford at the outset even the luxury of an adequate stockpile of consistent film negative. Because of the periodic need for Welles to raise additional funds, the shoot was repeatedly postponed and resumed. Principal shooting extended from July 1949 to March 1950 in various parts of Morocco and Italy. Welles prioritised obtaining the necessary shots of actors with limited availability, leaving his own close-ups as Othello to much later stages of production.[3] Welles became more reliant on editing to transform this technically, temporally, and geographically disparate footage into a cohesive assembly.

He later described the process in his essay film *Filming 'Othello'*:

> Iago steps from the portico of a church in Torcello, an island in the Venetian lagoon, into a Portuguese cistern off the coast of Africa. He's crossed the world and moved between two continents in the middle of a single spoken phrase. [...] A Tuscan stairway and a Moorish battlement are both parts of what in the film is a single room. Roderigo kicks Cassio in Mazagan, and gets punched back in Orvieto, a thousand miles away. Pieces were separated not just by plane trips but by breaks in time. Nothing was in continuity, I had no script girl, there was no way for the jigsaw picture to be put together except in my mind. Over a span sometimes of months I had to hold each detail in my memory, not just from sequence to sequence, but from cut to cut. And I had no cutter.[4]

Welles's new piecemeal method of multi-national filmmaking, variously described as 'patchwork' or 'jigsaw', would become his preferred *modus operandi*. The method was cheaper and gave Welles more flexibility and control. Sometimes it meant a significant sacrifice of the technical standards expected by Hollywood, particularly in synchronised sound. From this point Welles would himself dub the speaking parts of many of his minor (and sometimes major) cast members, which allowed him to rewrite the dialogue in the editing room.

Othello's triumphant completion (in several variant director-authorised cuts) was due to Welles's commitment, energy, technical mastery, and practical spontaneity. The film won the Palme d'Or at the Cannes Film Festival in 1952, which undoubtedly reassured Welles of the viability of the new patchwork method.[5]

None of Welles's mooted films for producer Alexander Korda came to pass in Europe, although he found great popular success as an actor in Korda's production of *The Third Man*. By 1953, Welles had numerous projects in the works: a Noah's Ark movie called *Capitan Noè* (also known as *Two by Two*), Wilde's *Salomé*, Shakespeare's *Julius Caesar*, and a life of Benvenuto Cellini. His original screenplays included *Operation Cinderella*, a comedy about the occupation of a small Italian town by a Hollywood film crew and the town's resistance, and *V.I.P.*, a farce about a Mediterranean island, the "last place on Earth without either a Pepsi or a Coca-Cola concession". There was also an original thriller, *Mr. Arkadin*.[6] Welles's old friend and political mentor Louis

Dolivet became a novice film producer. In December 1953 Dolivet incorporated Filmorsa, a Tangier-based company specifically designed to produce Welles's future films starting with *Mr. Arkadin*, and also to manage his career, which included paying off the debts incurred for *Othello*. Welles was under exclusive contract to Filmorsa until the end of 1956. Dolivet and Welles each invested in the venture, alongside various Swiss bankers. Filmorsa obtained a Spanish co-producer in a deal that would have seen Welles produce *Arkadin*, two additional films, and two television programmes. When that co-producer encountered financial difficulties, Filmorsa struck a new deal for *Arkadin* alone with Cervantes Films, another Spanish company.[7]

Under these circumstances Welles became one of the first American directors to make a film in postwar fascist Spain. The regime of Francisco Franco began to welcome international filmmakers as a useful source of foreign currency, although the local filmmaking infrastructure at the time was limited.[8] Nevertheless, there were considerable advantages to Spanish co-production. *Arkadin* was Welles's first experience incorporating the financial and technical resources of the state film industry of a European dictatorship. It would be years before this production strategy would deliver the artistic autonomy Welles sought.

Dolivet and Welles were profound ideological enemies of the Franco dictatorship, but they were not alone on the left in finding an acceptable accommodation with its state film industry. A year after Welles worked on *Arkadin* at Madrid's Sevilla Film Studios, the formerly blacklisted Robert Rossen, who had named names to the House Un-American Activities Committee in 1953, directed the epic *Alexander the Great*. Although the bulk of co-productions made in Spain in the 1950s and 1960s were Italian genre films, there were also a number of those large-scale US historical epics epitomised by Nicholas Ray's *King of Kings* (1961, narrated by Welles) and *55 Days in Peking* (1963) and Anthony Mann's *El Cid* (1961) and *The Fall of the Roman Empire* (1964). The producer of these roadshow spectaculars, Samuel Bronston, established his own studio in Spain, was granted favours and decorations by the Franco regime, and was active in efforts to propagandise a politically useful image of the country to the world.[9]

A limited form of censorship was imposed upon visiting filmmakers, but Welles seems to have avoided state interference. During a 1955 British television interview, he dismissed the question of whether filming in Spain implied a tacit support for the regime, fibbed that he had used Spanish locations only for those *Arkadin* scenes actually set in Spain, and claimed the film had no political component.[10] But later that year, in the Basque episodes of *Around the World* filmed on the French side of the border, he mocked the Franco regime for banning the use of the Basque language. The Basques, Welles explained, responded to the prohibition by simply speaking "a little bit more on the Spanish side".

* * *

Upon his return to live in Italy in 1958 after losing final cut on *Touch of Evil*, Welles found regular employment as an actor in European productions. Years later he explained to a Yugoslavian TV audience: "I often make bad films in order to live and I'm sorry to say quite a lot of these bad films were made in your country."[11] Unsurprisingly, few of these films are of lasting artistic merit, and although Welles's association added a measure of prestige, he rarely delivered good performances. Sometimes he blatantly mocked or sabotaged the films in which he appeared. But Welles was not merely exchanging his bankable name for lucrative paycheques. In addition to covering his considerable living expenses, he consistently diverted his fees into his own directorial projects, as he had on *Othello*.

In Mexico through the second half of 1957, Welles had begun shooting a television version of *Don Quixote* starring Francisco Reiguera in the title role and the stalwart Akim Tamiroff as Sancho Panza. He ran out of money before he could obtain all the required footage. Thereafter *Don Quixote* became a long-term personal project, always evolving in form, funded directly from Welles's acting fees or by diverting resources from other projects with which he was associated as an actor. A second-hand editing desk, which Welles installed in his house outside Rome, was payment for his small role in John Huston's *The Roots of Heaven* (1958). Welles's secretary, Audrey Stainton, recalled Welles deliberately contriving to slow down Emimmo Salvi's production of *David and Goliath* in Rome in 1959 in order to take advantage of a contractual convenience: he was able to shoot *Don Quixote* by day in nearby Manziana drawing on the resources of that pompous epic for as long as it continued.[12] Two years later Welles used a television commission from Italy's RAI – the nine-part family travelogue *Nella terra di Don Chisciotte* (*In the Land of Don Quixote*) – as the financial basis for shooting more of *Don Quixote* on location in Spain.

In 1982, to those who chalked up *Don Quixote* as another unfinished film, Welles insisted:

> I could finish the film whenever I want. I have financed it completely by myself. Nobody has the right to bother me about it. A novelist is not obliged to finish a book if he wants to interrupt it for awhile. It is my business and no one else had the right to meddle in it.[13]

He also promised on several occasions he would finally title the film *When Are You Going to Finish Don Quixote?*

Welles continued to develop film projects that never graduated to production. In December 1963 he published a story outline in Italian for an epic called *Saladin: Three Crusaders*, presumably as a prospectus for investors. In 1967 Welles and Oja Kodar adapted Edgar Allen Poe's 'The Masque of the Red Death' and 'The Cask of Amontillado' for the mooted Poe omnibus film *Spirits of the Dead*, which was finally produced with segments directed by Federico Fellini, Louis Malle, and Roger Vadim. Two years later Welles and Kodar adapted Nicolas Freeling's Dutch juvenile delinquency thriller *Because of the Cats* (1963). Around the same time Welles wrote a rollicking original pirate adventure comedy called *Santo Spirito*.[14]

As for the films that actually went into production through the 1960s and early 1970s, Welles operated on parallel tracks. He juggled personally owned 'private projects' like *Don Quixote* with work made with outside producers. In the latter category were *The Trial*, *Chimes at Midnight*, *The Immortal Story*, and *F for Fake*. In these cases Welles took advantage of the resources of film industries within dictatorships across the ideological spectrum: Tito's Yugoslavia, Franco's Spain, and the Shah's Iran. For a time this proved to be a successful strategy. Sometimes Welles found it necessary to employ creative subterfuges to get the films made, such as piggybacking *Chimes at Midnight* onto a commercially orientated *Treasure Island* adaptation he never really intended to make.[15] But the disasters that befell Welles in this period were merely financial, rather than due to the artistic interference of his producers. Despite low and unstable budgets – on *The Trial* it was necessary for Welles to pay some actors out of his own pocket – all of these films were commercially distributed in a form Welles approved. In this period he had created a viable though temporary path to completing his films his own way. This must be considered a significant achievement for a director whose films had met consistent commercial failure.

Welles was just one of many American filmmakers who took advantage of the opportunities offered by the film industries of autocratic governments. This kind of filmmaking for Welles coincided with a retreat from heedless political commentary. From 1963 to 1968 Welles and his family were based in Madrid. Despite Welles's now quiet ideological opposition to Franco, the Spanish film industry proved most consistently amenable to his projects, although he continued to move about the continent as a vagabond actor and director. A draft narration for *Orson's Bag* in 1969 reads:

> I made this show all over the world – because that's where I live, and because I tend to do a lot of different jobs all more or less at the same time, and in a lot of different places… Just movie-making keeps me on the jump all over the globe… We're like fruit pickers, we have to go where the work is.[16]

In 1967 Welles ventured beyond the Iron Curtain to attempt to work with Hungary's state film industry for an adaptation of Isak Dinesen's *The Heroine*, which would have formed an omnibus of Dinesen adaptations with *The Immortal Story* and the never-made *Full Moon*. But he lost faith in his financiers and aborted the film after a day's shooting in the Budapest Opera House.[17]

By the late 1960s Welles worked increasingly on the margins of independent European filmmaking, often taking seed money or other resources from unlikely sectors of the international film and television industries to allow him to commence shooting new projects without any locked-in funds for completion. *The Deep*, based on the 1963 thriller *Dead Calm* by Charles Williams, was shot on the Dalmatian Coast in 1967 and 1968. It was never quite finished. Welles began filming with very moderate support from the Yugoslavian state film industry in lieu of payment for outstanding work he had provided, including, he recalled, an otherwise unknown screenplay about the history of Sarajevo. *The Deep* was particularly small-scale for the usually ambitious Welles: five actors, two yachts, a drama set on water – his least urban film. Probably the key reason for its non-completion was that, as with *Don Quixote*, Welles was not facing external pressure to recoup the investments of other financiers. He was also dissatisfied with the result. Nevertheless, Welles kept promoting the film as an almost-finished product to producers well into the 1970s. Later, he admitted, "we just ran out of money" and the film "shows its poverty, and it looks like a TV movie".[18]

Despite frequent financial duplicity, Welles was a long-term beneficiary of the Yugoslavian film industry until the death of Josip Broz Tito in 1980. On Yugoslavian television in the late 1970s, he described Tito as "the greatest man in the world today".[19] Whether this was sincere admiration, deplorable cynicism, or a nuanced appraisal of Tito's 35-year rule of Yugoslavia between the pressures of the USSR and the West, the statement reflects badly on Welles in light of Tito's repression of Yugoslavian filmmakers. Back in 1969, just a month after Welles shot parts of *Orson's Bag* in Zagreb and attended the Belgrade premiere of the patriotic war film *The Battle of Neretva*, Tito had begun a round of cultural censorship, a 'counter-offensive', that included the banning of films and the exile (and even imprisonment) of filmmakers of the Yugoslavian 'Black Wave'.[20]

Welles ventured into even more dubious alliances in order to finance his films. His energy at the beginning of the 1970s focused on two radically new experiments: *The Other Side of the Wind* and *F for Fake*. Both films were produced and partly financed in a deal with Les Films de l'Astrophore, a French-based Iranian film company headed by Mehdi Boushehri, the brother-in-law of Mohammad Reza Shah Pahlavi. Welles also found it politically palatable to narrate a documentary celebrating the Shah in 1972.

F for Fake was completed quickly, although its worldwide release was staggered across several years and it failed to find commercial success or critical acclaim. *The Other Side of the Wind* began as one of Welles's private projects, its film-within-a-film shot piecemeal from 1970, and then became a commercial project when Welles signed up with Astrophore and a Spanish co-producer. Managing the American-based project from a great distance, Astrophore was initially far less insistent than previous producers that Welles conform to a rigid production schedule or professional accounting. The association gave Welles a freedom and relative financial security that he hadn't known for years. This freedom and Welles's elaborate innovations in shooting and editing, in addition to major budgetary embezzlement and personal tax problems, meant work on *The Other Side of the Wind* dragged on until 1976. With the breakdown of his relationship with his producers, and finally the Iranian revolution, the film was never completed.[21]

Despite many efforts, Welles was unable to find workable financing in Hollywood. The only film to see release in the last ten years of Welles's life was the low-budget essay *Filming 'Othello'*, financed by West German television. He died in Los Angeles on 10 October 1985, still working on new projects in cinema.

NOTES

1. From Jeanne Moreau's untitled poem on Orson Welles, 1975, reprinted at http://www.wellesnet.com/jeanne-moreau-on-a-free-man (accessed 11 August 2015).
2. *Press Conference* (1955), part I.
3. Berthome and Thomas, *Orson Welles at Work*, 169–75.
4. *Filming 'Othello'*.
5. I'm grateful to Stefan Drössler, director of the Munich Film Museum, for sharing with me his thoughts on this period of Welles's career.
6. Anile, *Orson Welles in Italy*, 267; Welles and Bogdanovich, *This Is Orson Welles*, 412–13.
7. François Thomas, 'The Filmorsa Years'.
8. Neal M. Rosendorf, *Franco Sells Spain to America: Hollywood, Tourism and Public Relations as Postwar Spanish Soft Power* (London: Palgrave Macmillan, 2014), 54.
9. See Rosendorf, *Franco Sells Spain to America*, 48–50, 56, 60–74.
10. *Press Conference* (1955), part I.
11. Welles quoted in the documentary *Druga strana Wellesa* (*The Other Side of Welles*, Daniel Rafaelic and Leon Rizmaul, 2005).
12. Audrey Stainton, 'Orson Welles' Secret', *Sight and Sound*, autumn 1988, reprinted at http://www.wellesnet.com/don-quixote-orson-welles-secret (accessed 11 August 2015).
13. Welles quoted in Esteve Riambau, 'Don Quixote: The Adventures and Misadventures of an Essay on Spain', in Drössler (ed.), *The Unknown Orson Welles*, 75.
14. Scripts and treatments survive in the Orson Welles–Oja Kodar Papers, Special Collections Library, University of Michigan.
15. Berthome and Thomas, *Orson Welles at Work*, 254.
16. In *Orson's Bag* (1968–70) (subseries), Draft pages (various scenes) (typescript, carbon, and photocopy, annotated), 10 April – 11 September 1969 (folder 1). Box 17, Orson Welles–Oja Kodar Papers, Special Collections Library, University of Michigan.
17. Drössler, 'Oja as a Gift', 42–3; Berthome and Thomas, *Orson Welles at Work*, 282–3.
18. Bill Krohn, 'My Favourite Mask Is Myself: An Interview with Orson Welles', in Drössler (ed.), *The Unknown Orson Welles*, 54.
19. Welles quoted in *Cinema Komunisto* (Mila Turajlic, 2010).
20. Anonymous, *Cinema Komunisto* (electronic press kit) (n.d.), 21, at http://www.cinema-komunisto.com/wp-content/uploads/2010/11/Cinema-Komunisto-EPK-ENGdec2011.pdf (accessed 11 August 2015).
21. See Josh Karp, *Orson Welles's Last Movie: The Making of the Other Side of the Wind* (New York: St. Martin's Press, 2015).

POSTWAR EUROPE

CHAPTER 10

SKIES AND RUBBLESCAPE
Mr. Arkadin/Confidential Report (1955)

> I am, have been, and will be only one thing – an American.
> – Charles Foster Kane

> I do not know who I am.
> – Gregory Arkadin

Through the 1950s and 1960s Welles was intensely interested in the operation of power, the problems of nationalism, and the meanings of freedom and justice in Europe. For a time Welles claimed to be writing a book on international government, possibly a collaboration with Louis Dolivet.[1] Although the book never materialised, his current political ideas found their idiosyncratic way into *Mr. Arkadin*, which was Pan-European in both its themes and its innovative mode of production. Any sort of coherence was lost, however, because once again Welles was unable to complete editing the film. It finally emerged in a set of bizarre variations seen by a limited audience.

The production of *Arkadin* began without a conventionally rigid shooting schedule and budget. Filming began in January 1954 and continued far beyond expectations, requiring Dolivet to repeatedly seek new funds. The production used Sevilla Film Studios in Madrid and locations in other parts of Spain, on the French Riviera, in Munich (on location and at Bavaria Studios), and in Paris (on location and at Photosonar studios in Courbevoie). Many of these locations doubled for international settings from Tangier to Acapulco.[2] Welles had shot and edited what became the largely self-financed *Othello* on two continents over a period of more than three years; on *Arkadin* he seems to have shifted his approach during filming towards the same multi-national patchwork method. This time he failed to find satisfaction. Welles remembered the shoot as "just anguish from beginning to end".[3] He and Dolivet quickly realised they were not suited to working together in the film business and agreed to wind up their joint business ventures after the completion of *Arkadin*.[4]

Even before all the necessary footage had been shot, a Spanish-language version of *Mr. Arkadin* had been assembled by August 1954 for finance-raising purposes. Presumably to qualify for the advantages of Spanish co-production status, two Spanish actresses, Amparo Rivelles and Irene López Heredia, gave performances that were later replaced in non-Spanish versions by Suzanne Flon and Katina Paxinou, respectively. Welles missed a September 1954 deadline to complete the English-language version of the film for a premiere at the Venice Film Festival; sporadic shooting was still going on in France as late as October.[5] A major falling out between Welles and Dolivet over the prolonged editing process – according to editor Renzo Lucidi, Welles was locking in a mere two minutes per week[6] – led to Welles's departure in January 1955. The editing continued under Lucidi, with some external input from Welles, who planned to return to make a final revision; as it turned out, he did not participate further. Even under these strained conditions, Filmorsa continued to work with Welles and insist he honour his exclusive contract. The company funded test material for *Don Quixote* in Paris and worked alongside a British company, Associated-Rediffusion, to produce Welles's documentary series *Around the World with Orson Welles* for ITV television. Welles eventually broke his contracts and returned to the United States in October 1955. He left behind incomplete film materials for only seven of the planned twenty-six episodes of *Around the World*.[7]

A lost English-language version of *Mr. Arkadin*, titled *Confidential Report*, had premiered in London in August 1955.[8] Another, probably slightly different, version – also now vanished – went into general release in the United Kingdom in November.[9] There are at least two surviving Spanish-language versions featuring Rivelles and López Heredia: one that strangely misattributes Robert Arden's performance to 'Mark Sharpe' and a later shorter version – the official Spanish release – which miscredits him as 'Bob Harden'.[10] A revised English-language version, also called *Confidential Report*, was released by Warner Bros. in Europe in the spring of 1956. This version has also survived. By this version much of the flashback structure, framed by a conversation between the characters Guy Van Stratten and Jakob Zouk, had been altered.[11]

In the very early 1960s the young American director Peter Bogdanovich investigated the holdings of a Hollywood television syndication company, M. & A. Alexander, and discovered a version of *Mr. Arkadin* that would become known as the 'Corinth' version, an early edit of mysterious origin that retained the flashback structure. Another US version, a crude reassembly in chronological order, lapsed into the public domain and for a long period was the most accessible version to the American public.[12]

The film (in its numerous variant versions) was not commercially or critically successful. The deep friendship of Welles and Dolivet may not have been irretrievably destroyed by the failure of the project, but for the following period their relationship was tumultuous. In 1958 Filmorsa unsuccessfully sued Welles for his behaviour during the production.[13]

As with many Welles films, determining what is the director's own work and what was compromised or reworked by the producer is difficult. Moreover, only some of *Mr. Arkadin*'s many variant versions are easily accessible. The three versions readily available are the 'Corinth', the 1956 European *Confidential Report*, and a posthumously assembled hybrid version called the 'Comprehensive Version', the work of Stefan Drössler of the Filmmuseum München and Claude Bertemes of the Luxembourg Cinémathèque.[14]

To add a little more to the elusiveness of a definitive *Arkadin*, there were also two versions published as prose fiction, both attributed to Welles's authorship. An obscure, very short, and not particularly effective five-part serial appeared in consecutive August 1955 issues of the UK's *Daily Express* to promote the film. The French novelisation, *Monsieur Arkadin*, serialised in *France-Soir* and published in book form by Gallimard in 1955, was attributed to Welles but actually ghostwritten by his French associate Maurice Bessy. The French novelisation was anonymously translated into English and published in the United States and United Kingdom in 1956 under Welles's name.[15] These publishing projects, like Bessy's earlier French novelisation of Welles's unmade script *V.I.P.* as *Une Grosse Légume* (1953), were part of Filmorsa's scheme to raise money for its doomed ventures.[16]

* * *

Mr. Arkadin had a complicated genesis. It's titular tycoon character led it to be compared unfavourably to *Citizen Kane* – a European self-parody or inferior knock-off, as John Huston's *Beat the Devil* (1953) was to his *The Maltese*

Falcon. But *Arkadin* is actually a distant cousin – or bastard step-nephew – of the very successful *Third Man* and is positioned within the generic lineage of the serious thriller, albeit in often bafflingly idiosyncratic and not particularly serious ways. Perhaps this tangential connection to a commercially successful property led Welles to claim in retrospect, rather bizarrely, that *Arkadin* had had the potential to be "a very popular film, a commercial film that everyone would have liked".[17] Things didn't work out that way. During post-production, Welles said, "it pretends to be a thriller – and it isn't".[18]

The Third Man had revived the serious thriller in the political context of postwar Europe. Graham Greene wrote it as a novella in preparation for his screenplay. Welles filmed the bulk of his performance as Harry Lime in Vienna in late 1948 as he scouted locations and made test shots for *Othello*.[19] *The Third Man*'s commercial and critical success made Welles even more famous, particularly in Europe.

The setting of *The Third Man* is the rubblescape of postwar Vienna, demarcated into zones by the Allied forces. The American Harry Lime, apparently dead at the outset, turns out to be a remorseless dealer in black market penicillin. His naive American friend Rollo Martin is confronted by his friend's ruthless criminality and sudden reappearance. The film ends with a famous chase through the sewers of Vienna. The expressionist cinematography of Robert Krasker – high-contrast, deep-focus black and white – is one of the reasons the film is often mistaken as the directorial work of Welles himself.

The Lives of Harry Lime (1951–52), a British radio prequel series, was ingeniously produced by Harry Alan Towers – "a famous crook", Welles recalled[20] – without the participation of the film's original producer, Alexander Korda, or director, Carol Reed. Towers separately secured Welles as an actor (and inevitably director and occasional writer) as well as the rights to use Greene's character and Anton Karas's 'Third Man Theme' for zither. Harry Lime's criminal psychopathy was toned down. The cosmopolitan settings – Europe, North Africa, India – could be achieved rather more economically on radio than on film. The episodes were pre-recorded, largely at Welles's convenience, in London, Rome, and Paris.[21]

Welles later said the *Arkadin* screenplay was created "from just throwing together a lot of bad radio scripts".[22] The film's central plot is drawn from one of Welles's *Harry Lime* episodes. 'Man of Mystery', the key episode that introduces Gregory Arkadian (note the slightly different spelling) and the investigation of his past, was recorded in Paris in 1951 and first broadcast on 11 April 1952.[23]

However, a Milan film magazine had reported some conception of a film screenplay (under its working title, *Masquerade*) already un[...] March 1951 while Welles was in Casablanca shooting more of *Othel*[...]

'Man of Mystery' introduces Arkadian as "one of the riches[t ...] in Europe". He has never been photographed. Arkadian wants the contract to build airbases in Portugal for what is implied to be NATO. Welles may have been inspired by the US-Portugal Defense Agreement, signed 6 September 1951, which codified US military rights to an airbase on the island of Lajes in the Azores.[25] Arkadian knows he will be subject to a thorough intelligence check by the United States Army. He hires Harry Lime, with his knowledge of the "continental underworld", to prepare an advance report on Arkadian's past. Arkadian claims he suffers from amnesia, remembering nothing prior to the winter of 1927, when he found himself in Lucerne possessing "only the suit I was wearing and a wallet with two hundred thousand francs... Swiss francs. It was with that money that my present great fortune was built." Lime investigates, discovers Arkadian had come to Switzerland from Warsaw, and decides to "look up a few Poles" now dispersed over the world. During Lime's interviews it emerges that Arkadian is really Akim Athabadze, a former member of a 'white slavery' and dope smuggling gang in interwar Poland. Closely tracking Lime's investigation, Arkadian murders the exiled Poles one by one as they are located. Arkadian seems to be a threat to Lime himself until the sordid history is revealed to Arkadian's beloved daughter, Raina. Faced with such exposure, Arkadian kills himself by jumping from his private plane.[26]

The radio episodes 'Murder on the Riviera' and 'Blackmail Is a Nasty Word' share additional plot elements with Welles's *Arkadin* screenplay.[27]

* * *

The origins of Gregory Arkadi(a)n, aka Akim Athabadze, recall the villains of Eric Ambler's early novels, who, according to Michael Denning,

> are of uncertain nationality and, like the villains of earlier thrillers, oppose any nationalism. "One should not," one of these entrepreneurs of information, Vagas, says [in *Cause for Alarm*, 1938], "allow one's patriotism to interfere with business. Patriotism is for the *café*. One should leave it behind with one's tip to the waiter." Business has no frontiers, it crosses national

boundaries with the best papers money can buy, and it crosses the frontier of legal and illegal without regard.[28]

When Welles announced *Mr. Arkadin* to *L'Écran français* in January 1952, he said it would "tell the misadventures of an arms dealer along the lines of Basil Zaharoff",[29] although later Welles described Zaharoff as "sly", unlike Arkadin, who nevertheless "occupies a similar position" to such mysterious tycoons.[30] Zaharoff, born in 1850 in Anatolia, was knighted by George V for providing arms to the Allied forces during World War I, although he was widely suspected of duplicity and even stoking war on both sides to create business. Welles played Zaharoff in a radio episode of *The March of Time* on the occasion of the tycoon's death in 1936.[31]

Another source for Gregory Arkadin was Josef Stalin, who shared the character's Georgian heritage. Welles elaborated that Arkadin was

> cold, calculating, cruel, but with that terrible Slavic capacity to run to sentiment and self-destruction at the same time. The beard came from a wig-maker and the character came partly from Stalin and partly from a lot of Russians I've known.[32]

Welles more generally reflected that

> Arkadin is the expression of a certain European world. He could have been Greek, Russian, Georgian. It's as if he had come from some wild area to settle in an old European civilization, and were using the energy and the intelligence natural to the Barbarian out to conquer European civilization, or Ghengis Khan attacking the civilization of China. And this kind of character is admirable; it's only Arkadin's ideology which is detestable, but not his mind, because he's courageous, passionate, and I think it's really impossible to detest a passionate man.[33]

This thoughtfulness might suggest that in Gregory Arkadin Welles had created a tycoon of human complexity, a character with an emotional life as richly conceived as Charles Foster Kane's. On the contrary, Arkadin is played by Welles with extreme artifice. His makeup, beard, hair, costumes, and accent are bizarre and affected. The performance is often singled out as the weakest aspect of the film.

Orson Welles as Gregory Arkadin

A key difference between 'Man of Mystery' and the film is the character of the investigator. Harry Lime is not simply renamed for legal reasons; he is transformed into Guy Van Stratten, a coarse and naive American "running American cigarettes into Italy", far less cosmopolitan and wily than Harry Lime. Robert Arden's performance as Van Stratten has also been widely criticised as inadequate. Jonathan Rosenbaum has defended Arden, locating the problem more in "the unsavoriness and obnoxiousness of the character rather than the performance itself"; Van Stratten is intended to be unattractive while "occupy[ing] the space normally reserved for charismatic heroes".[34] The character seems to have been reconsidered through successive drafts of Welles's screenplay. The *Masquerade* draft, completed on 23 March 1953, has a European hero named 'Guy Dumesnil'. The Van Stratten who narrates the English translation of Bessy's *Monsieur Arkadin* – apparently based on a Welles script draft *later* than *Masquerade* but predating the shooting script – is worldly and sardonic.[35]

The mood of artificiality is enhanced by the casting of supporting actors outside the ethnicity and mother tongue of their characters. The Jakob Zouk character provides the framing conversation with Van Stratten in most surviving versions, an invention by Welles early during shooting. In the European *Confidential Report* of 1956, Van Stratten's voice-over refers to Zouk as "a petty racketeer, a jailbird". In the 'Corinth' version, Zouk characterises his release as the jail wanting "to save themselves the price of the coffin". Although there are hints that Zouk is a Polish Jew – in the 'Corinth' he throws out such Yiddish reduplications as "gang schmang" and "killer schmiller" – it is inconceivable that a Jew would have emerged from a Munich prison circa 1954 after a fourteen-year stretch. Zouk is played by Akim Tamiroff, the brilliant Armenian comic actor who throughout his international film career specialised in 'ethnic' roles. For Welles alone he played an Italian gangster in *Touch of Evil*, a Mitteleuropean in *The Trial*, and Sancho Panza in *Don Quixote*.

The Polish diaspora characters were cast from all over Europe. Peter Van Eyck, who played Thaddeus, came closest to the character's source; he was born in Pomerania, historically part of Germany but post-1945 located in Poland. The others are played by an Englishman (Michael Redgrave), a Hungarian (Frederick O'Brady), a Russian (Mischa Auer), a Greek (Katina Paxinou), and an ethnic Armenian of obscure birth (Grégoire Aslan). Susanne Flon, who plays the Baroness Nagel, was French. Welles had originally intended to cast the Swedish Ingrid Bergman as the Baroness and the German Marlene Dietrich as Sophie.³⁶

Welles later claimed, "I wanted to make a work in the spirit of Dickens, with characters so dense that they appear as archetypes."³⁷ Critic William C. Simon remarks on the presentation of the film's characters through "hyperbolic caricature". Referring to Mikhail Bakhtin's concept of 'social speech types', Simon notes how in *Arkadin* these "speech types have a set of sociopolitical associations":

> Every character ... speaks their dialogue with a pronounced accent. [...] Their accents are drawn from conventionalised literary or social discourses of which there are a tremendous variety in the film. [...] [A]ll evoke a set of associations related to a particular culture by its literary and popular mythology. Especially significant is the notion of Eastern European world-weariness, a tremendous sense of philosophical resignation and ennui that animates all the characters in the film.³⁸

In Welles's films, *saudade* for vanished times and places is typically expressed in tender anecdotal monologues or by symbolic objects such as Rosebud. In addition to his numerous other foreign affinities, Welles was particularly fond of an antiquated Mitteleurope – particularly of the self-inventing Hungarians. The Polish characters in *Mr. Arkadin* are variously exiled to Munich, Naples, Paris, Mexico City, Acapulco, Tangier, Copenhagen, and Amsterdam; Van Stratten's interviews provide some of these lowlife refugees with the opportunity to voice their nostalgia for interwar Warsaw. Sophie, the former gang leader now married to a grotesquely mugging Mexican general, is particularly haunted by the memory of her Warsaw days with the dashing young Arkadin/

Athabadze: "I was crazy in love with him, mister!" she says, and later clutches her photograph album to her chest. And if there is a Rosebud in *Mr. Arkadin*, it is Jakob Zouk's traditional Christmas goose liver – "with applesauce, mashed potatoes, and gravy". Close to death, he names that dish, traditionally most popular in Hungary, as the price of allowing Van Stratten to save his life.

* * *

To add to the artificial mood, the first few minutes of all versions of the film – and the European *Confidential Report* in particular – present a startling clash of modes. The opening quotation from Plutarch, about a poet who is willing to accept any gift from a powerful king except the burden of a secret, promises a fable; Welles's narration over the aerial image of a pilotless plane purports to introduce a "fictionalised reconstruction" of scandalous true events; the credits, a montage of the colourful *dramatis personae* at their quirkiest, suggests a carnival of grotesques; and then Van Stratten's working-class American voice-over evokes the atmosphere of pulpy hardboiled detective stories. Rosenbaum has cited the stylistic mishmash in *Arkadin* as an influence on the imminent French New Wave.[39] The film was indeed praised in contemporary reviews by François Truffaut and Eric Rohmer, and in 1958 the critics of *Cahiers du cinéma* improbably selected the European release of *Confidential Report* as one of the twelve best movies of all time.[40]

Simon channels Bakhtin to explain Welles's method:

> Clearly, what Welles is doing in the opening moments of the film is to put into dialogic contact three diverse discourses: the fairy tale or legend of the paratext, the documentary reconstruction of the opening spoken lines, and a delirious hyperbolic aesthetic mode associated through the music score with a generalized Eastern European sensibility that will in fact prove to be the dominant mode of the film. This clash of discourses constitutes a positing of filmic heteroglossia and raises questions about the film's conception. Will it be a fairy tale? Will it be a docudrama? Will it be a most elaborate Polish joke?[41]

Paul Misraki's score is a collection of pastiches including Salvation Army brass band music (an original theme and 'Silent Night') and a buoyant orchestral dance theme with an Eastern European flavour. Misraki wrote the music without having read the screenplay or seen a cut of the film. Welles spliced together segments of Misraki's recorded cues in abrupt juxtapositions.[42]

So these are Welles's complicated generic, textual, and historical sources, the unconventional stylistic choices, and the production disasters surrounding *Mr. Arkadin*. In combination these factors left to posterity a confusing set of variant versions, none of them finished or approved by the director. And yet Welles's political critique of postwar Europe is still palpable across the versions. By updating the 'serious thriller' to the era of international air travel and the Iron Curtain – unprecedented speed and freedom of movement for the privileged, authoritarian restriction for the majority – Welles illustrates the new ways that space is controlled and experienced in a dizzying vision of erased distances that anticipates the internationalism of the James Bond films of the 1960s.

We also glimpse deliberately imagined urban terrains where traces of the past break through the material structures of the city. These palimpsestic spaces make for a suitable metaphor for postwar Europe. They reinforce Welles's privileging of antiquated cultural affiliations, idealised and evoked in nostalgic reverie or symbolic objects, over the arbitrary political divisions of nationhood and the ideological divide of the Cold War. This is most pronounced in the rubblescape of Munich.

* * *

In the best of today's films, there's always an airport scene, and the best yet is in *Confidential Report* when Arkadin finds the plane full and shouts out that he will offer $10,000 to any passenger who will give him his seat. It is a marvelous variation on Richard III's cry, "My kingdom for a horse," in terms of the atomic age.

– François Truffaut, 1956[43]

In the 'St-Germain-des-Prés' episode of *Around the World with Orson Welles*, filmed in 1955 after his departure from the *Arkadin* editing suite, Welles diplomatically lauds the airlines of Europe, but also voices nostalgia for "old-fashioned travel of all kinds. Not only old-fashioned trains … but old boats and barges and gondolas and canoes, ox-carts … anything that takes long enough to give you a chance to see where you're going before you get there."[44]

The port city of Naples was devastated during the war, but its rubble is not depicted in *Mr. Arkadin*. Welles shot at least part of the Naples sequence, the murder of Braco, in Madrid.[45] The sequence is built from expressionistic low-angle and canted shots which sometimes pan non-horizontally in a clever visual echo of the lopsided run of Braco's peg-legged assassin. Welles projects the assassin's distorted shadow against shipping crates. The montage does not maintain any sort of coherent spatial continuity in any version of the film. According to Lucidi, the first four sequences in the 'Corinth' version – which would therefore include the Naples sequence – appear as Welles intended.[46] The fictional space of Naples marries the iconography of ships and trains – two typical transitory settings of the 1930s 'serious thriller'.

But time has moved on and air travel now provides the dominant passage of movement for the powerful. The expansive international settings of *Mr. Arkadin* are only possible in the age of flight. The plane's centrality to the world of *Arkadin* is indicated by the opening image in all versions – an empty plane in the sky. Later, the incredible reach of Van Stratten's international investigation is conveyed by montage sequences incorporating images

The age of air travel in *Mr. Arkadin*

SKIES AND RUBBLESCAPE

of planes and airports. Key moments of drama occur at airports in Barcelona and Munich. In one deleted scene Van Stratten and Raina talk on a tarmac, presumably in Barcelona, and leave Raina's glum English suitor sitting alone on a ramp stairway leading nowhere.[47]

At the edges of the tarmac in Barcelona are half-completed concrete buildings that resemble the unfinished structures surrounding Sebastianplatz in Munich. Yet whereas rubble-strewn Munich exposes layers of its history, El Prat airport in Barcelona is a bland open tarmac in arid country.

The drama's climactic moment occurs in Barcelona's central air-traffic control tower. Here Raina communicates with her disembodied father, who is mostly represented by shots of a ceiling-mounted loudspeaker. With Arkadin's suicide the loudspeaker falls silent.

The variant versions of *Mr. Arkadin* indicate that the film's international settings were not fixed from conception but evolved over the long period of production. Apart from 'Man of Mystery', Welles left as evidence other early drafts (of sorts): the March 1953 *Masquerade* script, the ghostwritten novelisation, and the Spanish versions. This *Masquerade* script sets Arkadin's masked ball in Venice rather than its eventual location, Spain. In that version of the script Welles explicitly cites as precedent the ball thrown by the Mexican millionaire Carlos de Beistegui in Venice on 3 September 1951.[48] Welles was in attendance and reported on the event for the Italian weekly *Epocha*:

> Rehearsing at St. James's Theatre in London I thought about the costume I would wear to the ball. Impossible to move Othello into the eighteenth century. Too far. Cagliostro was just right. I got there without the costume, of course, which hadn't arrived from Rome. I get distracted, as everyone knows. Some think I do it deliberately. But that evening, at eight o'clock, I suddenly realized I had no costume. I had to improvise. At the [Hotel] Danieli they found me a turban, something between a lady's art nouveau hat and the headdress of a Sioux Indian chief…[49]

Other guests included Gene Tierney, Salvador Dalí, and Christian Dior. Winston Churchill, also in the city, had to skip the party lest he appear to his constituents as indulging in "conspicuous luxury".[50] When the film became a Spanish co-production, this long party segment was transferred to a castle whose exteriors were provided by the Castillo Alcázar in Segovia. Welles drew on Francisco de Goya to create the visual motifs of the ball.

The early incarnations use New York City as the setting for Arkadin's dinner with the Baroness Nagel. The Spanish versions include establishing shots of the New York City skyline and dialogue that describes the Baroness (played here by Amparo Rivelles) as a saleswoman on Fifth Avenue. The second confrontation scene between Arkadin, Van Stratten, and Raina also occurs in New York. The 'Corinth' version and *Confidential Report* shift these events to Paris, adding location shots of Van Stratten in Pigalle, outside Maxim's restaurant, and in conversation with a man played by Louis Dolivet in sight of the Eiffel Tower. Paris was the last of *Arkadin*'s locations to be filmed, although there seems not to be any particular dramatic reason for these scenes to have occurred in Paris rather than New York.

Hired by Arkadin to investigate the tycoon's amnesia-clouded origins, Van Stratten sets out with all expenses paid. Two variant versions of the same montage sequence contain totally different investigative itineraries. Van Stratten's variant voice-overs narrate a montage of cross-faded shots, some of which appear to be stock footage and others to be shot especially for *Arkadin*: the point of view inside a wheel well as a plane lifts off the ground, display boards listing international destinations, Van Stratten crossing the tarmac in front of a stationary Aerolíneas Argentinas jet, a taxiing TWA plane, and then Van Stratten's interviews with people in various outdoor urban locations. The interview shots are often concluded by a whip-pan (always to the right) that cuts mid-blur into the next shot. This transitional device goes back as far as the breakfast sequence of *Citizen Kane*, but Welles would use it extensively in *Around the World* the following year.

The images are identical in each version, but the voice-over varies. In the 'Corinth' version, Van Stratten narrates:

> I did a lot of travelling and asked an awful lot of questions before I learned the truth. From Helsinki to Léopoldville, Brussels, Belgrade, Beirut, Torino and Trieste, Marseille and Mogador. I talked to every crook who'd even been around in 1927. And a whole lot of other characters, besides.

And in *Confidential Report*:

> My travels took me from Helsinki to Tunis, Brussels, Amsterdam, Geneva, Zurich, Trieste, Marseille, Copenhagen. I talked to every crook who'd even been around in 1927. And a whole lot of other characters, too.

The variations are probably two alternative improvised takes from the same dubbing session. The cities Van Stratten visits have no particular political or historical significance; the names seem to have been plucked out of the air, in the first version for their alliterative value. But the striking impression gained from both versions is Van Stratten's ease and speed of movement while on Arkadin's payroll. Welles lived a similarly fast, peripatetic, aeroplane-enabled working life in the 1950s as he struggled to make films across Europe. And yet, even in Welles's privileged position as an international film star, he was frustrated by the limitations on his freedom of movement.

Shortly after making *Arkadin*, Welles filmed a television monologue denouncing "red tapism and bureaucracy" in relation to "freedom of movement".[51] The age of the Iron Curtain clearly restricted movement between East and West, but there were also numerous other bureaucratic restrictions of movement within Western Europe before the invention of the European Union.

Welles's essay 'For a Universal Cinema' lamented the logistical difficulties of Pan-European filmmaking in this era:

> I was developing the rushes of *Arkadin* in a French lab. Can you imagine that I had to have a special authorization for every piece of film, even if only 20 yards long, that arrived from Spain? The film had to go through the hands of the customs officials, who wasted their time (and ours) by stamping the beginning and end of each and every roll of film or of magnetic sound tape. The operation required two whole days, and the film was in danger of being spoiled by the hot weather we were then having. The same difficulties cropped up when it came to obtaining work permits.
>
> My film unit was international: I had a French cameraman, an Italian editor, an English sound engineer, an Irish script girl, a Spanish assistant. Whenever we had to travel anywhere, each of them had to waste an unconscionable amount of time getting special permissions to stay to work… Similar complications arose when, for example, we had to get a French camera into Spain…

Welles cited the problem of producers who "prefer the security of a limited but certain profit from a national or regional market to the infinitely wider possibilities of a world market, which would of course entail, at the outset, certain supplementary expenses".[52] He also wrote: "The challenge of time is one that I can accept… I am perfectly willing to fight that duel. But there is another, the futile and insidious struggle against the thousand and one formalities by which cinema finds itself chained down."[53]

The logistical torment of Welles's European co-production was foreshadowed in the film's very subject matter. The bureaucratic "importance of papers" that we see in the Ambler novels of the 1930s is updated to the Cold War. It is significant that at the outset Van Stratten is a petty smuggler jailed in Naples for bringing contraband American cigarettes into Italy (Bessy's novelisation gives more detail on Van Stratten's work for Thaddeus's smuggling operation out of Tangiers). Van Stratten acquires true freedom of movement only when he goes on Arkadin's payroll as an investigator. The moment is marked by a series of jump-cuts depicting different currencies thrown down onto a table. Arkadin's wealth and access to the network of air travel diminish the relevance of national borders.

Eric Rohmer recognised this at the time of the initial European release of *Confidential Report*:

> [Arkadin's] wealth resides less in possessions than in that most modern of powers, mobility, the ability to be present at practically the same time in every part of the globe. A life of travel, of palaces, seems gilded with a magic that sedentary luxury has lost … the power of money is depicted with a precision that only Balzac would not have envied.[54]

This 'power in mobility' is only possible in the age of air travel. As if to underscore that point, when Arkadin is unable to secure a seat on the Christmas Eve plane from Munich to Barcelona in order to prevent Van Stratten's revelations to Raina – his "My kingdom for a horse" moment, as Truffaut put it – he takes advantage of the luxury of a private plane that he pilots himself. When he believes his past has been exposed to Raina, Arkadin abdicates his metaphorical throne by jumping to suicide.

* * *

The city of Munich is at the centre of *Mr. Arkadin*, most particularly in the 'Corinth' version, which preserves the most extensive structural frame for flashbacks. Nevertheless, the 1956 *Confidential Report* offers a unique element in Van Stratten's opening voice-over, which specifically locates Jakob Zouk's attic at 'Sebastianplatz 16', a non-existent address in Munich; the location is actually the tenement behind Sebastianplatz 3. The film does not attempt architectural verisimilitude. A fictional cinematic space was constructed freely, and sometimes clumsily, from the material shot on location, quite possibly by Welles himself in the editing room. One example among many: in both the 'Corinth' version and *Confidential Report*, Van Stratten appears to enter the snow-blanketed courtyard of the tenement, cross the courtyard while gazing up to the attic, and then prepare to mount the stairs. In actuality he has entered the courtyard twice in successive shots from two entirely different entrances. Arkadin's later entrance into the same courtyard replicates this nonsensical movement and succession of shots.

In the various exterior shots of Munich, particularly around what purports to be Sebastianplatz, Van Stratten wanders through a 'berubbled *mise-en-scène*', a term I borrow from Robert R. Shandley's analysis of Germany's *Trümmerfilme* ('rubble film') cycle of 1946–49. Some of the better-known titles in that cycle include *Die Mörder sind unter uns* (*The Murderers Are Among Us*, Wolfgang Staudte, 1946) and *Zwischen Gestern und Morgan* (*Between Yesterday and Tomorrow*, Harald Braun, 1947).[55]

The rubble films have not been historically valued for their aesthetic qualities; after all, German films of this era were subject to the control of the occupying Allied military forces, intended to be a propaganda tool to ideologically rehabilitate the German public in the post-Nazi era. But recent critical re-evaluations have argued for the rubble films' ability to evoke the political complexities of their historical moment through their presentation of berubbled space. *Between Yesterday and Tomorrow* was shot at Munich's Regina Palast Hotel, which had been partially destroyed in the war. The film tells parallel narratives of pre- and postwar events, drifting between the damaged and surviving sections of the hotel. As Jennifer Fay observes, "the filmed images of the hotel signify both palimpsestically and spatially". Moreover, the film "encrypts the provisionality and temporality of life in catastrophe's wake. […] [It] participates in a materialist historical reckoning that is concerned with the erasure of history and the end of a corrupt social order whose remnants are everywhere."[56] Ironically, many other films in this cycle were shot in studios rather than in actual berubbled locations.[57]

While Shandley restricts his canon to German films made in the period 1946–49, the Munich sequences of *Mr. Arkadin* seem to constitute a kind of 'rubble film', even though *Mr. Arkadin* emerged from a completely different production model, censorship regime, and later period.

In a rubblescape the damaged structures reveal traces of the past. In Welles's Munich the bombed, broken walls reveal layers of historical strata – concrete, bricks, and stone. The city is a palimpsest. Partially destroyed buildings expose anachronistic relics from the past, such as the horse carriages of 'Sebastianplatz'. The unfinished prefabricated concrete buildings herald the future. But despite first appearances, *Arkadin* does not innocently or inadvertently document a passing historical moment in the postwar reconstruction of Munich. The 'berubbled *mise-en-scène*' was not merely found while shooting on location in Munich but instead contrived with exhilarating artfulness.

The Christmas setting is dramatically essential to provide a trigger for Zouk's nostalgia for goose liver. For many decades the shooting chronology, like so much other information concerning the *Arkadin* project, was obscure. Now it is known that the Christmas scenes were filmed in Munich during April and May of 1954 – mild springtime.[58] The wintry city is so convincingly faked with banked snow and billowing flakes – all the bitterness of a Bavarian winter – that few seem to have ever realised those scenes were not really shot in December.

Van Stratten in the Munich rubblescape

Welles hardly pursued the methods of the Italian neorealists when shooting on location. He did not seek to film some equivalent of documentary 'truth'. In the 1950s he pursued ways of transforming found urban structures – immovable streets and buildings – by embellishing them with powerfully symbolic detritus. Radically adapting what he found in real locations served Welles's dramatic, thematic, and ideological purposes. We see this again a few years later in *Touch of Evil*.

Welles had already publicly expressed the very criticisms of contemporary Germany at the centre of his imagined Munich in *Mr. Arkadin*. He had staged his theatrical revue *An Evening with Orson Welles* throughout Germany in the summer of 1950, and caused an uproar when he accused the country of lingering Nazism in a newspaper column.[59] That phenomenon is directly implied in *Arkadin* by the upside-down Hitler portrait and a swastika abandoned by a previous tenant in Jakob Zouk's attic. As Welles later told Peter Bogdanovich, "There's been instant de-Nazification, so of course the attics all over Germany filled up with such sacred relics."[60] The attic interior was a studio set in Madrid and the sequence was among the earliest filmed, shot long before the production moved on location to Munich.[61]

Van Stratten's search for the goose liver takes us into the streets of Munich by night. His comic quest allows Welles to emphasise again the bombed-out cityscape, its engulfing shadows and silhouetted ruins.

The Allies had bombed Munich numerous times during the war. Jeffrey Diefendorf's *In the Wake of War* recounts that Munich was left with five million cubic metres of rubble, supposedly double the matter contained within the Great Pyramid. It covered thirty-three per cent of the city. But of the big German cities, Munich was among the quickest to be cleared. Even by mid-1949, eighty per cent of its wartime rubble was gone.[62] Certainly by the time of *Mr. Arkadin*, Munich had overwhelmingly been rebuilt.

The Hollywood thriller *The Devil Makes Three* (Andrew Marton, 1952) was filmed partly on location in Munich a few years before *Arkadin*. It begins with a prologue, an authoritative direct-to-camera address by a United States military officer. He establishes a chronology of Munich's postwar reconstruction as of 1952, showing both the restoration of the city's traditional architecture and the construction of new Modernist buildings.

This prologue is followed by a flashback to the drama, set in the year 1947, when rubble still overwhelmingly dominated the city. *The Devil Makes Three*'s prologue corroborates Diefendorf's history of the pace of Munich's

Van Stratten in the Munich rubblescape

reconstruction. Considering that the Munich sequences of Arkadin were not shot until the spring of 1954, it seems Welles overemphasised material traces of the war, that he made a deliberate decision to 'berubble' his *mise-en-scène* just as deliberately and impressively as he had dressed the springtime streets in fake snow. Although *Mr. Arkadin* is ostensibly set in the present, the rubble evokes the grimmer condition of the Munich of the mid-to-late 1940s.

The Devil Makes Three (1952): Stills from the prologue including documentary footage of the rubble adjacent to the destroyed headquarters of the Nazi Party, the 'Brown House', in Munich

In short, *Mr. Arkadin* is an unreliable representation of the historical Munich of 1954. Welles's cinematic city is richer than what might have been captured through any realist approach, as it arose from the encounter of found Munich locations with Welles's political perspective on divided Germany. The palimpsestic rubblescape on screen not only is the bleak and unfriendly final stop for the dying Zouk, but also serves as a microcosm of Cold War Europe. Like Gregory Arkadin, Europe itself seems to be faking a condition of amnesia. Strictly policed national borders have divided politically obsolete cultural unities that nevertheless keep breaking to the surface via artefacts and nostalgic memories. Vehemently anti-nationalist, Welles makes a mockery of the fictions of nationhood.

The film was unfortunately botched by the circumstances of its making. Nevertheless, even in its unsatisfying variant versions, *Arkadin* is the closest Welles came to dramatising his vision of national identity and the operation of power in the cities and skies of 1950s Europe. The bureaucracy of borders and passports remains the means of controlling and dividing the common people; the wealthy obtain their power through an aerial mobility that circumvents such control.

NOTES

1. Thomas, 'The Filmorsa Years'; *Press Conference* (1955), part I.
2. Jonathan Rosenbaum, 'Welles's Anguish and Goose Liver' (DVD notes), *Confidential Report* (Melbourne: Madman DVD, 2009), reprinted at http://www.jonathanrosenbaum.net/2010/12/22958 (accessed 7 August 2015); Berthome and Thomas, *Orson Welles at Work*, 190, 191, 196; Thomas, 'The Filmorsa Years'.
3. Welles quoted in Welles and Bogdanovich, *This Is Orson Welles*, 226.
4. Thomas, 'The Filmorsa Years'.
5. Berthome and Thomas, *Orson Welles at Work*, 193–5.
6. Rosenbaum, *Discovering Orson Welles*, 155.
7. Thomas, 'The Filmorsa Years'.
8. This version has not been seen since 1962. Thomas, 'The Filmorsa Years'.
9. Berthome and Thomas, *Orson Welles at Work*, 196–7.
10. *On the Comprehensive Version* (Issa Clubb, 2006), in *The Complete Mr. Arkadin* (USA: Criterion Collection DVD, 2006).
11. Berthome and Thomas, *Orson Welles at Work*, 197.
12. *On the Comprehensive Version*.
13. Rosenbaum, *Discovering Orson Welles*, 156.
14. The 'Comprehensive Version', while making no claims to definitiveness – an impossibility, as Welles never finished the film – nevertheless attempted to assemble as much of the extant material as still existed in a coherent order that followed Welles's known intentions for the project. In *The Complete Mr. Arkadin*.
15. Rosenbaum, 'Welles's Anguish and Goose Liver'.
16. Thomas, 'The Filmorsa Years'.

17 Welles quoted in Rosenbaum, *Discovering Orson Welles*, 148.
18 *Press Conference* (1955), part I.
19 Berthome and Thomas, *Orson Welles at Work*, 169.
20 Welles quoted in Biskind (ed.), *My Lunches with Orson*, 90.
21 Frank Tavares, 'Orson Welles, Harry Alan Towers, and the Many Lives of Harry Lime', *Journal of Radio & Audio Media*, Vol. 17, No. 2, 2010, 168, 173.
22 Welles quoted in Welles and Bogdanovich, *This Is Orson Welles*, 237.
23 Berthome and Thomas, *Orson Welles at Work*, 189.
24 Anile, *Orson Welles in Italy*, 220.
25 See Luís Nuno Rodrigues, 'Crossroads of the Atlantic: Portugal, the Azores and the Atlantic Community (1943–57)', in *European Community, Atlantic Community?* (Paris: éditions Soleb, 2013), 457–67.
26 'Man of Mystery', *The Lives of Harry Lime* (Orson Welles, 1952). Original broadcast: 11 April. Included in *The Complete Mr. Arkadin*.
27 These episodes are also included in *The Complete Mr. Arkadin*.
28 Denning, *Cover Stories*, 75.
29 Welles quoted in Anile, *Orson Welles in Italy*, 265.
30 Welles quoted in Welles and Bogdanovich, *This Is Orson Welles*, 238.
31 Chuck Berg and Tom Erskine, *The Encyclopedia of Orson Welles* (New York: Facts On File, Inc., 2003), 434.
32 Welles quoted in Welles and Bogdanovich, *This Is Orson Welles*, 238.
33 Welles quoted in Bazin, Bitsch, and Domarchi, 'Interview with Orson Welles (II)', 71.
34 Rosenbaum, *Discovering Orson Welles*, 160.
35 Rosenbaum, *Discovering Orson Welles*, 152, 157.
36 Berthome and Thomas, *Orson Welles at Work*, 193.
37 Welles (1982) quoted in Rosenbaum, *Discovering Orson Welles*, 148.
38 William C. Simon, 'Welles: Bakhtin: Parody', *Quarterly Review of Film and Video*, Vol. 12, Nos. 1–2, 1990, 26.
39 Jonathan Rosenbaum during his commentary track with James Naremore on the 'Corinth Version' in *The Complete Mr. Arkadin*.
40 J. Hoberman, 'Welles Amazed: The Lives of *Mr. Arkadin*' (essay), *The Complete Mr. Arkadin*.
41 Simon, 'Welles: Bakhtin: Parody', 25.
42 Berthome and Thomas, *Orson Welles at Work*, 196.
43 François Truffaut, 'Confidential Report [*Mr. Arkadin*]', in Morris Beja (ed.), *Perspectives on Orson Welles* (New York: G. K. Hall, 1995), 27.
44 'St-Germain-des-Prés', *Around the World with Orson Welles* (Orson Welles, 1955). Original broadcast: 18 November.
45 This can be inferred because Rosenbaum reports that all of actress Patricia Medina's sequences were filmed in Madrid. Rosenbaum, *Discovering Orson Welles*, 154.
46 Rosenbaum, *Discovering Orson Welles*, 155.

47 A silent version of this deleted scene is included as a special feature in *The Complete Mr. Arkadin*.
48 Rosenbaum, *Discovering Orson Welles*, 152.
49 Welles quoted in Anile, *Orson Welles in Italy*, 230.
50 Welles quoted in Anile, *Orson Welles in Italy*, 229.
51 'The Police', *Orson Welles' Sketchbook*.
52 Orson Welles, 'For a Universal Cinema', *Film Culture*, Vol. 1, No. 1, January 1955, quoted in Rosenbaum, *Discovering Orson Welles*, 153.
53 Welles quoted in Brady, *Citizen Welles*, 472.
54 Eric Rohmer quoted in André Bazin (translated by Jonathan Rosenbaum), *Orson Welles: A Critical View* (Venice, CA: Acrobat, 1991), 120.
55 Robert R. Shandley, *Rubble Films: German Cinema in the Shadow of the Third Reich* (Philadelphia: Temple University Press, 2001), 8.
56 Jennifer Fay, 'Rubble Noir', in William Rasch and Wilfried Wilms (eds), *German Postwar Films: Life and Love in the Ruins* (New York: Palgrave Macmillan, 2008), 126–7.
57 Ramona Curry, 'Rubble Films', *Jump Cut: A Review of Contemporary Media*, No. 45, fall 2002, at http://ejumpcut.org/archive/jc45.2002/curry/index.html (accessed 8 August 2015).
58 François Thomas, 'Chronology' (essay), *The Complete Mr. Arkadin*.
59 Anile, *Orson Welles in Italy*, 196.
60 Welles quoted in Welles and Bogdanovich, *This Is Orson Welles*, 240.
61 Robert Arden later recalled his first days on the production in Madrid filming these scenes with Tamiroff, an actor of limited availability whose scenes needed to be completed quickly. Welles prioritised Tamiroff's close-ups and shot Arden's later (see the Arden audio interview with Simon Callow included in *The Complete Mr. Arkadin*). However, it does seem Tamiroff was present for some of the Munich filming later in the year, because he is shown descending the stairwell of 'Sebastianplatz 16' with Van Stratten.
62 Jeffry M. Diefendorf, *In the Wake of War: The Reconstruction of German Cities After World War II* (New York: Oxford University Press, 1993), 14–15, 29.

CHAPTER 11

LOST IN A LABYRINTH
The Trial (1962)

> I move from one kind of architecture to another in my dreams without any difficulty whatsoever.
>
> – Orson Welles, 1981

Continuing to make his living as an actor across Europe, Welles performed a small role in Abel Gance's Napoleonic epic *Austerlitz* (1960), produced partly in Yugoslavia by Michael and Alexander Salkind. The Salkinds, father and son, were a Russian dynasty of film producers with a reputation for fly-by-nightism. Sometime during the winter of 1960/61 they approached Welles to write and direct an adaptation of Nikolai Gogol's *Taras Bulba* (1835). Welles later explained that the producers arrived by long-distance taxi to offer him the job while he was vacationing in the Austrian Alps. After securing Welles's services, they asked to borrow their taxi fare back to Innsbruck. It was a harbinger of the lean season ahead, although Welles later said the Salkinds' plan to make a movie without any money was "wonderful".

Welles wrote a *Taras Bulba* script. When a rival motion picture adaptation went into production in Salta in the north of Argentina, the Salkinds presented Welles with an alternative list of story properties. He decided on Franz Kafka's *Der Prozess* (*The Trial*), which had been published posthumously in 1925.

The Salkinds set up a multi-national co-production – French, Italian, and German – that forced Welles to select actors and technicians from the different participating national film industries. He later said it was no great restriction. As on *Arkadin*, Welles worked with a limited budget and weathered unstable financial circumstances during shooting. He had to provide emergency funds to the budget himself. He also experienced again the frustrations of trying to work in collaboration with a fledgling state film industry, this time in Yugoslavia.¹ Through the 1950s Yugoslavia had gradually opened up its production facilities to international co-productions. For film producers, the Yugoslavian landscape promised "every kind of terrain and weather, from snow-covered Slovenian mountains to lush, blue Adriatic Ocean within hours of each other".²

Welles's patchwork methods and ability to improvise saved the project from cancellation. This time he was able to reconcile his editing process to the demands of his independent producers. Although he missed a deadline to finish the film in time for the 1962 Venice Film Festival, the Salkinds did not fire him.³ He finished his final cut immediately before the film's premiere in Paris that December. As such, *The Trial* is a fully realised Wellesian creation, the first film he was able to complete to his satisfaction in a decade.

Kafka's novel provided Welles with another opportunity to explore freedom, the law, and bureaucracy in the context of an invented postwar European city. Like *Arkadin*'s Munich rubblescape, the city of *The Trial* contrasts a grim present with the traces of a now divided, politically obsolete culture of Mitteleurope. But rather than reveal traces of the past palimpsestically in a rubblescape, the labyrinthine city of *The Trial* mashes wildly different built structures: monuments of the Austro-Hungarian Empire with Modern collectivist urban planning – architectural languages that expressed radically different ideologies.

Unlike *Arkadin*, *The Trial* lacks any typical Wellesian expression of *saudade* for this Mitteleuropean past. Welles's evocation of that past is limited to the material cityscape itself. This is part of the reason why, despite moments of comedy, *The Trial* is his bleakest movie, alongside *Macbeth*.

* * *

Kafka's novel recounts the trial of Joseph K., a bank clerk, who is arrested for unexplained reasons one morning. He is left at liberty for a time, and is determined to denounce the illegitimacy of the whole legal process to which he is subject. The nature of the charges against him are never revealed. Following a long series of unsuccessful attempts to resolve his case, K. is led to a quarry outside the city and executed in such a way "as if he meant the shame of it to outlive him".⁴

Although in most cases faithful to the source text, at least as the unfinished novel had been published and translated, Welles departed from Kafka and personalised the material. He rearranged the chapters and changed the ending of K. submitting meekly to execution, because it "stank of the old Prague ghetto" and was untenable to Welles after the Holocaust. He also instructed Anthony Perkins to play K. as a socially ambitious schemer.[5]

The parable 'Before the Law', which originally appeared during Kafka's lifetime in his collection *Ein Landarzt* (*A Country Doctor*, 1919), is also told to K. by a priest towards the end of *The Trial*, as part of "the writings which preface the Law". A man from the country comes begging "for admittance" to the law, which is patrolled by a guard. After making the man wait until he is near death, the guard finally admits: "No one but you could gain admittance through this door, since this door was intended only for you. I am now going to shut it."[6] Welles narrates this haunting, fatalistic parable as the prologue to his film, illustrating it with a series of 'pinscreen' illustrations by Alexander Alexeieff and Claire Parker that follow Kafka's hints by visualising the abstract law as a closed city or fortress.

"Before the Law"

Following the prologue, K. attempts to navigate a labyrinthine city which is almost reduced to the spaces of his nonsensical trial – its courts, law offices, and, finally, execution site. Kafka's setting is a non-specific Mitteleuropean city in which time and space are vague. The unfinished nature of the manuscript only enhances its vagueness. K.'s search for a resolution to his case has been described as "an exploratory journey through the 'phantasmagoria' of the modern city, a space defined by surfaces, theatrical scenarios, and unreadable representations". He is an alienated individual in the modernist tradition, unable to contain a total vision of the city.[7]

Welles reinvents Kafka's city setting for the screen. *The Trial*'s frequent spatial absurdity is licensed by Welles's explanation at the outset that the film follows the "logic of a dream... a nightmare". His screenplay contained a longer, more explicit narration that did not make the final cut: "Do you feel lost in a labyrinth? Do not look for a way out, you will not be able to find it. There is no way out."[8]

The unnavigable labyrinth, implicit in the source material, happily chimed with Welles's Pan-European patchwork method. He filmed through the first half of 1962 in at least three different European countries and, as with *Othello*, sometimes cut together shots acquired from disparate locations. The illogical spaces of the city are flaunted in the dialogue. When K. exits through a tiny door in the studio of the court painter Titorelli, he finds himself back in an uncomfortable place he'd only recently escaped: "This is the law court office," he says in bewilderment. It forces him to admit his surprise at the extent of his ignorance of "everything concerning this court of yours". Moreover, spatial relationships between the characters and objects are sometimes malleable from shot to shot. In another scene K. exits the Interrogation Commission Hall; in the counter-shot from outside the door looms absurdly large over K.'s tiny figure:

This is not to imply that Welles was indifferent to visual continuity; in fact, Welles's meticulous work with cinematographer Edmond Richard ensured an aesthetically consistent image of extremely deep contrast so as to allow Welles flexibility in editing.[9] The film's expressionist aesthetic – its deep focus and abysmal darkness – is a major triumph in a body of work that always demanded the best of cinematographers.

* * *

Welles did not make a period film set in Kafka's late 1910s. He freely blended nineteenth- and early twentieth-century buildings with the unmistakably contemporary architecture of Europe. The wild internationalism of *Mr. Arkadin* was succeeded by a single imagined urban setting that was intended to evoke the flavour of Kafka's Prague but that follows the author's example in blurring its exact location. The cast again provided a smattering of accents – American, French, English, German, Italian, and Akim Tamiroff's Akim Tamiroff. Welles shot the film by combining footage from Zagreb, Paris, and Rome. In Zagreb he sought the "flavor of a modern European city, yet with its roots in the Austro-Hungarian empire". At the time he said, "I never stopped thinking that we were in Czechoslovakia":

> It seems to me that the story we're dealing with is said to take place 'anywhere.' But of course there is no 'anywhere.' When people say that this story can happen anywhere, you must know what part of the globe it really began in. Now Kafka is central European and so to find a middle Europe, some place that had inherited something of the Austro-Hungarian empire to which Kafka reacted, I went to Zagreb. I couldn't go to Czechoslovakia because his books aren't even printed there. His writing is still banished there.[10]

The Austro-Hungarian Empire, politically united in 1867, had collapsed with the end of World War I, around the time Kafka wrote *The Trial*. Vienna and Budapest had been the joint political and cultural capitals of the dual monarchy. Welles knew both cities intimately as a boy in the 1920s and had soaked up the surviving ambience of a recently vanished age. He later recalled old Vienna with idealistic affection in two short television documentaries, and had a particular fondness for Hungarians of the period such as art forger Elmyr de Hory and producer Alexander Korda; eccentric, self-inventing exiles born in the dying days of the dual monarchy.

But Kafka's Prague had been overshadowed by the cultural centrality of the dual capitals – and Zagreb even more so. By the 1940s the territory of the former dual monarchy had been bisected by the Iron Curtain. Croatia was now contained within the Federal People's Republic of Yugoslavia. It has been said that for much of its history Zagreb had the character of a capital city that lacked an enveloping nation; its complicated history was representative of a long-term disjunction between the spaces of political power and the spaces to which people attached their identity.[11] As one historian writes:

> Culturally, Zagreb has been defined by its strategic position as a crossroads between cultures and identities. Situated at the 'centre of the edge' of the great European empires and multinational states: Rome and Byzantium, Habsburg and Ottoman, the USSR, Yugoslavia, and, now, the European Union, Zagreb has occupied a strategic position at the intersection of north and south, orthodox and Roman Catholicism, Slavic and Mediterranean cultures.[12]

Josip Broz Tito broke relations with Stalin and the Soviet Union in 1948, but even before that Zagreb's development reflected the Yugoslav state's distinct urban planning trajectory. While communist Europe was generally forced into embracing Socialist Realist architecture, Zagreb remained committed to the international Modernist avant-garde, a style "untainted by associations with past imperial subjugation or politically-charged vernacular traditions".[13]

Even after the Salkinds' original plan to construct sets in a Zagreb studio was abandoned, Welles persisted with the city for its locations. In his words, postwar Zagreb's urban topography provided "both that rather sleazy modern, which is a part of the style of the film, and these curious decayed roots that ran right down into the dark heart of the nineteenth century".[14] In fact, only a few scenes in the final cut depict architectural remnants of the Austro-Hungarian epoch: a brief scene inside the Croatian National Theatre (which opened in 1895), outside the Zagreb Cathedral (restored in a neo-Gothic style in 1906), and K.'s forced march through the old streets towards his execution on the periphery of the city.

Otherwise Zagreb's Modernist topographies are emphasised. Welles's attitude towards Modernist architecture was unwaveringly negative. It had crept into the periphery of Welles's *mise-en-scène* as early as the pre-fabricated concrete shells rising above the rubble of Munich and in the arid fields surrounding

K. at the Croatian National Theatre and the Zagreb Cathedral

The march to execution

the Barcelona airport in *Mr. Arkadin*. Welles disliked Michelangelo Antonioni – he called him a "solemn architect of empty boxes",¹⁵ presumably in reference to the austere postwar Italian cityscapes of *La Notte* (1961), *L'Eclisse* (1962), and *Il deserto rosso* (*The Red Desert,* 1964). Later, the film-within-a-film in *The Other Side of the Wind* was apparently intended as a parody of Antonioni's ponderous style. Welles screened one sequence in a rough cut at the 1975 AFI Lifetime Achievement Award ceremony: a young man (Bob Random) in pursuit of a woman (Oja Kodar) through Los Angeles's Century City, a then still-embryonic Modernist redevelopment of the former Twentieth Century Fox backlot. Welles invented his own Modernist cityscape through reflections in glass and mirrors.¹⁶ And at the climax of Welles's late script *The Big Brass Ring*, a presidential candidate murders a blind beggar in Madrid in the vicinity of "some ghastly housing scheme, new in the last days of the Generalissimo, and already fallen into the sordid decay of cheap construction... Buildings like big ugly boxes are crammed together on the barren earth where not a tree or blade of glass is growing."¹⁷

In the 1930s Zagreb's planning authorities embraced the utopian tenets of the Congrés internationale de l'architecture moderne (CIAM), guided by a belief in the ability of Modernist architecture and town planning to transform society.¹⁸ With the postwar federation of communist Yugoslavia came Vladimir Antolić's General Plan of Zagreb (1947). Antolić inherited the city's pre-war regulation plans and synthesised them with other architectural influences, including Le Corbusier. He created an ambitious scheme for a socialist city centre to be built around what was temporarily called Moscow Avenue, and eventually became the Avenue of the Proletarian Brigades.¹⁹ The ideological thrust of the Antolić General Plan was to organise space for the collective, "according to a different set of spatial hierarchies from the traditional bourgeois city".²⁰ Due to the expense of its implementation, the Antolić General Plan was never officially accepted, only went ahead in piecemeal stages around the Avenue of the Proletarian Brigades through the postwar era, and was never finished.²¹

Welles arrived to film *The Trial* in 1962 in the midst of this slow, ideologically guided transformation of Zagreb's urban landscape. Despite his nuanced appreciation of Yugoslavia's non-Soviet form of communism, Welles saw little distinction between Yugoslav and Soviet urban planning. In 1962 he described filming the "hideous blockhouse, soul-destroying buildings [of Zagreb],

Figs 1-3: Frames from the tracking shot from Madame Grubach's boarding house to the Avenue of the Proletarian Brigades; Fig. 4: K. stands at the edge of the Avenue

which are somehow typical of modernist Iron Curtain architecture".²² It's hardly surprising that the self-defined "man of the Middle Ages" recognised the oppressive quality of the postwar cityscape of Zagreb, despite its ostensible ideological basis in anti-bourgeois collectivist social relations. Welles lamented the loss of much older forms of social organisation.

In *The Trial* Welles consistently uses Modernist spaces as the context of alienation. One comic scene of miscommunication was filmed in a tracking shot that follows K. and Miss Pittl across an urban wasteland at dusk. The characters move from the concrete slab where Madame Grubach runs her boarding house to the Avenue of the Proletarian Brigades, the principal thoroughfare and tram route of the socialist city plan.²³

Welles was particularly happy to be able to film inside a cavernous exhibition hall at the Zagreb Trade Fair because it provided a filming space on a scale unavailable in France or England.²⁴ These halls, on the other side of the Sava River, were built in the late 1950s and became a rare trade crossroads for the antagonists of the Cold War, the only trade fair to host the innovations of the United States, the Soviet Union, and the developing world.²⁵

Zagreb Trade Fair interior sequence in *The Trial*

Inside the hall Welles filmed hundreds of typists working at rowed desks. K. apparently lords over this surreal factory of typing minions, dehumanised and regulated by a clock. And yet even with the material shot within this open-plan interior, Welles's editing blatantly ignores the true layout of the space. In one sequence K. finds the storeroom where his investigators are being flogged as a result of his complaints. The storeroom is located under a staircase. K. escapes the room, crosses the floor of typists, and sits with his uncle in his unpartitioned office. But when the typists depart en masse, K. marches further away from the staircase; yet somehow he quickly finds himself right back there.

* * *

Welles combined Zagreb locations with material shot in other cities. A bold use of the patchwork technique comes in a sequence following K.'s panic attack in the law court offices. Welles lines up successive shots from different locations. Despite no evident spatial connection between these locations, the scene is given continuity by the movements and continuing dialogue between K. and his niece Irmie.

K. encounters Irmie outside Rome's Palace of Justice (fig. 5); Irmie follows K. across the wide landing of a stone staircase clearly not in the same vicinity (fig. 6). As K. turns back to speak face to face with Irmie, Welles cuts to a long

5

6

7

8

9

234 AT THE END OF THE STREET IN THE SHADOW

shot that positions the pair no longer on the staircase, but instead in front of a complex of office buildings (fig. 7), possibly filmed in Rome's Esposizione Universale Romana district, originally a Mussolini-era project (Welles had location scouted there as far back as 1952 for a mooted *Julius Caesar*; Antonioni had only recently used the area in parts of *L'Eclisse*[26]). K. continues to walk alone towards what is supposed to be his office building (fig. 8). Welles did not use the trade fair for the exteriors but instead used the Zagreb Workers' University on the north side of the river, two kilometres west of K.'s lodgings further along the Avenue of the Proletarian Brigades. The counter-shot of Irmie places her in front of yet another steel and glass edifice of an unknown location (fig. 9). A contemporary photograph of the Zagreb Workers' University shows this building is not in the vicinity of the university's front staircase.

The low-ceilinged interiors of Mme Grubach's boarding house, where investigators transgress into K.'s private room and arrest him as he wakes, were built inside the Studios Boulogne in Paris. The first scenes for the film were shot here from 26 March 1962.[27] Welles remembered having to pay the English actress Madeleine Robinson himself to prevent her walking off the set, indicating the shaky state of the Salkinds' finances from the beginning of production.[28]

The film was only finished due to its director's magnificent ability to "preside over accidents". Welles had designed additional sets with the assistance of art director Jean Mandaroux intended to be constructed in Zagreb, presumably at Jadran Film Studios. Welles explained at the time of the film's release:

> I had planned a completely different film that was based on the absence of sets. The production, as I had sketched it, comprised sets that gradually disappeared. The number of realistic elements were to become fewer and fewer and the public would become aware of it, to the point where the scene would be reduced to free space as if everything had dissolved.[29]

That concept had to be abandoned. In later years Welles often told an anecdote about how he solved a budget crisis that forced him to abandon the sets and threatened the picture's very continuation. A creative epiphany emerged from an almost hallucinatory urban misperception in Paris. The epiphany led him to shoot large portions of *The Trial* inside the Gare d'Orsay.

Welles gave contradictory explanations for the budget crisis. In some versions he blamed the financial problems of the Salkinds: they either had no money for set construction, or else had been blacklisted by the Yugoslavian industry because they still hadn't paid off their debts for *Austerlitz*.[30] But years later, Welles blamed corruption within the state film industry. He explained that Yugoslavian producers, "like all people who have lived under occupation for a long time – the Yugoslavs had lived for four hundred years under the Turks – [...] [they] learn, as an act of honour, to steal from strangers."

In this version the Yugoslavians played a "trick" they'd "played on hundreds of Italian co-producers". They waited until shooting was imminent to announce they had "miscalculated" the cost of building the sets, and hence demanded more money – or else partial ownership of the film. The Salkinds "didn't even have the money to pay our hotel bill in Zagreb", let alone pay the additional demands; so Welles put the entire cast and crew on a night train out of the country.[31] Welles later acknowledged that the Salkinds ran out on the company's bill at the Hotel Esplanade in Zagreb. He also recalled a narrow escape a few years later from the Zagreb hotel manager, who tried to apprehend Welles while he was shooting Denys de La Patellière and Raoul Lévy's *Marco the Magnificent* in Belgrade, four hundred kilometres away. A Yugoslavian snowstorm prevented the manager's arrival.[32]

Whatever the cause of the cancellation of set construction for *The Trial*, Welles's solution was inspired. Drinking with actress Jeanne Moreau in the early hours of the morning at the Hôtel Meurice on the Rue de Rivoli, Welles gazed out of his window and saw a puzzling image in the sky of Paris: two moons. Moreau pointed out he was really looking at the twin clock faces of the Gare d'Orsay across the Tuileries and the Seine. They crossed the river to the empty train station, where Welles said he

> discovered the world of Kafka. The offices of the advocate, the law court offices, the corridors – a kind of Jules Verne modernism that seems to me quite in the taste of Kafka. There it all was, and by eight in the morning I was able to announce that we could shoot for seven weeks there.[33]

The Gare d'Orsay had been built in 1900 in the French Beaux Arts style. By 1962 it was largely out of use. Welles was conscious of its historical resonance:

> If you look at many of the scenes in the movie that were shot there, you will notice that not only is it a very beautiful location, but it is full of sorrow, the kind of sorrow that only accumulates in a railway station where people wait.

The Gare d'Orsay, Paris, circa 1900

> I know this sounds terribly mystical, but really a railway station is a haunted place. And the story is all about people waiting, waiting, waiting for their papers to be filled. It is full of the hopelessness of the struggle against bureaucracy. Waiting for a paper to be filled is like waiting for a train, and it's also a place of refugees. People were sent to Nazi prisons from there, Algerians were gathered there, so it's a place of great sorrow. Of course, my film has a lot of sorrow too, so the location infused a lot of realism into the film.[34]

The interiors of the Gare introduced another distinct architectural element to Zagreb's Modernism and its Austro-Hungarian monumentality. Welles later explained, "I wanted a nineteenth-century look to a great deal of what would be in fact expressionistic".[35] Because of the Gare's glass ceiling, the scenes had to be shot at night.[36] The near-abandoned station provided a variety of useful spaces. Here Welles created the advocate's office, various waiting rooms, and the interior of the cathedral. Welles dressed these settings with bureaucratic detritus – files, papers, old books, even the wet washing of the accused.

Welles freely combined shots filmed inside the Gare with footage from the streets of Zagreb, even within the same scene. Immediately following his brief attendance of a concert inside the Croatian National Theatre, K. is led by the investigator out of the concert hall to meet his future executioners. On the way he passes from the concert hall's lobby into a labyrinthine passageway filmed inside the Gare. The executioners wait for K. inside one of the Gare's dark and claustrophobic industrial rooms. In the reverse angle, however, K. appears standing in an open street. The spatial relations of the characters are maintained by their positions and the prop of the hanging lamp above K.'s head.

Welles's imagined city is nightmarish yet palpable. Brimming with cinematic invention, *The Trial* has remained underrated within Welles's body of work.

NOTES

1   Welles presented his version of these events in an audience question-and-answer session following a screening of *The Trial* at the University of Southern California on 14 November 1981. Welles's cinematographer Gary Graver shot the session for a mooted documentary that was never made. The unfinished material was restored in 2001 by the Filmmuseum München as *Filming 'The Trial'*. Viewed 17 June 2013 at the Filmmuseum München, Germany.
2   Gerald Peary, 'Hollywood in Yugoslavia', in Graham Petrie and Ruth Dwyer (eds), *Before the Wall Came Down: Soviet and East European Filmmakers Working in the West* (Lanham, MD: University Press of America, 1990), 172.

3   Anile, *Orson Welles in Italy*, 284.
4   Franz Kafka (translated by Willa and Edwin Muir), *The Trial* (New York: Everyman's Library, 1992), 251.
5   *Filming 'The Trial'*.
6   Kafka, *The Trial*.
7   Rolf J. Goebel, 'The Exploration of the Modern City in *The Trial*', in Julian Preece (ed.), *The Cambridge Companion to Kafka* (Cambridge: Cambridge University Press, 2002), 42–4 (quote: 42).
8   Quoted in Berthome and Thomas, *Orson Welles at Work*, 239.
9   See Berthome and Thomas, *Orson Welles at Work*, 245.
10 *Monitor* (1962).
11 Eve Blau, 'City as Open Work', in Eve Blau and Ivan Rupnik (eds), *Project Zagreb: Transition as Condition, Strategy, Practice* (Barcelona; New York: Actar, 2007), 14–15.
12 Uncredited, 'Mapping Project Zagreb', in Blau and Rupnik (eds), *Project Zagreb*, 26.
13 Blau, 'City as Open Work', 16.
14 *Monitor*.
15 Orson Welles, 'But Where Are We Going?', *Look*, 3 November 1970, reprinted at http://www.wellesnet.com/orson-welles-but-where-are-we-going (accessed 1 September 2015).
16 Unfinished material compiled as *Scenes from the Other Side of the Wind* by the Filmmuseum München. Viewed 17 June 2013 at the Filmmuseum München, Germany; Karp, *Orson Welles's Last Movie*, 74–5.
17 Orson Welles with Oja Kodar, *The Big Brass Ring: An Original Screenplay* (Santa Barbara: Santa Teresa Press, 1987), 131.
18 Blau and Rupnik (eds), *Project Zagreb*, 163.
19 Uncredited, 'Case Study 11: The 1947 General Plan: The Communist Functional City', in Blau and Rupnik (eds), *Project Zagreb*, 176.
20 Uncredited, 'Case Study 11', 180.
21 Uncredited, 'Case Study 11', 176.
22 Welles quoted in Uncredited, 'Prodigal Revived', *Time*, Vol. 79, No. 26, 29 June 1962, reprinted at www.wellesnet.com/pacific-film-archive-to-present-an-orson-welles-retrospective-march-7-april-13-2008/ (accessed 16 August 2015).
23 The buildings survive at the intersection of what are now Avenija Marina Drzicá and Grada Vukovara (the former Avenue of the Proletarian Brigades).
24 *Monitor*.
25 Uncredited, 'Case Study 12: The Zagreb Fair: Urban Laboratory', in Blau and Rupnik (eds), *Project Zagreb*, 216.
26 In any case, Welles shot at least some of *The Trial* in the EUR district. See Anile, *Orson Welles in Italy*, 284.
27 Welles and Bogdanovich, *This Is Orson Welles*, 428.
28 *Filming 'The Trial'*.
29 *Monitor*.

30 Welles quoted in 1964 in Cobos, Rubio, and Pruneda, 'A Trip to Quixoteland', 98.
31 *Filming 'The Trial'*; a similar situation seems to have occurred in Budapest in 1967, leading Welles to abandon shooting of *The Heroine* after one day. See Drössler, 'Oja as a Gift', 42–3.
32 Biskind (ed.), *My Lunches with Orson*, 91.
33 *Monitor*. For Jeanne Moreau's participation, see her comments in 'Jeanne Moreau on Orson Welles's *The Trial*', *Wellesnet*, 31 March 2010, at http://www.wellesnet.com/jeanne-moreau-on-orson-welless-the-trial (accessed 16 August 2015); the Salkinds seem to have ran out on their Paris debts, too. Welles admitted in the early 1980s, "To this day I can never go to the Meurice." See Biskind (ed.), *My Lunches with Orson*, 91.
34 *Monitor*. The Gare had been used to receive French citizens repatriated from Nazi prison camps in 1945. See Antony Beevor and Artemis Cooper, *Paris After the Liberation, 1944–1949* (New York: Penguin, 2004 [1994]), 147.
35 *Filming 'The Trial'*.
36 Berthome and Thomas, *Orson Welles at Work*, 243.

IMMORTAL STORIES

CHAPTER 12

TO ADORE THE IMPOSSIBLE

Although Orson Welles never dropped his ambition to make films about the contemporary world, he was also frequently drawn to stories set in a mythical past free of the trappings of the twentieth century. This tendency led him to work on cinematic cities that would communicate his personal vision of an age rather than the material specifics of a precise historical moment, as he had done for *Citizen Kane* and *The Magnificent Ambersons*.

For such projects Welles drew on a core group of writers. The sea tales of Herman Melville, Joseph Conrad, and Isak Dinesen provided adventure, moral complexity, and cosmopolitan encounters in the ports of a vanished, much larger world. Welles frequently pursued experimental adaptations of *Moby Dick*, including an acclaimed London stage production, *'Moby Dick' Rehearsed* (1955), and filmed himself reading the work in the early 1970s. Welles was never able to bring Conrad's work to the screen, but in addition to his contemporary adaptation of *Heart of Darkness*, he wrote screenplays based on *Lord Jim* and the island drama *Victory* (under the name *Surinam*).

Many of Dinesen's tales were located in a vague, static middle nineteenth century. In 'The Dreamers', which Welles adapted in the last years of his life, the narrator says: "It happened just as I tell it to you. But as to names and places, and conditions in the countries in which it all took place, and which may seem very strange to you, I will give you no explanation."[1]

In his introduction to another Dinesen adaptation, this time of the story 'The Old Chevalier', Welles explained:

> If these stories don't seem to be quite true to life, it's because they aren't concerned with ordinary life today. They belong to a life we've left behind us in another century; they have to do with honour and irony ... as well as love.[2]

Welles departed from the twentieth-century mania for progress, disinclined to view that obsession as compatible with a civilised life. He defended his nostalgia for what he knew to be an idealised past, lamenting that "the optimists are incapable of understanding what it means to adore the impossible".[3]

Dinesen proved almost as central to Welles's artistic sensibility as Shakespeare and Cervantes. Welles wrote:

> there is almost nothing I wouldn't give to have spent one of those evenings on her farm at the foot of the Ngong hills. She would, she tells us, have been sitting cross-legged, like Scheherazade herself – 'telling a long tale, from where it began, to where it ended...'[4]

Dinesen's story 'The Old Chevalier' was originally planned for inclusion in a Welles omnibus project, *Paris by Night*, in the early 1950s.[5] Like all the projects he developed for Alexander Korda, it was never made, but for years afterwards Welles tried to film that tale as well as others. In the end only *The Immortal Story* made it to the screen. It was produced by Albina Films in collaboration with the French television station ORTF, and was intended for joint theatrical distribution and television broadcast. This chamber drama abandons itself completely to Dinesen's elegiac, melancholy Scandinavian mood. In the late 1960s Welles began to consciously avoid his distinctive visual signatures as he shifted into colour filmmaking. A few years later *The Other Side of the Wind* combined a style attributed to work of the fictional director Jake Hannaford with pseudo-documentary footage; Welles also proudly boasted of *F for Fake* that "there isn't a Wellesian shot in it".[6]

The scenario of *The Immortal Story* has the clear simplicity of a fable. Mr Clay (Welles), an elderly and wealthy merchant, employs his accountant, Levinsky (Roger Coggio), to re-stage an 'immortal story' frequently told among seafarers: that a rich old man hired an impoverished young sailor to impregnate his young wife. Clay wants to make this myth real. Levinsky convinces the beautiful but ageing Virginie (Jeanne Moreau) to participate in the re-enactment as the wife. Her father's financial downfall and suicide were caused by the ruthless, money-mad Clay, who now occupies her original family home. A young virginal sailor named Paul (Norman Eshley) is selected in the streets, and the couple make love under Clay's surveillance. But Clay's plan is ruined when Paul falls in love with Virginie. Paul rejects the payment and refuses to share the story in the future. Clay dies with the arrival of dawn.

Filming began in Paris in September 1966 and then moved to Spain. Welles changed Dinesen's setting of Canton to the old Portuguese colony of Macau – the "wickedest city in the world", according to *The Lady from Shanghai*'s Mike O'Hara, another wandering, impoverished sailor hired by a rich man. This nineteen-century incarnation of Macau is rather more sedate, a quiet port city. Welles created it by transforming parts of several medieval Spanish villages. In Brihüega he created the illusion of a harbour without depicting water, simply by filming tattered sails in false perspective against an ancient stone wall – a trick he'd invented on *Othello*. The village of Pedraza, previously used for the London of *Chimes at Midnight*, furnished him with a main square and that favoured architectural form, colonnades, which he painted with Chinese characters.

Shot by Willy Kurant, *The Immortal Story* was Welles's first completed film in colour. Welles edited the film at Jean-Pierre Melville's Jenner studios in Paris and again overran his deadline. There were financial problems as the relationship between the production company and the distributors broke down, and Welles attempted to film additional Dinesen adaptations to expand the hour-long film into a more marketable feature-length omnibus. One segment was to be 'The Heroine', which he began shooting in Budapest in April 1967 but abandoned immediately.[7] *The Immortal Story*'s scheduled premiere at Cannes was cancelled due to the protests of May 1968. It finally premiered at the Berlin Film Festival in June and for many years remained in obscurity.

* * *

While Dinesen's static past allowed Welles to indulge in pure storytelling, he found more profound resonance in depicting change, the ruthless shedding of old values, the obliteration of the spirit of an age for a modernity that was somehow smaller in human terms – what Welles described as a "moral takeover".[8] Early on he'd found the theme in Tarkington's *The Magnificent Ambersons*, but in later years he explored the idea of this "takeover" in the more distant European past. In several cases he used contrasting models of urban spaces to emphasise the transition.

Welles declared himself a "Man of the Middle Ages, with implications due to the barbarity of America".[9] One of his most powerful sequences is the meditation in *F for Fake* on Chartres Cathedral, emblem of anonymous medieval ingenuity, "the premier work of man perhaps in the whole western world":

> You know it might be just this one anonymous glory of all things, this rich stone forest, this epic chant, this gaiety, this grand choiring shout of affirmation, which we choose when all our cities are dust, to stand intact, to mark where we have been, to testify to what we had it in us to accomplish.

An idealised conception of the Middle Ages had emerged in Marxist circles in postwar America, particularly through revivals of early community-based music and liturgical drama.[10] But Orson Welles's medieval enthusiasms were of a different, much more personal order. Bill Krohn has argued for the profound importance of the period to the filmmaker. The culture of the Middle Ages offered favoured artistic forms including the carnivalesque and the types of storytelling that were forged in encounters between the sailor and the farmer in medieval trading cities.[11]

Welles was fascinated by the concept of chivalry. "What interests me is the *idea* of these dated old virtues," he said, "and why they still seem to speak to us when, by all logic, they're so hopelessly irrelevant." The obsessions of Welles's middle period were two characters representative of a romanticised medieval past who have somehow washed up, comically and tragically, into a period of bitter obsolescence. Don Quixote is a lunatic self-styled model of romantic chivalry who sets forth not into Cervantes's brutal and fallen seventeenth century of brigands, unchaste ladies, and windmills, but into the brutal and fallen twentieth, encountering the urban junkyard, women on Vespas, and the lies of the cinema screen. Welles explained that "the anachronism of Don Quixote's knightly armor in what was Cervantes' own modern time doesn't show up very sharply now. I've simply translated the anachronism."[12]

The other figure was Shakespeare's Falstaff, to Welles "the greatest conception of a good man, the most completely good man, in all drama. [...] His goodness is like bread, like wine."[13] This relic of medieval 'Merrie England' is rendered obsolete by a colder epoch creeping over London around 1400 following the usurpation of the crown by Henry Bolingbroke. Welles believed "When the last of the Plantagenets was gone that magic was gone out of England. Chivalry died with it. The very moment of the death of chivalry is the death of Hotspur – the last of the true knights."[14]

Welles never went long without returning to Shakespeare, whether on stage, on radio, or in film.[15] Simon Callow assesses that Welles had "no interest ... in Elizabethan stage conventions, but was increasingly gripped by the Elizabethan lived experience".[16] Welles recognised Shakespeare as close to the origins of his own culture: the language he wrote had just been formed; the old England, the old Europe of the Middle Ages, still lived in the memory of the people of Stratford. He was very close, you understand, to quite another epoch, and yet he stood in the doorway of our 'modern' world. His lyricism, his comic zest, his humanity came from those ties with the past.[17]

Chimes at Midnight, at the peak of Welles's achievements in cinema, was the final stage of his long-evolving Falstaff project. Welles created a new play by reworking both parts of *Henry IV*, *The Merry Wives of Windsor*, *Richard II*, and *Henry V*, re-structuring the material around Falstaff and Prince Hal.[18] Welles produced a version of this project in 1939 with the Mercury Theatre as *Five Kings (Part One)*. He revived the concept as *Chimes at Midnight* in 1960 at the Dublin Gate Theatre. By 1964 Welles had managed to cobble together a small budget working with producers Emiliano Piedra and Ángel Escolano in a Spanish co-production. He sold the project on the promise of concurrently making a version of *Treasure Island*, but after a few weeks plundered that production's resources and finished only *Chimes at Midnight*.[19]

The drama of *Chimes at Midnight*: Sir John Falstaff (Welles) is an ageing glutton, a drunkard, a casual conman, and a petty thief. Prince Hal (Keith Baxter) is his willing companion in debauched revelry, to the disapproval of his austere father, King Henry IV (John Gielgud). The drama, set at the commencement of the fifteenth century, centres on Hal's wavering between the life-loving hedonism represented by Falstaff and his father's call to royal duty. War comes between the King and the Percys, led by Hotspur (Norman Rodway). Falstaff drafts a pathetic army. Many die in the bloody Battle of Shrewsbury, but the King prevails. Hal kills Hotspur on the field of battle; Falstaff makes a mockery of Hotspur's death by claiming, in the presence of the King, that he was Hotspur's killer. Upon the death of his father, Hal assumes the crown and publicly renounces Falstaff – "I know thee not, old man" – and banishes him. Falstaff, grief-stricken, dies.

A completely fictional London of 1400 was created by a patchwork of shots from various locations around Spain, the type of composite cinematic city that had by now become Welles's trademark. Welles once nominated the Spanish city of Ávila as his favourite place in the world; he found it a "very strange, tragic place".[20] The walls of Ávila stand in for the ramparts of the King's castle. Welles found further useful locations in the villages of Calatañazor and Pedraza outside Madrid.[21]

The medieval streets of 'London'

The dying spirit of Merrie England is embodied most corpulently by Falstaff, and Welles's imagined London is an earthy city of material contrasts that symbolise the "moral takeover" on the cusp of the Renaissance. The two principal settings – the Boar's Head Tavern in Eastcheap and the King's castle – reflect this contrast and face off across a field that Prince Hal must cross on several occasions.

Many critics have observed the symbolic contrast between the wood of the tavern and the cold stone of the castle. Andrew Davies writes:

> The interaction throughout the film of wood and stone as seminal spatial elements sustains the central conflict between the waning world of organic spontaneity on the one hand, and the emerging world which is to be rational, detached, opportunistic and essentially inorganic, on the other.[22]

Falstaff in the Boar's Head Tavern, watching Hal walk towards the ramparts of the castle

The Boar's Head Tavern set was built inside a warehouse in Carabanchel, a suburban district of Madrid.[23] This "bawdy house" is the centre of the Falstaffian community, of mischief and fun, of play acting and practical jokes, of drunkenness and fornication. Welles does not idealise the setting but immerses his characters in its earthiness. To James Naremore, the tavern is not an unambiguously warm environment but rather "a bare, rough, excremental atmosphere filled with pansexual displays of affection, where, in the latter parts of the film, imagery of disease and death predominates".[24]

* * *

Welles had earlier tapped into the conflict between the Middle Ages and the Renaissance for his cinematic interpretation of *Othello*. In his essay film *Filming 'Othello'*, Welles agreed with critic Jack J. Jorgens that he had "tried to depict a whole world in collapse, a world that is a metaphor not just for Othello's mind but for an epic, pre-Modern age".[25]

The play is split between two locations symbolic of this division. The first act takes place in Renaissance Venice and the rest in wild Cyprus. Paraphrasing the critical judgments of Jorgens and André Bazin, Welles explained:

> In Venice, Iago's attempts to sow discord are frustrated, he's but a shadow on the canal, or a lurking whisperer, a threat, a possibility. The civilized order of Venice is embodied in rich harmonious architecture, placid canals, and in the symmetrical altar at which Othello and Desdemona are married. In Cyprus, at the frontier of the civilized world, the restraints of Venice are lifted – art, luxury, and institutions are taken away, and the longer we're in Cyprus, the more the involuted Iago style triumphs over the heroic and lyrical Othello style in the film.

Welles drew on the Renaissance paintings of Vittore Carpaccio as "the source for the costumes and the general aesthetic of the movie". But the final realisation of the two settings was the result of Welles's creative responses to the production's financial problems. In 1948/49, when *Othello* was still to be a French-Italian co-production by Michele Scalera, Welles planned totally different cityscapes with the Hungarian art director Alexandre Trauner. According to Welles, Trauner designed Cyprus as "a grimly handsome fortress of a place, starkly poised between Veneto and Byzantium, and for our movie much more right than anything real which might still be standing in this century".[26] It would have been built at the Victorine Studios in Nice, along with Venice itself.[27] Welles reasoned that

> if for three fourths of our film we were to inhabit an invented world [Cyprus] rather than a series of real locations, then our version of reality would have

been merely mocked by those famous and familiar old stones of Venice. There could be no stylistic integrity unless Venice too would be a Venice by Trauner, a city totally undeveloped by the tourist industry.

But Scalera soon withdrew and Welles had to rely on his own resources to fund the film. Thereafter "nothing was designed; everything had to be found, hence all that globe-trotting".[28] He used real locations in Venice, and elsewhere. Welles not only avoided the cinematic clichés of Venice, but was totally unfaithful to the city's real geographic layout, making his own city out of disparate found

The Venice of *Othello*

elements. Welles began to deprioritise typical editing continuity, welding the film together by the force of his vision.[29] In this mishmash, Welles created a Venice almost as fictional as Trauner's unrealised studio version.

*　*　*

Welles reimagined Venice again – an eighteenth-century version – for another radical Shakespearean adaptation that he shot in 1969.[30] An unfinished and much-abridged version of *The Merchant of Venice*, which his script calls 'The Shylock Story', was to be part of the *Orson's Bag* television special.[31] For decades most of the edited workprint was thought stolen, but it eventually turned up in a cache of lost Welles films in Pordenone, Italy, enabling a reconstruction from the original negative by Cinemazero and the Munich Film Museum in 2015.[32]

Welles again canvased the European palimpsest to find a variety of urban locations, which were combined into the cinematic Venice of 'The Shylock Story'. He filmed in Italy and Yugoslavia. Peter Bogdanovich writes that Welles believed "the Dalmation coast, having once been part of the Venetian Empire, is full of the right sort of architecture".[33]

Welles's scripted introduction defines this Venice as a "light-hearted, cold-hearted city ... something hard and cruel lurking under the brilliant carnival facade".[34] The film contains haunting scenes of a near-empty city. Welles again uses colonnades as an architectural element. The colonnades hide masked figures who track Shylock's slow progress.

In *Filming 'Othello'*, again paraphrasing critical commentary, Welles explained the use of a key motif in his earlier Shakespeare film:

An eighteenth-century Venice

In the play, one of Iago's favorite images is that of the net, the snare, the web, making him a fisherman, a hunter, a spider. "With as little a web as this, will I ensnare as great a fly as Cassio," he says. Our camera holds that image before your eyes and plays variations on it. We see it through the grate which Desdemona passes to escape her father, the net that holds her hair in Cyprus, the ships' rigging, the rack of spears in the fortress, and the windows and doors of Othello's bedroom. In the end Iago is caught in his own mesh; always hovering above him is the iron cage where the sun will scorch him and the gulls will peck at his flesh.[35]

In 'The Shylock Story' the motif returns, now suggesting both Jessica's imprisonment by her father, Shylock, and his imprisonment as a Jew in an anti-Semitic city. Welles specifies the motif in the pages of the script: a shot of Lorenzo fixing a mask to Jessica's face is to be through an "iron grill", and as Shylock moves through the streets he is seen through a "grilled window".[36] On film Welles uses a variety of diagonal cross-bars and an echo of this in the pattern of paving stones on the edge of the canal.

In some ways 'The Shylock Story' recalls *The Trial*. Welles reconceived the Jewish themes of both source texts. On US television in 1967, introducing a performance of the "Hath not a Jew eyes?" monologue, Welles argued that "on the matter of bigotry nobody has ever spoken out as well as [Shakespeare] did three hundred years ago". Joseph McBride notes that the "cold fury" of this performance of the speech was "consistent with his rewriting of Kafka to make *The Trial*'s post-Holocaust version of Joseph K. defiant at the end rather than acquiescent in his own execution".[37]

In 'The Shylock Story', the moneylender encounters stationary figures in carnival masks on the edge of the canal: a chilling *tableau vivant*.[38] It recalls the unsettling moment in *The Trial* when Joseph K. walks through a field of emaciated, half-naked stationary figures wearing numbered signs and waiting – a clear evocation of the Holocaust.

Tableaux vivants in 'The Shylock Story' and *The Trial*

NOTES

1   Isak Dinesen, *Seven Gothic Tales* (New York: Vintage, 1991), 279.
2   Uncredited [Orson Welles], *The Old Chevalier*, Script (mimeograph, 1978), 1. Box 11, Orson

Welles–Oja Kodar Papers, Special Collections Library, University of Michigan.
3   Welles quoted in Welles and Bogdanovich, *This Is Orson Welles*, 211–12.
4   Orson Welles, *The Dreamers* 'Ninth Revised Screenplay' (photocopies of annotated typescript, 1980-85), 2. Box 12, Orson Welles–Oja Kodar Papers, Special Collections Library, University of Michigan.
5   Rosenbaum, *Discovering Orson Welles*, 82.
6   Welles quoted in Krohn, 'My Favourite Mask Is Myself', 56, 64.
7   Berthome and Thomas, *Orson Welles at Work*, 270–9.
8   Welles quoted in Welles and Bogdanovich, *This Is Orson Welles*, 102.
9   Welles quoted in Bazin, Bitsch, and Domarchi, 'Interview with Orson Welles (II)', 71.
10 See Kirsten Yri, 'Noah Greenberg and the New York Pro Musica: Medievalism and the Cultural Front', *American Music*, Vol. 24, No. 4, winter 2006, 421–44.
11 Bill Krohn, 'The Force of the Work', quoted in Rosenbaum, *Discovering Orson Welles*, 112.
12 Welles quoted in Welles and Bogdanovich, *This Is Orson Welles*, 96.
13 Welles quoted in McBride, *Orson Welles*, 168.
14 Welles quoted in Welles and Bogdanovich, *This Is Orson Welles*, 102.
15 In the early 1980s Welles scripted a *King Lear*, created a video presentation for potential investors, and had a professional photographer seek out locations in France. Test photographs of Hautacam, Pierrefitte, and the fortress at Carcassonne survive in Welles's archives. Even after a production deal with the French government broke down in early 1985, Welles continued to work on a draft of the script and a shot-by-shot breakdown for the first half. See *King Lear* (1983–85) (subseries), Photographs, 1983–85?, box 15, Orson Welles–Oja Kodar Papers, Special Collections Library, University Of Michigan; *King Lear* (subseries), Script (20 September 1985), box 2, Orson Welles–Alessandro Tasca di Cutò Papers, Special Collections Library, University Of Michigan; and Welles and Bogdanovich, *This Is Orson Welles*, 452, 511–12.
16 Callow, *Orson Welles: Hello Americans*, 387.
17 Welles quoted in Welles and Bogdanovich, *This Is Orson Welles*, 211–12.
18 Michael Anderegg, '"Every Third Word a Lie": Rhetoric and History in Orson Welles's *Chimes at Midnight*', in Bridget Gellert Lyons (ed.), *Chimes at Midnight: Orson Welles, Director* (New Brunswick: Rutgers University Press, 1988), 327.
19 *Treasure Island* was finally produced as a feature starring Welles from his pseudonymous script in 1972. He did not direct. See Berthome and Thomas, *Orson Welles at Work*, 250–66; Welles and Bogdanovich, *This Is Orson Welles*, 268–9.
20 *Orson Welles: The Paris Interview* (Allen King, 1960) (USA: Kultur Video DVD, 2010).
21 Berthome and Thomas, *Orson Welles at Work*, 256.
22 Andrew Davies, *Filming Shakespeare's Plays: The Adaptations of Laurence Olivier, Orson Welles, Peter Brook and Akira Kurosawa* (New York: Cambridge University Press, 1988), 127.
23 Berthome and Thomas, *Orson Welles at Work*, 256.
24 Naremore, *The Magic World of Orson Welles*, 222.

25 *Filming 'Othello'*.
26 *Filming 'Othello'*.
27 Berthome and Thomas, *Orson Welles at Work*, 167.
28 *Filming 'Othello'*.
29 See Berthome and Thomas, *Orson Welles at Work*, 173, 179.
30 See Krohn, 'My Favourite Mask Is Myself', 46.
31 In *Orson's Bag* (1968–70) (subseries), Draft pages (various scenes) (typescript, carbon, and photocopy, annotated), 10 April – 11 September 1969 (folder 1). Box 17, Orson Welles–Oja Kodar Papers, Special Collections Library, University of Michigan; Berthome and Thomas, *Orson Welles at Work*, 285–7.
32 I viewed the 2001 partial assemblage *Orson Welles' Shylock* on 17 June 2013 at the Filmmuseum München, Germany. The reconstructed film premiered at the Venice Film Festival on 1 September 2015. See also Anonymous, 'Orson Welles Stars on Eve of Venice Film Festival', Agi.it, 7 August 2015, at http://www.agi.it/en/people/news/orson_welles_stars_on_eve_of_venice_film_festival- 201508071640-spe-inw0004 (accessed 6 September 2015).
33 Welles and Bogdanovich, *This Is Orson Welles*, 30.
34 In *Orson's Bag* (1968–70) (subseries), Draft pages (various scenes) (typescript, carbon, and photocopy, annotated), 10 April – 11 September 1969 (folder 1).
35 *Filming 'Othello'*.
36 In *Orson's Bag* (1968–70) (subseries), Draft pages (various scenes) (typescript, carbon, and photocopy, annotated), 10 April – 11 September 1969 (folder 1).
37 McBride, *Whatever Happened to Orson Welles?*, 236.
38 McBride writes that some of the masked figures were "full sized wooden puppets". McBride, *Whatever Happened to Orson Welles?*, 235.

CHAPTER 13

IN THE LAND OF DON QUIXOTE

Among the films commercially released during Welles's lifetime, Spain appears as a setting only in parts of *Mr. Arkadin* and *F for Fake*, and as a travel destination in two relatively obscure television documentary series. This group of films does not comprehensively communicate the profound significance of Spain across decades of Welles's creative life; a fuller appreciation can only be reached by examining his numerous unfinished or unproduced projects. Although he often located the action of these films in the pastoral countryside and the village, Welles also frequently filmed, or planned to film, Spanish cities – particularly Madrid, Seville, and Pamplona.

The setting appeared early on, long before Welles had the opportunity to film on location in the country. Sometime in the mid-1940s Welles developed a film based on Prosper Mérimée's *Carmen* (1845). There seem to have been alternative conceptions, one set in Latin America and another retaining the original Spanish settings – the Upper Andalucian sierras, the Basque Country, Cordoba, and Triana, the Gypsy quarter of Seville, where Welles had lived for a spell the century after Carmen.[1] Welles sent a Spanish-set treatment written by Brainerd Duffield to Columbia Pictures studio head Harry Cohn, appending a note promising "not the operatic dilution, but the original melodrama of blood, violence, and passion".[2] Although Welles's *Carmen* never went beyond pre-production, Rita Hayworth co-produced her own version, *The Loves of Carmen* (Charles Vidor, 1948), without her by-then ex-husband's involvement.[3]

Mérimée's *Carmen* was an early classic of the *españolada* form, a folklorish vision of Spain populated by familiar characters and a range of melodramatic actions rooted in the stasis of a feudal, patriarchal, and superstitious society.[4] Years later Welles claimed to "hate anything which is folkloric",[5] so it's intriguing to imagine how he would have renovated the source text.

In addition to providing colourful story material for European opera and operetta, the *españolada* was exploited by Hollywood in adaptations of Vicente Blasco Ibáñez's bullfighting novel *Blood and Sand* (Fred Niblo, 1922; Rouben Mamoulian, 1941), Rudolf Friml's operetta *The Firefly* (Robert Z. Leonard, 1937), and *The Adventures of Don Juan* (Vincent Sherman, 1948). The form had been propagated at home in early Spanish cinema in films such as Florián Rey's *Nobleza baturra* (*Nobility of the Peasantry*, 1935) and *Carmen, la de Triana* (1938). In the Franco era such "nostalgic and uncritical recuperation of the past" proved politically useful, even as the *españolada* form was ridiculed within Spain; see, for example, Luis García Berlanga's comedy *¡Bienvenido, Mister Marshall!* (*Welcome, Mister Marshall!*, 1952).[6] But the old stereotypes died hard. Spain's supposed cultural timelessness licensed Hollywood films to blend the folkloric and the contemporary in films such as *The Barefoot Contessa* (Joseph L. Mankiewicz, 1954).

In 1953 Welles visited Spain for the first time in two decades.[7] Ernest Hemingway, another public opponent of the Franco regime, also came back to see bullfights and visit the Prado. Hemingway later rationalised:

> I had never expected to be allowed to return to the country that I loved more than any other except my own and I would not return so long as any of my friends there were in jail. But in the spring of 1953 in Cuba I talked with good friends who had fought on opposing sides in the Spanish Civil War about stopping in Spain on our way to Africa and they agreed that I might honorably return to Spain if I did not recant anything that I had written and kept my mouth shut on politics.[8]

In 1954 Welles shot part of *Mr. Arkadin* in the city of Segovia. He used the exterior of the Alcázar de Segovia as Gregory Arkadin's Spanish residence ("Well, that's a castle in Spain for sure!" notes Guy Van Stratten). Arkadin's masked ball, much of it clearly shot in a studio, featured costumes based on the art of Goya.

Although *Arkadin*'s brief depiction of Spain is merrily unrealistic, the film avoids the obvious folkloric clichés. Welles would continue to explore his own personal vision of Spain for the rest of his career.

Welles lived with his third wife, Paola Mori, and their young daughter, Beatrice, in Aravaca near Madrid between about 1963 and 1968, the period of filming *Chimes at Midnight* and *The Immortal Story*.[9] He seemed cautious

Mr. Arkadin: The Alcázar de Segovia and the masked ball

about flaunting his Spanish residency except for a period in the summer of 1966 when he was following the season of *corridas*, shooting yet more parts of *Don Quixote* in Pamplona, and pitching a bullfighting film called *The Sacred Beasts*. The Welleses relocated to England in 1968, although they did not yet sell their Aravaca residence. Part of that house caught fire in August 1970, while the Welleses were absent, and some of Welles's documents and possessions were destroyed.

* * *

Welles had visited Spain and France to film episodes of *Around the World with Orson Welles* in early 1955, shortly after his loss of editorial control on *Mr. Arkadin*. His ambitious agreement with Associated-Rediffusion called for twenty-six half-hour television episodes, an opportunity to renew his cosmopolitan public persona in a new medium. But in October Welles broke his contracts and departed Europe without notice. Associated-Rediffusion completed and broadcast the material as a six-part series. Another episode on the Dominici murder case near the village of Lurs, France, was not completed, possibly due to censorship concerns; it was reconstructed as part of a documentary in 2000.[10]

The series as it was broadcast represents an innovative development of Welles's 'first person singular' approach for the medium of television, a technique that would mature by the time of *F for Fake*. He conducted interviews on location, but his responses in counter-shot where obvious reshoots; he also tended to restructure the conversations in the editing room.[11] In 1958's *Viva Italia* (aka *Portrait of Gina*), an unshown television pilot made in much the same energetic style as *Around the World*, the editing recasts interview subjects such as actor Rosanno Brazzi as agreeable commentators on what edges close to a Welles monologue.

Two episodes of *Around the World* focus on the "contented, grounded Basques, who have lived for centuries satisfied in a static, agrarian society".[12] The village of Ciboure, legally in France, had preserved the Basque language and culture. The documentary allowed Welles to again ridicule the political fiction of national borders by celebrating the endurance of a culture that predated the French and Spanish nations and straddled the territory of both. It also gave Welles another opportunity to celebrate an Arcadia, an idealised pastoral counterpoint to the corruptions of modern urban life. In fact, the sequence of a procession of Basques through the hills almost exactly resembles in its framing shots in the staged funeral Welles filmed thirteen years earlier in the fishing community of Fortaleza, Brazil, but was never able to edit.

Throughout the episodes Welles praises the Basque village's isolation from the mania for technological progress but, ever the inclusive diplomat, is at pains

'Pays Basque I (The Basque Countries)', *Around the World With Orson Welles* (1955)

'Four Men on a Raft' in *It's All True* (1942)

to avoid offence: "If we appreciate the Basques," he says, "it doesn't *depreciate* what is often called the 'American way of life'." Welles admires the Basques' independent attitude, *joie de vivre*, and stoicism during the recent war. But only his charisma and enthusiasm offset a tendency to infantalise the Basque people, particularly in some of his 'interviews' with the welcoming villagers.

Welles with a Basque couple

One of the episodes features a conversation with Lael Tucker Wertenbaker, an expatriate American writer raising a son in Ciboure. Wertenbaker is motivated by a belief that "what we need are intervals – all of us – in backwaters". Although education is much more demanding than in the United States, in Ciboure the children are "kings of their kingdom" and free of "mechanical aids to amusement". In his counter-shot Welles nods and opines:

> An aid to amusement seems to me to be at the centre of a great part of the moral crisis that we're faced with all over the world now. I don't think we need aids to amusement. I think we have to amuse ourselves.

He also tells Wertenbaker:

> I don't think progress and civilisation go together particularly… I think if you move forward you are not very likely to be civilised in the process and the most civilised countries are likely to be those where progress is not considered a very important preoccupation. And I think it's awful good for a kid – and awfully good for us, too – occasionally, to get away from those areas where moving somewhere and getting something done seems to be more important than living in a certain way and being a certain thing.

IN THE LAND OF DON QUIXOTE

Despite his diplomatic disclaimers, it's difficult not to read this as a statement that civilisation is lacking in progress-mad America. But neither does he grant Basque society that status. Wertenbaker makes a summary statement that the Basques are "proud of their past, and they're easy in the present, and they're not afraid of the future". Welles calls it "a beautiful phrase and a wonderful formula" but criticises part of it. The Basques may be easy in the present, he allows, but "very few civilised people are". He explains: "I don't think the Basques are totally civilised in the pure sense of that word, because civilisation does imply city culture, by definition, and these people don't have a city culture."

Welles also disagrees that the Basques have any justification to be "proud of their past", because despite their longevity they've not "done a lot. You can only be proud of your past if … you've built a pyramid or have a library full of books to show for your past." Welles probably didn't read Basque fluently enough to come to this final conclusion on its literature, and was ignoring obvious figures such as Maurice Ravel, a Basque composer born right there in Ciboure. But the fact that the Basques had created a culture of their own, which endured despite decades of official repression, is almost beside the point. In many ways the Basque episodes say more about Orson Welles in the mid-1950s than they do about the Basques. The Spanish documentary *Orson Welles en el país de Don Quijote* (2000) concludes:

> In front of Welles's camera, the Basque country of the 1950s became transfigured into a curious mix of mythological nationalistic imagery and the rural folkloric fantasy used by the Franco regime to try to hide the complex reality of these lands. [...]
>
> Orson Welles toured Spain from the perspective of an Anglo-Saxon Hispanist, who with liberal progressive convictions tried to delve into the traditions that fascinated him while accommodating the reality appearing before him to the view he himself formed of the country.[13]

It's true that Welles's introduction of critical nuance to his otherwise celebratory picture of life in the Basque country upsets the easy clichés of the television travelogue. Becoming a Basque may not be a plausible option for the modern city-dweller, but to seek "an interval in a backwater" is a most welcome antidote to the forward-looking obsessions of modernity. Both Welles and Wertenbaker value Ciboure as a pastoral retreat, a place free of both progress and civilisation, an escape from urban society rather than a totally fulfilling alternative way of life in itself.

Around the World finds Welles at a pivotal point in his long-term fascination with Spain – or, to be more accurate in this case, an archaic Pyrenees culture divided arbitrarily between fascist Spain and the French Fourth Republic. Just a few months earlier in Paris he had made the first test shots for his adaptation of *Don Quixote*, which would become his obsession for decades and evolve alongside changes in Spain. From now on Welles would frequently make films inside Spain.

* * *

> [A] romantic strain lives on in the American character, and this finds expression in that minority among expatriates who do indeed make quite determined (if futile) efforts to participate in the social and cultural life of the country where they find themselves.
>
> – from *Crazy Weather*, a treatment by Orson Welles and Oja Kodar, circa late 1973[14]

Ernest Hemingway had vividly communicated his personal appraisal of Spanish culture in novels, non-fiction books, and journalism. In 1932, the year before Welles's brief spell training as a *torerito* in Seville, Hemingway published *Death in the Afternoon*, his now classic book on bullfighting. Although widely mocked by Spaniards during his lifetime for his pretentions to the status of cultural authority,[15] Hemingway served as a popular explicator of Spain for the English-speaking world. In his fictional protagonists and his ever-more frequent media appearances, he also created the prototype for the macho expatriate American *aficionado*. Of Hemingway and the *corrida*, Welles later joked, "He thought he invented it, you know."[16]

In Welles's telling, their first encounter, during the recording session for *The Spanish Earth* in 1937, was marked by Hemingway's easily provoked homophobia and his blustering machismo. They seem to have later mixed in the same social circles in Venice in the late 1940s and in Paris in the late 1950s.[17] And even if in retrospect Welles dubiously claimed Hemingway as "a very close friend of mine" – he said he was "enormously fond of him as a man" for his humour – Welles's public expression of his Spanish enthusiasms departed in significant and critical ways. Welles's celebration of Spain was open and inclusive, typical of his cosmopolitan persona. Hemingway invited his readers to share his contempt for foreigners of less serious *afición* or for those who deviated from his code of stoic machismo. By 1959, in declining physical and mental health, Hemingway was trailing an entourage of sycophants while reporting on the bullfighting season for the mainstream American media. "I never belonged to his clan," Welles explained, "because I made fun of him. And nobody ever made fun of Hemingway."[18]

Welles was interested in types of courage beyond macho physical posturing. In 1981 he told students at UCLA that he valued bravery above all other virtues, but insisted, "don't call me a macho, that's not what I'm talking about".[19] Nevertheless, he saw bullfighting at its best as an exhibition of bravery, and remarked that "it's always rewarding to observe this rare commodity in action".[20]

A further distinction was that Welles proved capable of self-criticism and re-evaluation of his Spanish enthusiasms, particularly in relation to the *corrida*. He said in 1974:

> I've turned against it for very much the same reason that my father, who was a great hunter, suddenly stopped hunting. He said "I've killed enough animals and I'm ashamed of myself." [...] Although it's been a great education to me in human terms and in many other ways, I begin to think that I've seen enough of those animals die. [...] Wasn't I living second-hand through the lives of those *toreros* who were my friends? Wasn't I living and dying second-hand? Wasn't there something finally voyeuristic about it? I suspect my *afición*. I still go to bullfights, I'm not totally reformed, and I can't ask for the approval of the people who have very good reasons to argue about stopping it.[21]

Welles's growing disdain for the voyeuristic American macho in Spain had found expression in a string of related projects: *The Sacred Beasts*, *The Other Side of the Wind*, and *Crazy Weather*. But none of these projects – nor the Spanish-set *Don Quixote*, *Mercedes*, *The Dreamers*, or *The Big Brass Ring* – reached cinema screens. Neither were Welles's earlier Spanish television documentaries broadcast outside Europe. Yet while Welles's vision of Spain had none of the public visibility of Hemingway's, it can be traced in Welles's surviving papers and unfinished films as a long-term critical engagement. That vision informed how he came to reimagine Spanish cities in his work.

***

Welles claimed to be that rare *aficionado* more interested in bulls than bullfighters. In the season of 1966, when interviewed by the novelist James A. Michener in Seville, Welles explained:

> What it comes down to is simple. Either you respect the integrity of the drama the bullring provides or you don't. If you do respect it, you demand only the catharsis which it is uniquely constructed to give. [...] What you are interested in is the art whereby a man using no tricks reduces a raging bull to his dimensions, and this means that the relationship between the two must always be maintained and even highlighted. The only way this can be achieved is with art. And what is the essence of this art? That the man carry himself with grace and that he move the bull slowly and with a certain majesty. That is, he must allow the inherent quality of the bull to manifest itself.[22]

Norman Foster's abandoned 'My Friend Bonito' aside, Welles first put a *corrida* on film for another 1955 episode of *Around the World*. In 'Spain: The Bullfight', Welles strides like a giant through the milling crowds outside Las Ventas in Madrid. He made insert shots in a studio that recreated his arena seat, from where he pretended to observe and film the action close to the alley ringing the arena.[23] When Welles abandoned the series, writers Kenneth Tynan and Elaine Dundy were subbed in to pad out the too-short episode with an introduction and commentary.[24]

Compared to his stylistically inventive television travel documentaries of the 1950s, the nine episodes of *In the Land of Don Quixote* are conventional and largely tedious, and much less effective for the lack of Welles's first-person presence as presenter and narrator. Welles exploited this commission from RAI in Italy as another piggyback ride for the ever-evolving *Don Quixote* and reportedly dismissed the series as "just a travelogue".[25] These silent 16mm movies of Welles's family on vacation are not particularly successful even in that undemanding genre, despite their extensive view of the cities of Spain. Welles shot material in Madrid, Seville, Pamplona, Córdoba, Cádiz, Gibraltar, Algeciras, Granada, Ronda, Guadix, Jerez, Toledo, Aranjuez, Alcalá de Henares, Ávila, and Segovia.[26] His executive producer Alessandro Tasca di Cutò recalled, "We had no script other than the one in his mind, and his idea of how he would assemble it in the cutting room."[27]

Welles worked on the editing at his wife's family villa in Fregene outside Rome.[28] His original material was supplemented by stock footage from the archives of NO-DO, Franco's propaganda newsreel service.[29] Individual segments within the episodes are divided by a repeated shot of a Quixotic windmill accompanied by a flamenco guitar punctuation. Most of the music was provided by the young virtuoso Juan Serrano.

Welles's notes indicate he planned to use bullfighting as the unifying theme of the series. In June 1961 he explained to an editorial assistant who was compiling reels of usable footage:

> The idea is not to do a single programme on bullfighting, but to use this theme in several of the programmes as we follow the different *ferias*. Following the *ferias* gives us an excuse to see the different towns and to examine the aspects of Spanish character and countryside.

Bullfighting and its rituals are indeed prominent in the broadcast version, although the ultimate significance of each *corrida* is sometimes obscure within the casual assemblage and minimal commentary. Welles explained to the editorial assistant, "I just have a lot to say about bullfighting in general and in particular, and will use the best of the material to illustrate my remarks,"[30] but in the end RAI commissioned another writer to provide an Italian narration that was voiced by actor Arnoldo Foa. It is unclear to what extent RAI tampered with Welles's edit, although Tasca di Cutò called the final product a "flat, distorted ghost of the original".[31] Juan Cobos, the assistant director of *Chimes at Midnight*, said, "I cannot imagine that [Welles] ever approved the final cut that was shown on RAI-TV in 1964. I think he only partially cut the series, and he certainly didn't want the spoken narration that was used." Welles attempted to import the negative back into Spain later in the 1960s to reedit and record a narration but was impeded by Spanish bureaucracy.[32]

Left-wing critics in Italy at the time of original broadcast criticised Welles's lack of political engagement with the political situation under Franco.[33] During the filming Tasca di Cutò encountered Franco in person at the Seville *feria* and was given permission to film the dictator, but the material did not make the series.[34] The series expresses an American tourist's point of view unlikely to have offended the regime or to have contradicted the folkloric image of Spain the dictatorship promoted to the world. In comparison to Welles's later Spanish explorations, *In the Land of Don Quixote* is without much depth. Nevertheless, one city sequence rises above the mundane and is worth examining.

* * *

Hemingway had made the fiesta of San Fermín famous in the English-speaking world with *The Sun Also Rises* (1926). Back in 1923 he had reported to the *Toronto Star*: "As far as I know we were the only English-speaking people in Pamplona during the Feria." The *encierro* or 'running of the bulls', "the Pamplona tradition of giving the bulls a final shot at everyone in town before they enter the pens", had "been going on each year since a couple of hundred years before Columbus had his historic interview with Queen Isabella in the camp outside of Grenada". Hemingway claimed the amateur fight following the *encierro* created "a casualty list at least equal to a Dublin election".[35]

It has been said, probably apocryphally, that tickets for the 1961 fiesta sat on Hemingway's desk in Sun Valley, Idaho, on 2 July, the day he took his own life with a shotgun. That summer's fiesta began just four days later. Unless he relied entirely on a second-unit crew, Welles was on location in Pamplona, historical capital of the Basque country, to film the *encierro* for an episode of *In the Land of Don Quixote*. The coincidence of these events has been little noticed, but Hemingway's suicide had a profound effect on Welles's subsequent work. He used the date of Hemingway's suicide for the date of Jake Hannaford's death (and seventieth birthday) in *The Other Side of the Wind*.[36]

The episode about the *encierro* of San Fermín is also one of the few parts of the travelogue series to have inspired Welles's creativity.[37] Cobos, who reports that Welles incorporated some stock footage, agreed that "here you can see him at his best on the editing room".[38]

The structure of the *encierro* episode suggests a revival of the spatial conceit of Welles's unrealised samba sequence in 'Carnaval', the mapping of a city by illustrating human movement from the periphery to the centre in the context of a mass cultural ritual.

In the *encierro* episode, three loose stages lay out a trajectory from the countryside to the city of Pamplona. The first begins with images of ancient paintings of bulls in the caves of Altamira. This is followed by footage of bulls chased, corralled, and branded on ranches, in encounters with humans in small rural bullrings, and marched through the countryside. The second stage depicts an *encierro* through the streets of a provincial town. Runners scramble to safety by hoisting themselves onto the grates of windows or ward off angry bulls with chairs. In the amateur fight in the Plaza de Toros, men are knocked aside and thrown, dozens of women face the bulls, and a range of spectators gawk with voyeuristic pleasure from the safety of their seats.

The third stage is the longest: the *encierro* of San Fermín. It's a stunning and terrifying montage lasting six minutes. The sequence has been too long obscure, buried within the nearly four hours of this generally unremarkable series. If not as magnificently realised as the Battle of Shrewsbury in *Chimes at Midnight* – its technical limitations are considerable by comparison, and the many clumsy edits and sound mix give the impression the sequence was never actually finished – it shares a little of that sequence's energy and violence.[39]

At the launch of a rocket flare, the bulls are released from their corral. In the rush several bulls knock each other over and slide on their backs before again finding their feet. Men are lifted by the horns, thrown aside, trampled underfoot. Welles creates a moment of macabre comedy by cutting away from a bull's charge on a fallen man to a pair of nuns observing from the safety of a high window. The soundtrack is repetitive drumming and dubbed-in human screams.

The density of the crowd mounts as it nears the entrance to the Plaza de Toros. Finally the charge compounds into a mass of bodies blocking the entry. The bulls leap and scramble across the writhing human mass. Welles explores an innovative visual concept by intercutting the live-action footage with dynamic still photographs. The stills pause on moments of fear or pain, when runners are crushed in the crowd or meet the horns of a bull. The camera either roves across these photographs or cuts to small details. Guitar music punctuates the drumming during these interpolations.

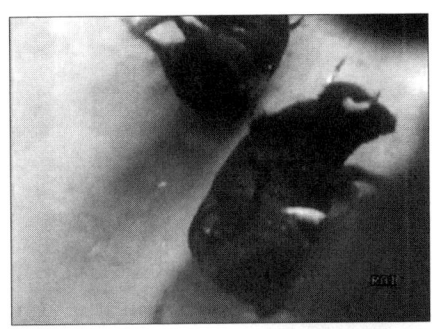

Scenes of the encierro at the Fiesta de San Fermín in Pamplona (*In the Land of Don Quixote*)

One man died in the event that year, and Welles unflinchingly depicts on screen the exhilaration and violence of an old Spanish ritual that had become, thanks to Hemingway's writings, a major international tourist attraction. Welles's documentary reconstruction neither romanticises nor particularly criticises the *encierro*. But by beginning the episode with images of the Altamira caves he entrenches the ritual in ancient Spanish traditions. Welles emphasises the majestic natural force of the bulls, the fear they provoke, in images of raw nature flooding the streets of the city of Pamplona.

* * *

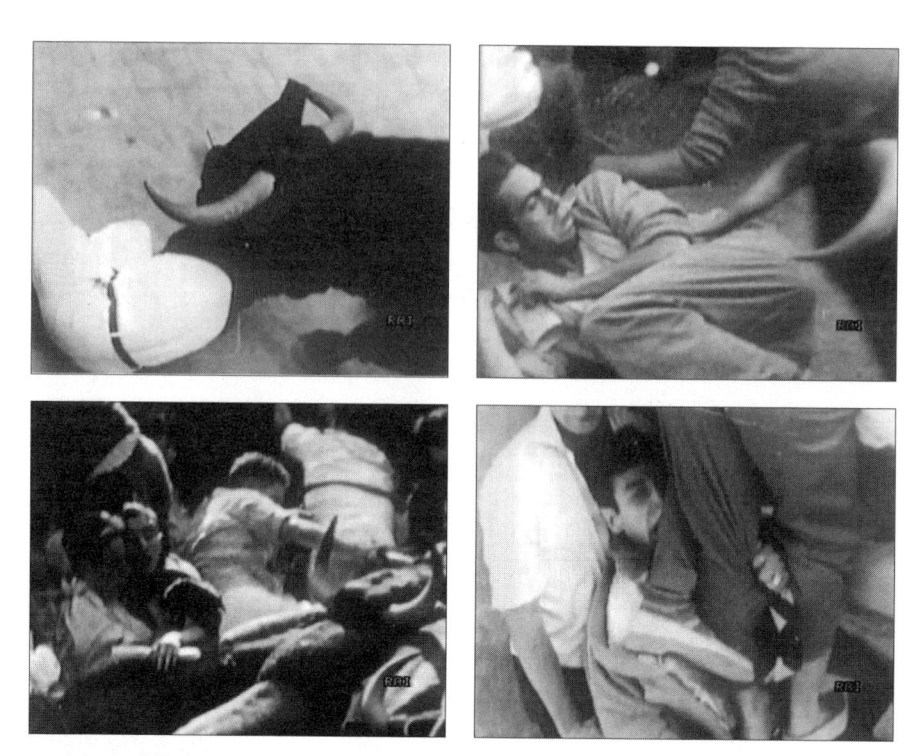

Still photographs used in the *encierro* sequence (*In the Land of Don Quixote*)

Barely a month after Hemingway's suicide, columnist Leonard Lyons reported in the *Hollywood Citizen News* that Welles was at work on a screenplay about a bullfighter that was probably an embryonic version of his project *The Sacred Beasts*.[40] This script seems to be Welles's first cinematic attempt to interrogate American interest in Spanish culture.

Welles explained the project to documentarians Albert and David Maysles in the summer of 1966:

> It has to do with a kind of voyeurism, a kind of ... emotional parasitism. And it has to do with the whole mystique ... of the he-man. This picture we're going to make is against he-men.
>
> [It's about] the people who go to bullfights not occasionally as tourists do but who are passionately addicted to it as *aficionados*. That part of the *aficionados* who have the Hemingway mystique, who got hooked through Hemingway. And our story is about a pseudo-Hemingway. A movie director who belongs to that league that in Spain they call the *macho* ... a fellow that you can hardly see through the bush of the hair on his chest.[41]

Welles's project evolved, lost its bullfighting background, and transplanted its drama to Los Angeles, where it was shot as *The Other Side of the Wind*. Nevertheless, the theme of American *aficionados* in Spain did not recede from Welles's interest but reappeared in *Crazy Weather*, an unmade treatment project of the early 1970s.[42] Oja Kodar remembered she began writing the story, and "whenever something had to do with Spain, [Welles] wanted to be involved ... he managed to introduce something about bullfighting into the story although I hated bullfighting."

Kodar admitted that no ending was ever written. The surviving draft is a consistently numbered 144-page composite combining treatment and formatted screenplay material, often with variant versions of the same scenes and some missing parts. References within that draft date it to late 1973. Kodar remembers collaborating on the project in Paris while Welles was editing parts of *The Other Side of the Wind*.[43] This would have been prior to his return to the USA to film John Huston's performance as Jake Hannaford.

Like *The Sacred Beasts*, *Crazy Weather* is a scathing attack on he-men, American ignorance, and cultural appropriation. There is also a new emphasis on women's subjective experience of urban space. The story centres on a love triangle. Welles and Kodar introduce Jim Foster, one of those romantic Americans who make "quite determined (if futile) efforts to participate in the social and cultural life of the country where they find themselves".

> He lives and works in Spain, and he's fallen head over heels with everything Spanish... Spain has a very strong appeal for his sort of American; their special vision of the so-called Spanish way of life seems to combine the prestigious dignity of an antique civilization with something of the tense simplicity of a good cowboy movie. Jim Foster never read Mérimée, but he's well-grounded in Hemingway – a key to his character, he cherishes Spain as a 'man's country'. [...]
>
> The corrida has never had so many fans among non-Spaniards. Hundreds of foreigners follow the bulls with studious enthusiasm from the beginning to the end of one *temporada* after another. Jim, of course, is one of these.[44]

Despite his Spanish wife and years living in Spain, Jim speaks only "limited and rather stilted" Spanish.

The key setting is an unnamed provincial town on the road to Madrid where Jim and his wife, Amparo, plan to attend a *corrida*. Amparo, driving towards the town, accidentally injures a nameless foreign youth with her car and offers him a lift. The boy's arrogance and aggressive sexuality disrupt Jim and Amparo's marriage. He taunts Jim about his misogyny and flirts with Amparo. Along the road Jim is forced to hike to a filling station to replace gasoline the boy has intentionally drained from the tank. The boy later sabotages the car's tyres. It's an open question whether Amparo and the boy committed adultery on the banks of a river. After driving Jim to the point of rage, the boy exits the car and limps off alone.

When the couple arrive in town, Jim gets out at a motel bar to drink Scotch. Amparo drives on alone towards the Plaza de Toros in the town's outskirts and is overwhelmed by traffic. The treatment focuses on Amparo's dazed experience of the street celebrations of the *feria*, a ritual that had been depicted with touristic detachment in *In the Land of Don Quixote*.

In *F for Fake*'s 'girl-watching' title sequence, Welles made gentle mockery of men leering at Kodar as she walked through a city during summer. That sequence was shot in Rome circa 1969 for "quite another film" – probably *Orson's Bag* – but incorporated into Welles's essay film around the same period he and Kodar wrote *Crazy Weather*.[45]

In that 'girl-watching' sequence Welles turns the camera's gaze back on the observers. By contrast, *Crazy Weather*'s treatment, sketchy as it is, suggests an approximation of Amparo's subjective encounter with the spaces of a town, her encounter with its heat, dust, and crowds, while in emotional distress. Apart from George's brief 'last walk home' in *The Magnificent Ambersons*, approximations of subjective experience are rare among Welles's realised city sequences.

The boy accosts Amparo outside the Plaza de Toros and insists on using Jim's ticket. Amparo acquiesces, and then finds herself crushed by the mob. She is forced against the boy:

F For Fake

It takes the two in a sort of huge embrace, holding them tightly against each other... If before she's had any thought of resisting, it's too late... The crowd is acting as the boy's accomplice, cutting off all possibility of retreat, forcing a prolonged physical intimacy. [...] The narrow arched corridor inside the Plaza is jammed to suffocation – to near paralysis – by a steaming mass of humanity crammed so densely together that the effect is not so much of numbers as of a single heavy-breathing beast.[46]

Meanwhile, Jim has a cornily macho response to his wife's possible infidelity, which he later admits to her. His voiced-over confession presents a flashback to his meeting with a young tourist – "as dumb a female as ever came out of Germany", the treatment notes. With "the considerable stimulant" of the "mounting *allegria* in the streets", he takes her on a carousel ride. The boy appears in time to join the couple, and Jim broods with anger at how he has been made to feel middle-aged in their company. The boy, however, assumes "a certain vague air of the pimp" and leads the couple to the girl's tent in an open hippie camp field outside the town. Then he leaves them alone.

Later, somehow wounded by a bull's horn – the treatment's continuity is lost by this point – the boy criticises Jim's Spanish fetish with a frankness that is remarkable considering Welles's earlier television documentaries: "He's got these picturesque notions, and a mind like a post-card. For good old Jim, Spain is granddaddy's land. The clock stopped here somewhere in the middle of a Victorian novel..."[47]

Crazy Weather joined the many other Welles projects of this period that were developed but never produced. *The Other Side of the Wind*, almost completely shot but not fully edited, descended into legal entanglements that were not resolved during Welles's lifetime, and Welles's exploration of the Hemingwayesque figure remained unseen. Yet Spain remained a setting in at least four additional works-in-progress towards the end of Welles life: early incarnations of *Mercedes* (aka *House Party*), a new essayistic conception of *Don Quixote*, *The Dreamers*, and *The Big Brass Ring*.

* * *

In 1961 Welles had gone to Seville to shoot the April *feria* for two episodes of *In the Land of Don Quixote*. In addition to more bullfighting scenes, including the graphic goring and tossing into the sand of a *torero*, Welles filmed the city in moving shots as the family Mercedes crawled through the narrow streets of the city (the accompanying music in the broadcast version is Bizet's "operatic dilution" of *Carmen*). The family visit the Plaza de España and the Casa de Pilatos, Seville locations that would in the coming months double for parts of the Middle East in David Lean's *Lawrence of Arabia* (1962). In another scene Welles and Beatrice drive a horse-drawn cart into the Barrio de Santa Cruz, the traditional Jewish quarter, to the accompaniment of flamenco music.

Seville returned as an imaginative setting at the end of Welles's career in the screenplay of *The Dreamers*. It is a much more ambitious adaptation of Isak Dinesen's work than *The Immortal Story*, which had been restricted to four speaking parts, Mr Clay's house, and the largely empty streets and colonnaded squares of Welles's imagined Macau. That said, *The Dreamers* continues Welles's faithful embrace of Dinesen's sombre aesthetic and her vague mid-nineteenth-century settings.

The screenplay, written in collaboration with Kodar in the late 1970s, combines 'The Dreamers' and 'Echoes', two Dinesen tales about the character Pellegrina Leoni. With its frame story set off the coast of Africa, 'The Dreamers' has been described as "a curious cultural inversion of Joseph Conrad's *Heart of Darkness*" in which European events are related as an exotic tale to its African and Arabic listeners. The cinematic potential had already been recognised: Truman Capote had wanted to make it with Greta Garbo.[48]

Dinesen established a structure of flashbacks within flashbacks. In the Welles-Kodar adaptation, a man named Lincoln tells the Pellegrina story on "a full moon night in 1870" on a dhow headed for Zanzibar. He recalls how in 1863 he met two other abandoned lovers of Pellegrina by coincidence at an inn on a high mountain pass in winter. They each tell the others a story of their

Welles in Seville, 1961 (*In the Land of Don Quixote*)

obsession for a vanished lover. They conclude they have all loved the same woman. What's more, Pellegrina promptly arrives at the inn with her Jewish "shadow", Marcus Kleek – a breathtaking moment of dreamy illogic anticipated by one of the lovers. They chase after her through a snowstorm. She leaps from a cliff. As Pellegrina lies on her deathbed at a nearby monastery, Kleek recalls her history: she had been an opera star who had lost her voice when a theatre in Milan caught fire during a performance. Presumed dead, she abandoned her identity. The loyal Kleek followed, watched, and provided for her when it was necessary. She moved to a village in the mountains, and fell slowly in love with a young boy, Emanuele, her singing student, until cast out as a suspected witch (this village episode is the plot of 'Echoes'). Pellegrina then set out to wander into "the great world of cities and men". Changing her name as she pleased, she took and abandoned many lovers. And then we learn that one of the young monks in the monastery where she lies dying is Emanuele.

The screenplay relocates parts of the Pellegrina story to cities of autobiographical significance to Welles, personalising what is an otherwise faithful adaptation of the two tales. In Dinesen's story, Lincoln's hunt for Pellegrina takes him from Rome to Basel, Amsterdam, and finally the Alps. The screenplay makes this a brisk *Arkadin*esque journey through Santiago de Compostela, to Amsterdam, Dresden, Odessa, Prague, and then the Venice Carnival, where Lincoln encounters Donna Lucetta Boscari, "notorious from Vienna to Palermo, expert in poisons and aphrodisiacs, procuress to the higher clergy". According to Kodar, Jeanne Moreau might have starred as Donna Lucetta.[49] Welles had filmed documentary footage of the Venice Carnival back in 1969, possibly for incorporation into *Orson's Bag*, but his interest in Venetian masques dates back to his attendance of the Beistegui ball in 1951.

The Roman scenes in Dinesen's story, where Lincoln first meets Pellegrina, are moved to Triana in Seville. Welles stirred in a sizeable helping of Merimee's Carmen. Welles makes Pellegrina's character the daughter of a Spanish baker whom one character describes as having "a little bit of gypsy phosphorescence".[50] In the sierras of Andalucía, Pellegrina wears riding clothes "still unchanged since Goya".[51] Dinesen, however, who felt a kinship with Pellegrina, once described her in terms of another Spanish archetype long familiar to Welles – she was a "Donna Quixote".[52]

In the Land of Don Quixote had presented several panoramic shots of Seville, and Welles evidently intended to return to this vantage to film the cityscape for *The Dreamers*. Lincoln is said to observe Seville "as though all of

Spain were laid out under his feet". His narration remarks: "It seemed to me that I might lift the very tower of the great Cathedral in Seville between my two fingers."[53] In the Dinesen story he fantasises it is St Peter's Basilica in Rome. A *Carmen*esque version of mid-nineteenth-century Seville is palpably evoked by the script, with occasionally specific ideas for visuals. The first image was to have been the naked silhouette of Pellegrina through the window of a Triana brothel, juxtaposed ironically with a male voice singing a *saeta* to a Madonna in a Holy Week procession. Lincoln remembers "the many smells there in that street… If ever I were to smell them again, I'd feel that I'd come home."[54] But as their romance progresses, he glimpses the ever-observant Kleek "at the far end of the street … a tall figure all in black [who] stands motionless in the shadows"[55] – a very Wellesian image. Pellegrina soon vanishes.

Struggling to find funding for this ambitious project, Welles shot several scenes at his home in Los Angeles between 1980 and 1982. He played Kleek and cast Kodar in the role of Pellegrina. Gary Graver, a young and selfless collaborator in this period, was the cinematographer. The scenes have survived and have been posthumously assembled for screening by the Munich Film Museum.[56] Despite the poverty of their making, they are beautiful fragments of one of Welles's final unfinished works.

* * *

By 1974 Welles was despairing of the modernisation of Spain:

> In the last six months it's joined the glory of the present world to such an extent that you don't know whether you're in Los Angeles or not in half the streets in Madrid. And a great deal of the grace and the pleasure of life, at least in the big cities, is gone.[57]

Franco would die the next year, clearing the way to Spanish democracy. But rather than celebrate the fall of a regime he had opposed ideologically from its very beginning, Welles was ambivalent about the change. In 1982 he reflected, "in a curious way the liberation of Spain and the fragile democracy has rather done away with both Don Quixote and Sancho Panza, and it's a sad point I've got to make… Spain is losing its Spanishness."[58]

Welles spoke of transforming the ever-evolving *Don Quixote* into an essay film on this very subject called *When Are You Going to Finish Don Quixote?*

It was never made, but thoughts on post-Franco Spain found their way into another project called *The Big Brass Ring*, which he wrote at the urging of filmmaker Henry Jaglom in 1981 and 1982. Material from a story by Oja Kodar called 'Ivanka' was incorporated into the original concept. Welles and Jaglom set up a deal with producer Arnon Milchan but were unable to find a star actor willing to play the lead role for a fee of two million dollars.[59]

The Big Brass Ring is both a half-serious political thriller and another *Arkadin*esque romp. It concerns the friendship between Blake Pellarin, a US senator and as-yet failed presidential contender, and his political mentor, Kimball Menaker, a former Roosevelt advisor and Harvard professor whose homosexuality has been publicly exposed.

Recovering after the election of Ronald Reagan, Pellarin is letting his beard grow while sailing off the coast of North Africa with his wealthy wife, Diana. When he catches Tina, a Brazilian manicurist, stealing his wife's emerald necklace, he decides in a rash moment to help her fence it. He vanishes into Africa to seek Menaker's help. Diana, who desperately wants to be First Lady, marshals a team of flunkeys and intelligence operatives to track down her husband and keep tabs on his activities. At the airport in Tangier Pellarin is accosted by the famous journalist Cela Brandini, who has just interviewed Menaker as background research on a story about the senator.

Menaker's present situation is even more absurd than that of the exiled Polish crooks of *Arkadin*. He lives in virtual captivity as an advisor to an African despot in the fictional Republic of Batunga, is guarded by two beautiful "mother-naked" black lesbians, and cares for an incontinent monkey. After securing Menaker's help, Pellarin takes the monkey out of Batunga and onboard his yacht, which is docked in Barcelona. Alas, the monkey leaps overboard with the emerald necklace in its paws, disappearing forever into the depths and leaving Pellarin with the bizarre responsibility of finding cash to pay off the manicurist. But he persists. "I think the craziest promise is the sacred one," Pellarin explains to Menaker, who joins him in Madrid.

Spain is marching into European modernity. Menaker hears that the "paint [is] peeling off the Goyas" at the Prado because of the smog. Old cafés have become banks, even as the Gran Via's "nineteenth century eccentricities" still show "their silhouettes against its pallid sky".[60]

Menaker's romantic history is recalled in the memory-haunted spaces of the Retiro park. There the men will pay off Tina through her brother (Tina has not been allowed to enter Spain). Pellarin arrives at the park with a briefcase of cash. In an unpublished alternative version of the script in the form of a novella, Menaker instructs Pellarin to meet him at "the equestrian statue of some forgotten Spanish hero". Pellarin doesn't find it, and only after enquiries does he discover that "the statue has been gone for almost forty years".[61] In the script, Menaker is hiding behind a bush, captivated by the sight of a homeless young man asleep on a park bench. The man reminds Menaker of his crippled lover Vanni, who "caught it not far from here" more than forty years earlier in the Civil War.[62] Vanni was seriously wounded but lived on for decades in Florida as an invalid.

The Civil War comes back to life with this memory trigger. Menaker recalls to Pellarin that Madrid was the "first city that was ever bombed. And how the world was shocked. In those days we were innocent. We still believed mass murder from the skies was quite a sin." During the war "you could take a street car to the front line. But not the subway – on the subway you could end up on the wrong side." Menaker was staying at the Gran Via Hotel alongside "Malraux, Ehrenberg, Dos Passos", waiting for his fighting lover to return. He pointedly notes twice that "Hemingway wasn't there that year."[63]

Menaker and Pellarin take pity on the sleeping homeless man and stuff money into his shoes. Shortly after three "tough-looking sailors" approach, but rather than make off with the cash, they wake up the young man and insist he take better care of his money. "Where on earth could that happen except here in this dumb country?" says Menaker.[64]

Pellarin's romantic past comes to light in another part of the city. Nine years earlier, after a tour of duty in Vietnam, he had temporarily abandoned Diana to live with a French-Cambodian woman in Paris. The woman mysteriously vanished, and although Pellarin returned to Diana, he has obsessively searched for her ever since. But Menaker reveals he has kept in contact with the woman, and leads Pellarin to a rendezvous with her in a house, "once the home of some prosperous merchant in another century",[65] in the vicinity of the celebrations of the Verbena de San Juan.

The screenplay provides a vivid visual and aural sketch of the setting. Pellarin and Menaker's cab passes through "canned music, loud and various, blaring out… there's a great yelping of barkers, the clatter of shooting galleries, the clickety rattle of the wheels of fortune … the cab has moved into the glare of many lights."

When they turn a corner, the "large, dark house blots out much of the light and baffles much of the sound … the muted growl and clatter of the Verbena

Fair" is "weirdly echoed from the other side of the dark house".[66] As Pellarin prepares to enter the house, recalling his obsessive search for the woman, "the noises of the feria are muted now, melting together, like the murmur of some crazy ocean".[67] A dreamlike encounter awaits.

Pellarin enters the house and finds the woman waiting naked for him. The script is vague as to specific visual ideas: "The scene is strange, almost surreal … (the action must be given in synopsis … The climax of this sequence is strong erotic: to spell out its specific details would be to risk pornography)."[68]

Menaker walks to the *feria* and rides a Ferris wheel. His passenger car passes a window of the house and he spies the couple making love. When the Ferris wheel stops its motion, Menaker's eyes meet the naked Pellarin's.

The mysterious French-Cambodian woman vanishes immediately after the love-making. Pellarin searches the house for her. By now he has figured out Menaker sabotaged the adulterous relationship in Paris to protect Pellarin's presidential chances. He promptly renounces the old man to his face. Then he has another run-in with Cela Brandini, who reveals that Menaker has for years been harbouring a sexual obsession for Pellarin, which involved a semen-stained handkerchief he had sent to Vanni in Florida. In rather opaque plotting, this causes Pellarin to utter "a sudden, terrible groan" and "wander through the dark streets of the city, searching … for his friend".[69] In a state of despair, Pellarin beats a helpless blind beggar to death under a concrete overpass in a wasteland of late-Franco Modernist architecture.

In an outrageous *dénouement* at the Madrid railway station, the inspector of police returns the briefcase full of money Pellarin left at the murder scene and refuses to implicate this American VIP in the case. Pellarin is then unexpectedly reunited with Menaker on the rapid train. There will be no stops for six hours until they reach the French frontier. Pellarin buys a bottle of brandy and the men sing cheerfully together as the train departs.

It's a dark and strange conclusion to one of Welles's final projects in cinema, yet another that would not be realised beyond the page. Perhaps by way of explanation Welles ends his script with:

If you want a happy ending, that depends, of course, on where you stop your story.

NOTES

1 Brainerd Duffield, 'Carmen Treatment', n.d. Box 22, folder 21, Lilly Library; Heylin and Wood both cite a Latin American version. See Heylin, *Despite the System*, 202; and Wood, *Orson Welles: A Bio-Bibliography*, 206–8.
2 Orson Welles, Memo to Harry Cohn, n.d. Box 22, folder 21, Lilly Library.
3 Welles and Bogdanovich, *This Is Orson Welles*, 400.
4 Román Gubern's definition in Marsha Kinder, *Blood Cinema: The Reconstruction of National Identity in Spain* (Berkeley: University of California Press, 1993), 22.
5 Parkinson, 1974.
6 Eva Woods Peiró, 'Rehearsing for Modernity', in Joan Ramon Resina (ed.), *Burning Darkness: A Half Century of Spanish Cinema* (Albany: State University of New York Press, 2008), 14.
7 Esteve Riambau, 'Don Quixote: The Adventures and Misadventures of an Essay on Spain', in Drössler (ed.), *The Unknown Orson Welles*, 71.
8 Ernest Hemingway, *The Dangerous Summer* (New York: Scribner's, 1985), 43.
9 Leaming, *Orson Welles: A Biography*, 469.
10 Berthome and Thomas, *Orson Welles at Work*, 198–202.
11 The documentary *The Dominici Affair* (Christophe Cognet, 2000) illustrates how extensively Welles re-structured his interviews during the editing process.
12 Welles quoted in Tarbox, *Orson Welles and Roger Hill*, 247–8.
13 *Orson Welles en el país de Don Quijote* (Carlos Rodríguez, 2000). Viewed 17 June 2013 at the Filmmuseum München, Germany.
14 Uncredited [Orson Welles and Oja Kodar], *Crazy Weather*.
15 See Jeffrey Herlihy-Mera, '"He Was Sort of a Joke, in Fact": Ernest Hemingway in Spain', *Hemingway Review*, Vol. 31, No. 2, spring 2012, 84–100.
16 *Parkinson*.
17 See Valerie Hemingway, *Running with the Bulls: My Years with the Hemingways* (New York: Ballantine Books, 2004).
18 *Parkinson*.
19 *Filming 'The Trial'*.
20 Welles quoted in James A. Michener, *Iberia: Spanish Travels and Reflections* (New York: Random House, 1968), 304.
21 *Parkinson*.
22 Welles quoted in Michener, *Iberia*, 302.
23 Berthome and Thomas, *Orson Welles at Work*, 200.
24 See Kenneth Tynan, letter to John Appleton, 29 October 1955, in Kathleen Tynan (ed.), *Kenneth Tynan Letters* (Random House Ebooks, 2012).
25 Juan Cobos in Cobos and Lawrence French, 'Juan Cobos on Orson Welles' Spanish Travelogue *In the Land of Don Quixote*', *Wellesnet*, 18 June 2008, at http://www.wellesnet.com/juan-cobos-on-orson-welles-spanish-travelogue-in-the-land-of-don-quixote

(accessed 6 September 2015).
26 *Nella terra di Don Chisciotte* (*In the Land of Don Quixote*), Documentary 1961 (subseries), Production notes June 1961. Box 1, Orson Welles–Alessandro Tasca di Cutò Papers, Special Collections Library, University of Michigan.
27 Alessandro Tasca di Cutò, *A Prince in America* (Smashwords ebook, 2011), 109.
28 Anile, *Orson Welles in Italy*, 289.
29 Cobos and French, 'Juan Cobos on Orson Welles' Spanish Travelogue *In the Land of Don Quixote*'.
30 Orson Welles, letter to editor (name illegible), 5 June 1961, in *Nella terra di Don Chisciotte* (*In the Land of Don Quixote*), Documentary 1961 (subseries), Production notes June 1961. Box 1, Orson Welles–Alessandro Tasca di Cutò Papers, Special Collections Library, University of Michigan.
31 Tasca di Cutò, *A Prince in America*, 112.
32 Cobos and French, 'Juan Cobos on Orson Welles' Spanish Travelogue *In the Land of Don Quixote*'. In 2005 a new version of the series without the narration was prepared by Ciro Giorgini and broadcast by RAI.
33 Anile, *Orson Welles in Italy*, 289.
34 Tasca di Cutò, *A Prince in America*, 110.
35 Ernest Hemingway, *By-Line: Ernest Hemingway – Selected Articles and Dispatches of Four Decades*, ed. William White (New York: Scribner's, 1967), 95, 103, 105.
36 McBride, *Whatever Happened to Orson Welles?*, 180.
37 'Cierro di Pamplona', *Nella terra di Don Chisciotte* (Orson Welles, 1964).
38 Cobos and French, 'Juan Cobos on Orson Welles' Spanish Travelogue *In the Land of Don Quixote*'.
39 Jess Franco's universally loathed posthumous edition of *Don Quixote* (1992) intercuts Welles's 16mm footage of the 1961 San Fermín *encierro* from *In the Land of Don Quixote* with what appears to be 35mm *Don Quixote* footage featuring Akim Tamiroff at the 1966 San Fermín festival. See Rosenbaum, *Discovering Orson Welles*, 203; and Riambau, 'Don Quixote: The Adventures and Misadventures of an Essay on Spain'.
40 McBride, *Whatever Happened to Orson Welles?*, 180. According to novelist Peter Viertel, Welles had been developing the project as early as 1958. Karp, *Orson Welles's Last Movie*, 10.
41 *Orson Welles in Spain*.
42 An undated private letter from Welles to Kodar confirms their co-writing of *Crazy Weather* and another project based on Kodar's story 'Blind Window' (known as *Mercedes*, *House Party*, and *Mercy*). Name and topical (series). Box 21, Orson Welles–Oja Kodar Papers, Special Collections Library, University of Michigan.
43 Oja in Drössler, 'Oja as a Gift', 43.
44 Uncredited [Welles and Kodar], *Crazy Weather*, 32–3.
45 Lawrence French, 'Truth and Lies About Orson Welles' *F for Fake*', *Wellesnet*, 11 February 2008, at http://www.wellesnet.com/truth-and-lies-about-orson-welles-f-for-fake/ (acces-

sed 7 September 2015).
46 Uncredited [Welles and Kodar], *Crazy Weather*, 30–1.
47 Uncredited [Welles and Kodar], *Crazy Weather*, 130.
48 Susan C. Brantly, *Understanding Isak Dinesen* (Columbia: University of South Carolina Press, 2002), 56.
49 Peter Tonguette, 'From the Beginning: Notes on Orson Welles' *The Dreamers*', in Drössler (ed.), *The Unknown Orson Welles*, 92.
50 Orson Welles, *The Dreamers* (undated draft), 14, at http://www.scribd.com/doc/149698063 (accessed 9 July 2013).
51 Welles, *The Dreamers* (undated draft), 9.
52 Dinesen quoted in Susan Hardy Aiken, *Isak Dinesen and the Engendering of Narrative* (Chicago: University of Chicago Press, 1990), 294n8.
53 Welles, *The Dreamers* (undated draft), 10.
54 Welles, *The Dreamers* (undated draft), 4–5.
55 Welles, *The Dreamers* (undated draft), 7.
56 Viewed 17 June 2013 at the Filmmuseum München, Germany.
57 *Parkinson*.
58 Welles quoted in Krohn, 'My Favourite Mask Is Myself', 62.
59 Jonathan Rosenbaum, 'Afterword', in Welles with Kodar, *The Big Brass Ring*, 140. A very loose adaptation of the Welles–Kodar script was directed by George Hickenlooper in 1999 with a screenplay by F. X. Feeney and Hickenlooper.
60 Welles with Kodar, *The Big Brass Ring*, 126.
61 Orson Welles, *The Big Brass Ring* (novella), [Final?] Novella draft (photocopy of typescript) (copy 1), n.d. (3 folders). *The Big Brass Ring* (1981–82) (subseries), Scripts. Box 14, Orson Welles–Oja Kodar Papers, Special Collections Library, University of Michigan.
62 Welles with Kodar, *The Big Brass Ring*, 75.
63 Welles with Kodar, *The Big Brass Ring*, 81–2.
64 Welles with Kodar, *The Big Brass Ring*, 84.
65 Welles with Kodar, *The Big Brass Ring*, 114.
66 Welles with Kodar, *The Big Brass Ring*, 109–10.
67 Welles with Kodar, *The Big Brass Ring*, 114.
68 Welles with Kodar, *The Big Brass Ring*, 115.
69 Welles with Kodar, *The Big Brass Ring*, 131.

INDEX

A Country Doctor see Ein Landarzt
Adventures of Don Juan, The 258
Albina Films 244
Alexander the Great 195
Ambler, Eric 49, 78, 82–3, 90, 93–4, 131, 183, 207, 217
American Civil War 10, 21, 28, 68; post-Civil War 24, 26, 29; *see also The Magnificent Ambersons*
American historiography 40
American Magazine 89
An Evening with Orson Welles (play) 220
Antolic´, Vladimir 232
Antonioni, Michelangelo 231, 235
Argentina 133, 146, 182, 184–5, 189, 225; *see also* Good Will tour and Nazism and *The Other Man*
Armstrong, Louis 101–3
Arnold, Jack 166
Around the World in Eighty Days 17, 145, 160
Around the World in Eighty Days (novel) 127
Around the World in Eighty Days (play) 127
Around the World with Orson Welles (TV series) 165, 204, 259–60; 'St-Germain-des-Prés' (episode) 212; 'Spain: The Bullfight' (episode) 265; *see also* Basque Country and Europe and Spain

Asphalt 169
Assassin 181
Association for the Protection of the Individual Against Officialdom 165
audience 8, 28–9, 51, 53, 64, 87, 169, 203, 238n.1
Austerlitz (Welles as an actor) 225, 236
Austro-Hungarian empire 1, 3, 83, 165, 226, 229; *see also The Trial*
avant-garde 4, 230

Badge of Evil (novel) 166
Bakhtin, Mikhail 210–11
Barefoot Contessa, The 258
Basque Country 165, 196, 257, 260–2, 268
Battle of Neretva, The 199
Baudelaire, Charles 70
Bazin, André 249
Beat the Devil 206
Because of the Cats 197
Berlin Film Festival 245
Berlin: Symphony of a Metropolis 4
Bessy, Maurice 205, 209, 217
Between Yesterday and Tomorrow see Zwischen Gestern und Morgan
Beyond the Limit see Other Man, The
¡Bienvenido, Mister Marshall! 258

283

Big Brass Ring, The 11, 84, 231, 264, 273, 277; and *Madrid* 11, 231
Big Money, The (novel) 22
Big Sleep, The 169
Black Irish 145
blacklist 128, 160, 195, 236
'Blackmail Is a Nasty Word' (radio episode) 207
Black Rose, The 193
Black Wave *see* Yugoslavia
Blake, Nicholas *see* Day-Lewis, Cecil
blaue Engel, Der 169
Blasco Ibáñez, Vicente 258
Blind Window see Mercedes
Blood and Sand 258
Blue Angel, The see blaue Engel, Der
Bogdanovich, Peter 2, 18, 54, 191n.35, 205, 220, 251
Border Incident 165
Brazil 50, 80, 89, 101–2, 105–6, 115, 118, 120, 260, 277; Afro-Brazilian 100, 110–11, 116; *see also It's All True* and *jangadeiro* and Rio de Janeiro
Breen, Joseph 92, 146
Bronston, Samuel 195
Budget Script *see Journey into Fear*
Buenos Aires 81, 133, 184; *see also* Argentina and Good Will tour and *The Stranger*
bullfighting 14, 181, 258–9, 263–4, 266, 271, 273; aficionado 263, 265, 270–1; *corridas* 104, 168, 259, 263–6, 271; *see also Crazy Weather* and *The Sacred Beasts*

Cabinet of Dr. Caligari, The 168
Cahiers du cinéma 22, 211
Camille (TV programme) 17
Campbell Playhouse 38
Campbell Playhouse, The (radio play) 15, 50, 65

Cannes Film Festival 194, 245; Palme d'Or 194; *see also Othello*
Capitan Noè 194
Carmen 257, 274, 276
Carmen (novel) 257
Carmen, la de Triana 258
Carnaval (segment) *see It's All True*
Carne, Sturges 154
Carringer, Robert L. 36, 38, 54
Cause for Alarm (novel) 83, 207
CBS radio 16, 50, 65, 145
Cervantes Films 195
Cervantes, Miguel de 183, 244, 246
Chimes at Midnight 6, 14, 197, 245, 247, 258, 266, 268; Falstaff 11, 14, 247, 248; Madrid 245, 247–8; *see also* Europe and Spain
chivalry 129, 147, 246
Cid, El 195
Cinédia Studio 54, 106
Citizen Kane 6, 10, 13, 16, 21–30, 31n.22, 33–47, 49, 51, 59, 61–4, 77–82, 84, 86, 89–90, 99, 104, 108, 128–9, 139, 184, 193, 203, 205, 208, 215, 243; capitalism 10, 21; Colorado 25–6, 28–9, 35, 59; Depression 34, 43; Kane-as-Hearst 38; New York 3, 21–2, 34–7, 42–7, 59, 81, 90; megalomania 22–3, 34, 44, 46; *New York Inquirer* 34, 37, 44; Rosebud 27, 29, 31n.22, 33, 35, 39–40, 57, 210–11; semi-documentary realism 128; Xanadu 33, 35, 47, 63; *see also* and expressionism and Gregg Toland and San Francisco and William Randolph Hearst
Cobos, Juan 266, 268
Cohn, Harry 17, 148, 159, 162, 257
Cold War 1, 160, 212, 217, 221, 233; nationalism 10; *see also* Vienna and Zagreb
Columbia Pictures 257

Communism 24, 40, 42, 125–6, 143n.10, 230, 232; anti-communism 128, 130; non-Soviet form of 232; pro-communism 24
Comprehensive Version see Mr. Arkadin
Confidential Report see Mr. Arkadin
Conrad, Joseph 16, 78–9, 81, 243, 274
Corinth version *see Mr. Arkadin*
Cortez, Stanley 49, 64
cosmopolitanism 4, 99–100
Cotten, Joseph 16, 35, 51; *see also Citizen Kane* and *The Magnificent Ambersons*
Cradle Will Rock, The 15, 23, 80
Crazy Weather 181, 189–190n.2, 263, 264, 271, 272, 273; American macho in Spain 264; *see also* bullfighting
Cyrano de Bergerac 127

Danton's Death (play) 16
Dassin, Jules 77, 128, 148, 169–70
David and Goliath (play) 196
Day-Lewis, Cecil 83
Dead Calm 198
Death in the Afternoon (novel) 14, 236
Deep, The 5, 198
Devil Makes Three, The 220–1
Dinesen, Isak 10, 198, 243–5, 274–6
Dmytryk, Edward 128, 133, 169
Doctor Faustus (play) 15
Dolivet, Loui (Ludovicu Brecher) 126–7, 160, 195, 203–5, 215
Don Quixote 5, 11, 17, 196, 197, 198, 204, 210, 246, 257– 79; *see also* Europe and Pamplona and Spain
Don't Catch Me 80, 89–90, 104, 127; *see also* comic thriller
Don't Catch Me (novel) 83
Dos Passos, John 4, 22–3, 30n.2, 278
Dreamers, The 264, 273–4, 276
'Dreamers, The' (tale) 243, 274
Dublin Gate Theatre 14, 247

Duffield, Brainerd 79, 257
Dupont, Ewald André 169

'Echoes' (tale) 274–5
Ein Landarzt (book) 227
Escolano, Ángel 247
Esquire (magazine) 6
Europe 2–3, 6, 22, 26, 40, 82, 90, 99, 110, 119–20, 163–5, 193–9, 203–13, 216–17, 222, 225, 229–30, 245, 251, 258–9, 264, 274, 277; Mitteleurope 210, 226–8; mythical 10; ancient/old 10, 129, 247; postwar 10, 206, 212, 226; romantic nostalgia 4; seaport town 81; self-exile 10, 128; Welles as an actor in 196; European spy novel 83; *see also* Cold War and fascism
European Union 216, 230
Everybody's Shakespeare (play) 14
Expressionism 3, 148, 168–70, 175, 213, 228, 237; expressionism-within-realism 175; expressionist lighting 5; German 4, 18n.5, 37, 128, 130; shadows 137, 175

Fall of the City, The (play) 15
Fall of the Roman Empire, The 195
Fante, John 79, 101, 103–4, 156
Fellini, Federico 197
Ferguson, Perry 36–7, 47, 49, 89, 139
Fessier, Michael 79, 156
F for Fake 5–6, 181, 197, 199, 244–5, 257, 259, 272; pseudo-documentary 244; *see also* Europe and Spain
55 Days in Peking 195
Filming 'Othello' 6
Filmorsa 195, 204–5
Films de l'Astrophore, Le 199
Final Draft see Take This Woman
First Person Singular (radio play) 15
Five Kings (Part One) (play) 14, 16, 247
Fleet's In, The (musical) 53

Foreign Correspondent 83
Forster, Norman 50
42nd Parallel, The (novel) 22
Fountain of Youth, The (TV programme) 17
Franco, Francisco 266; post-Franco 277, 279; Pro-Franco committee 147; regime 23, 147, 195–6, 197–8, 231, 258, 262, 266, 276; *see also* Spain
Freed, Donald 181
Freeling, Nicolas 197
Full Moon 198
Fully Dressed and In His Right Mind (novel) 79, 156, 157

Gance, Abel 225
García Berlanga, Luis 258
Gare d'Orsay *see Trial, The*
Gilda 146
Gillette, William 4, 15, 35
Gogol, Nikolai 225
Goldwyn, Samuel 37
Good Neighbor Policy 10, 78, 86, 88–9, 99, 115, 125; pre-Good Neighbor Policy 101; Welles as ambassador of 17, 50, 100, 110, 129, 160, 183; Good Will tour 133; *see also* Franklin Delano Roosevelt and *It's All True*
Goosson, Stephen 154
Grand Detour (Illinois) 57
Green Goddess, The (play) 16
Greene, Graham 82–3, 181–9, 190n.5, 206
Grosse Légume, Une see V.I.P.
Grune, Karl 169

Hammett, Dashiell 130, 169
Hampton, Christopher 182
Hannaford, Jake 244, 268, 271
Hathaway, Henry 193
Hath not a Jew eyes? (TV programme) 253
Hawks, Howard 169
Hayworth, Rita 17, 90, 146, 160, 257

HBO 185
Hearst, William Randolph 16–17, 23–4, 30, 38–47, 184; proto-fascist 23; *San Francisco Examiner* 39; yellow journalism 39; *see also Citizen Kane*
Heartbreak House (play) 15
Heart of Darkness 90, 66, 79–80, 86, 102, 131, 149, 173, 243
Heart of Darkness (novel) 16, 78, 272
Heart of Darkness (radio play) 79
Heart of Darkness (play) 82
Hearts of Age 15
Hemingway, Ernest 11, 14, 23, 131, 258, 263–4, 267–71, 273, 278; *see also* bullfighting
Heroine, The (book) 198, 240n.31
Heroine, The (segment) 245
Herrmann, Bernard 16, 53–4
Heston, Charlton 166
Heyman, John 182
His Honor, the Mayor (radio play) 24
Hitchcock, Alfred 83–5, 87, 89–90, 138
Honorary Consul, The (novel) 181–4, 186, 190n.5
Hopper, Hedda 126
Horse Eats Hat (play) 15
House Party see Mercedes
House Un-American Activities Committee 128, 160, 195
Huston, John 17, 131, 133, 138, 169, 196, 206, 271

If I Should Die Before I Wake (novel) 145
Immortal Story, The 6, 81, 197, 198, 244–5, 274; Spain 197, 258; *see also* Europe
Imperial Hearst (novel) 38
International Pictures 17, 131
In the Land of Don Quixote (TV programme) 196, 265–70, 272–5; Madrid 265
Iron Curtain 198, 212, 216, 230, 233
It's All True 10, 17, 49–50, 78–80, 89,

99–121, 122n.47, 133, 146, 156, 186, 189, 260; Carnaval footage 109, 119, 127; 'Carnaval' (segment) 79, 100, 108, 115, 268; and samba and *saudade* and Rio de Janeiro; semi-documentary 17, 78, 108; *see also* Brazil
It's All True: Based on a Film by Orson Welles 104, 107, 112

Jadran Film Studios 235
Jaglom, Henry 277
Jangadeiros 101
jangadeiros 106, 117–18, 120; and Fortaleza 4, 100–1, 106–7, 117–18, 120, 147, 260; *see also* Brazil
jazz 80, 101–3, 110; *see also* The Story of Jazz
Jew Süss (play) 14
Jorgens, Jack J. 249
Journey into Fear (novel) 49, 78, 83, 90, 183
Journey into Fear 50, 81–2, 89–93, 95, 97n.58, 104, 131; Istanbul 93; *see also* thriller
Joyce, James 4, 23
Julius Caesar (play) 15, 37, 235

Kael, Pauline 38
Kafka, Franz 3, 225–9, 230, 236, 253; *see also* Prague and *The Trial*
Kammerspiel 130, 168–9
Karas, Anton 206
Keller, Harry 167, 175
KGB 126
King of Kings 195
King, Sherwood 145
Killers 138
Kirk, Mark-Lee 49
Kodar, Oja 181–9, 190n.5, 197, 231, 263, 271–2, 274–7, 281n.42; *see also Crazy Weather* and *The Other Man* and *The Other Side of the Wind*

Koerner, Charles 53
Korda, Alexander 127, 194, 206, 229, 244
Kracauer, Siegfried 168
Krasker, Robert 206
Krohn, Bill 1, 246
Kurant, Willy 245

Lady from Shanghai, The 17, 78, 80–1, 90, 103–4, 129–31, 145–61, 164, 168–9, 187, 245; Acapulco 81, 131, 156, 147–8, 153–6, 203, 210; anti-authoritarianism 129, 164; hall-of-mirrors 157, 168–9; labyrinthine spaces 168–9; New York 80, 131, 146–8, 151–3, 158; San Francisco 81, 104, 131, 146–8, 151–3, 155–9; *see also* expressionism and Naples and noir and thriller
Lang, Fritz 168
Larrinaga, Mario 37
Last Laugh, The see letzte Mann, Der
Latin America/South America 10, 17, 50, 81, 88–9, 92, 95, 100–1, 103–4, 110, 118, 130–5, 138, 173, 181–6, 189, 257; *see also* Good Neighbor Policy
L'Eclisse 231, 235
left-wing: activism 130; critics 23, 266; filmmakers 128; left-wing serious thriller 183; melodrama 25
letzte Mann, Der 169
Little Prince, The (book) 127
Lives of Harry Lime, The (radio play) 206
Lloyd, Harold 35
Lord Jim 243
Los Robles see Touch of Evil
Loves of Carmen, The 257
Love Story 104, 156; *see also It's All True*
Lucidi, Renzo 204

Macbeth 15, 17, 54, 160, 226; *see also* expressionism
machismo 183–4, 263–4

Mackenzie, John 182
Magnificent Ambersons, The 10, 13, 16, 21, 24, 26, 35, 49–71, 72n.27, 77, 89, 92, 99–101, 107, 243, 272; African Americans 57; distant European past 245; Indianapolis 10, 27–9, 52, 54, 56–7, 60–3, 65–7, 70, 100; mansion 52, 56, 62–6, 69–70, 73n.54; *see also* New York
Magnificent Ambersons, The (novel) 13
Malle, Louis 197
Maltese Falcon, The 169, 206
Mancini, Henry 173, 178n.24
M. & A. Alexander 205
Mandaroux, Jean 235
Manhattan Transfer (novel) 22
Man in the Shadow, The 166
Mankiewicz, Herman J. 16, 25, 31n.22, 32, 38–41, 79
Mankiewicz, Joseph L. 258
Mann, Anthony 77, 128, 165, 169, 195
'Man of Mystery' (episode) 206–7, 209, 214; *see The Lives of Harry Lime*
Man with a Movie Camera 4, 117
March of Time, The (radio play) 84, 208
Marco the Magnificent 236
Marx, Karl 15, 40, 89, 126, 132, 182, 246
Masquerade see Mr. Arkadin
Masterson, Whit 166
Mayer, Louis B. 23
May, Joe 169
Maysles, Albert and David 270
McCarthy, Joseph 127, 160; and Cold War
Meltzer, Robert 105, 110, 119
Melville, Herman 245
Melville, Jean-Pierre 245
Mercedes 181, 264, 273–4
Merchant of Venice, The 251
Mercury Theatre 15–16, 23, 247
Mercury Theatre on the Air, The (radio play) 15

Mercy see Mercedes
Mérimée, Prosper 257, 271, 275
Merrie England 2, 24, 28, 58, 246, 248
Metty, Russell 137, 170, 175
Mexican Melodrama see Way to Santiago, The
Mexican Spitfire Sees a Ghost 53
Midlander, The (novel) 56
Miller, William *see* Masterson, Whit
mise-en-scène 5, 46, 60, 77, 82, 139, 166, 183, 219, 221, 230
Misérables, Les (play) 15
Misraki, Paul 211–12
Moby Dick (novel) 243
'Moby Dick' Rehearsed (play) 243
Monash, Paul 166
Monsieur Arkadin (novel) 205, 209
Monsieur Verdoux 50
Moreau, Jeanne 236, 275
Mori, Paola 258
Mr. Arkadin 3, 6, 10, 29, 81, 87, 126, 155, 163, 165, 175, 187, 194–5, 203–14, 217–21, 224n.62, 229, 231, 257–9; Barcelona 214, 217, 231, 277; flashback structure 204–5; Madrid 195, 203, 213, 220, 224n.62, 257–8, 277; Munich 3, 144n.27, 203, 210, 212, 214, 217–21, 226; Spanish-language version 204; *see also* Europe and impressionism and Naples and Spain and thriller
multi-national filmmaking 194
Munich Film Museum 251, 276
Murder, My Sweet 169
Murder on the Riviera (radio episode) 207
Murnau, F. W. 168, 169
Musketeers, The (TV programme) 17
'My Friend Bonito' (episode) 49; *see also It's All True*

Naked City, The 77, 148, 169, 170; semi-documentary realism 148

Naked Lady, The (TV programme) 17
Naples 81, 87, 210, 213, 217
Naremore, James 8, 25, 40–1, 86, 148, 248
Native Son (play) 16
Nazism 79, 85, 87, 90–92, 119, 132–3, 136, 220–1; in Argentina 133, 135; death camp 132, 139; de-Nazification 220; Germany 80, 131, 168 ; Nazi-hunter 129, 143n.20; post-Nazi era 218; prisons 237, 240n.34
Nella terra di Don Chisciotte 5
New Orleans 102
New York 4, 10, 14, 22–3, 28, 34, 41–2, 80, 90, 102–3, 130, 149, 170; *see also Citizen Kane* and *The Lady from Shanghai* and *Mr. Arkadin*
New Yorker 38, 149
New York Post 125
New Wien (segment) 1, 3, 9
Night and the City 170
Night Train to Munich 83
Nobility of the Peasantry see Nobleza baturra
Nobleza baturra 258
noir/film noir 4, 10, 78, 128–31, 146, 154, 164–5, 168–70, 183, 189; cinematic cities 130, 164; labyrinths 170; postwar noir 129; private-detective-centred 169; worldview 130
Noriega, Jose 88–9, 127
Nosferatu 168

OCIAA 50, 99, 115
Office of the Coordinator of Inter-American Affairs *see* OCIAA
Old Chevalier, The 253n.2
'Old Chevalier, The' (short story) 43, 244
One-Man Band see Orson's Bag
Operation Cinderella 194
Orson's Bag 2, 9, 11n.n.3,8, 198–9, 251, 272, 275; and Vienna and Zagreb
Orson Welles en el país de Don Quijote 262

Orson Welles #4 see Way to Santiago, The
Orson Welles Show, The (radio play) 50
ORTF 244
Otello, Grand 105, 111, 116–17, 119
Othello 6, 120, 163, 168, 175, 193–6, 203, 206–7, 214, 228, 245, 249–50–2; *see also* Cannes Film Festival Palme d'Or and Europe
Other Man, The 181–9, 190n.5; *see also* Oja Kodar and Pan-American cities and thriller
Other Side of the Wind, The 84, 157, 181, 199, 231, 244, 268, 271, 273; American macho 264
Out of the Past 138

Pamplona 4, 257, 265, 267–9; *encierros* 267–8; San Fermin 267–9, 281n.39; *see also In the Land of Don Quixote*
Pan-American films 10, 77–181, 189; anti-fascist 50, 78, 106; Carnaval 116; cities 99, 181; identity 101, 165; port city 165; propaganda 116; thrillers 78, 128, 163, 184
Paris by Night 244
Paul, Elliot 79, 101–2
Photosonar studios 203
Piedra, Emiliano 247
Poe, Edgar Allen 197
political films 77
port cities 4, 77, 131, 148, 184
Portrait of Gina see Viva Italia
Prague 3, 227, 229, 230, 275; Holocaust 227
Prince of Foxes 193
Prozess, Der see Trial, The
Pulitzer Prize 25, 57

RAI-TV 266
Ray, Nicholas 195
Reed, Carol 2, 83, 193, 206

Rio de Janeiro 1, 4, 50, 71, 101, 106–7, 109–10, 112, 119, 186; bidonville 187–9; Carnaval, 4, 50, 71, 79, 100–12, 115–19, 127; *see also* Brazil and *It's All True*
Rivelles, Amparo 204, 215
RKO 13, 16–17, 21–4, 37, 49–51, 53–6, 59–60, 63–7, 69, 77–84, 86, 88–93, 100–4, 107–9, 115, 118–19, 122n.47; RKO-Pathé Studio 64
Rockefeller, Nelson 50, 183
Rohmer, Eric 211, 217
Roosevelt, Franklin D. 40, 50, 78, 86, 99, 125, 127–9, 277; Depression era 15, 22; *see also* Good Neighbor Policy
Roots of Heaven, The 196
Rosenbaum, Jonathan 6, 8–9, 18, 54, 209, 211, 281n.39
Rossen, Robert 128, 195
rubble films 218
Ruttland, Walter 4

Sacred Beasts, The 109, 259, 264, 270–1; *see also* bullfighting
Safety Last 35
Saladin: Three Crusaders 197
Salome 119, 127, 194
samba 100, 104–5, 109–17, 119, 268; *see also* Brazil and Rio de Janeiro
Samba 119
saudade 1, 71, 113–15, 165, 210, 226
Scalera, Michele 193, 249–50
Schaefer, George 16, 23, 53
Sevilla Film Studios 195, 203
Shadow of a Doubt 138
'Shadow, The' (radio episode) 15
Shakespeare, William 2, 14, 160, 180, 244, 246, 251, 253
Shoemaker's Holiday, The (play) 15
Shylock Story, The 251, 253; *see also* The Merchant of Venice
Side Street 77, 169

silent film 4, 15, 28, 35, 101, 120
Siodmak, Robert 131, 168
Sirhan Sirhan 181
Sleepy Lagoon Defense Committee 164
Smiler with the Knife, The 80, 82, 84, 86, 88, 90
Socialist Realism 22–3
Spain 10–11, 14, 23, 43, 87–8, 155, 165, 195–7, 203, 214, 216, 245, 247, 25–9, 262–7, 270–3, 276–8; *españolada* 14, 257–8; Stalinist influence in 23; *see also* bullfight and Ernest Hemingway and Francisco Franco and John Dos Passos
Spanish-American War 10, 26, 29, 40, 43
Spanish Civil War 15, 93, 129, 147, 258; International Brigades 151; Popular Front 15, 22–3, 82–3; postwar 165, 195; *see also* fascism and Spain
Spanish Earth, The 23
Spiegel, Sam 131
Spirits of the Dead 197
Stamboul Train (novel) 83
Sternberg, Josef von 169
Stewart, James G. 81
'St-Germain-des-Prés' (episode) *see Around the World with Orson Welles*
Story of Jazz, The 101–3
Stranger, The 17, 78, 81, 125–42, 153, 168, 175, 189; film noir postwar thriller 30; Puerto Indio 133–5, 137, 141, 175, 189; *see also* Argentina and expressionism and noir
Straße, Die 169
Street, The see Straße, Die
Street with No Name, The 169
Sun Also Rises, The (novel) 14, 267
Surinam *see Victory*

Take This Woman 146, 161n.17
Tamiroff, Akim 144n.27, 196, 209, 224n.62, 229, 281n.39

Taras Bulba (novel) 225
Tarkington, Booth 13, 24–5, 50, 54, 56–71, 245
Tasca di Cutò, Alessandro 265–6
Temporary Draft 131
Third Draft see Black Irish
Third Man, The 2, 141, 183, 193–4, 206; and expressionism and postwar Europe and thriller and Vienna
Third Man (theme) 206
thriller 5, 10, 17, 49, 77–95, 118, 127, 138, 148, 156, 165, 181–3, 185, 194, 197–8, 206–7, 220; anti-fascist 78, 90, 95; comic 104; Pan-American 78, 128, 146, 163, 184; political 277; postwar 30n.2; serious thriller 82, 206, 212–13; spy thriller 78
Tito, Josip Broz 2, 197–9, 230
Toland, Gregg 36–7, 49; *see also Citizen Kane*
Too Much Johnson 12n.11, 22, 36, 47n.5, 108; and Madrid 47n.5
Too Much Johnson (play) 4, 15, 35
Touch of Evil 3, 6, 17, 46, 78, 80, 85, 95–96n.12, 142, 155, 163–77, 177n.7, 178n.21, 179n.26, 185, 187, 196, 210, 220; US/Mexican border 3–4, 77, 155–68, 170–4, 177, 178n.21; cinematic spaces 78; expressionist use of shadows 137, 175; Los Angeles 78, 164; Los Robles 3, 78, 81, 164, 166–8, 170, 174–5, 177, 178n.24, 179n.26; Venice Beach 78, 164, 168, 175, 177; *see also* expressionism and noir and thriller
Tourneur, Jacques 138
Towers, Harry Alan 206
Trauner, Alexandre 249–51
Treasure Island 197, 247, 254n.19
Trial, The 3, 6, 10, 157, 168, 197, 210, 225–38, 238n.1, 239n.31, 240n.33, 253;

Gare d'Orsay 3, 235–7; post-Holocaust 253; *see also* Europe and expressionism and Prague and Vienna and Zagreb
Trivers, Paul 79, 89
Turmoil, The (novel) 56–7
Twelfth Night (play) 14
Twentieth Century Fox 118, 139, 154, 156, 231
Two by Two see Capitan Noè

United Nations 125–7, 176
Universal Pictures 17, 128, 139, 166
Unnamed Mexican Story 89
urban spaces 5, 11, 36, 46, 78, 95, 102, 245

Vadim, Roger 197
Varieté 169
Variety see Varieté
Veiller, Anthony 17, 131, 138
Venice Film Festival 160, 204, 226, 255n.33
Vertov, Dziga 4
Victory 243
Vidor, Charles 146, 257
Vienna 1–2, 206, 229, 275; Riesenrad Ferris wheel 2, 279; *see also The Third Man*
V.I.P 205
Viva Italia 259

Wade, Robert *see* Masterson, Whit
Walked by Night 169
Walker, Vern 81
War and Peace 127
Warner Bros. 118, 204
War of the Worlds (radio programme) 16
Washington Evening Star 160
Way to Santiago, The 49, 83, 86, 88–90; *see also* thriller
Webb, Roy 53
Welcome, Mister Marshall! see ¡Bienvenido, Mister Marshall!
Wertenbaker, Lael Tucker 261–2

When Are You Going to Finish Don Quixote? 197, 276
Wilde, Oscar 119, 127, 194
Wilder, Billy 168
Williams, Charles 198
Wilson, Richard 102, 105, 120
Winter of Our Discontent, The 14
World War I 40, 62, 82, 208, 229
World War II 10, 91, 131; fascist Spain 195; postwar period 10, 30, 27, 127–9, 131, 153, 165, 169–70, 201–22, 226, 230–3, 246; Soviet-style internationalism 125; *see also* fascism and Good Neighbor Policy and *The Lady from Shanghai*

Yugoslavia 197–9, 225–6, 230, 232, 236, 251; TV audience 196; *see also* Black Wave and Josip Broz Tito

Zagreb 2–3, 11, 199, 229–34, 236–7; General Plan of Zagreb 232; *see also Orson's Bag* and *The Third Man* and *The Trial*
Zugsmith, Albert 166
Zwischen Gestern und Morgan 218